SpringerWienNewYork

Editors:
Andrea Gleiniger, Angelika Hilbeck, Jill Scott

Produced by:
Zurich University of the Arts (ZHdK)
Institute for Cultural Studies in the Arts – Z-node
Jill Scott
Juanita Schläpfer-Miller

Research Associate:
Juanita Schläpfer-Miller
Alain Rickli

Graphic Design:
Karin Schiesser
Philippe Kipper
Marianna Prenger

Copy Editors:
Juanita Schläpfer-Miller
Susanne N. Hillman

Images on cover:
Frem Proteins: Images Courtsey of Prof Dr. Ian Smyth: Developmental Biology of the Skin. Monash University. Australia
Swiss Norway Spruce Forest and Water draught analysis on a cellular level: Images Courtsey of Dr. Norbert Kräuchi WSL Birmensdorf: Forest and Climate Research. ETHZ

Printed in Austria

SpringerWienNewYork is part of
Springer Science+Business Media
springer.at

Printed on acid-free and chlorine-free bleached paper
SPIN 80015359

With 69 colour figures and 15 black and white figures

Library of Congress Control Number 2010933593

ISBN 978-3-7091-0287-9 SpringerWienNewYork

TRANSDISCOURSE 1

MEDIATED ENVIRONMENTS

EDITED BY ANDREA GLEINIGER • ANGELIKA HILBECK • JILL SCOTT

Z hdk

Zürcher Hochschule der Künste

SpringerWienNewYork

OUTLOOK: THE TRANSDISCOURSE SERIES

Juanita Schläpfer-Miller

TRANSDISCOURSE – is a term that embraces emergent meanings around the multifarious interpretations of the word 'transdisciplinarity'. This book series not only reflects upon the idea of an intersectional discourse of all creative media-arts disciplines, with the various disciplines of life science, physics, engineering and computing, but it creates a dialogue for the purpose of exploring and critically addressing the ethical implications of art within society, and for our environment. Together, the resulting set of focused publications will act as 'nodes'. Each designed to instigate research trajectories where individual investigative pathways intersect, form new branches, and diverge. The series aims to create a critical transdisciplinary space where combined artistic, technological and scientific approaches call for embodied practical, as well as theoretical solutions. The aim is also to create an intersectional discourse between research within the art disciplines – architecture, fine arts, media, sound, and theatre; the humanities – history, psychology, and sociology; and science – life sciences, physics, computing, and engineering.

Each book in this series provides an integrated textual and visual showcase for innovative material projects and related arguments that challenge and provoke transdisciplinary discourses. We have adopted a format of a theoretical essay section as well as a colour gallery section for invited curators. While the essays are critical reflections, the gallery pages are either for related audiovisual explorations, or artworks, which represent these potentials in a non-verbal manner.

This book *Trasndiscourse: Mediated Environments* is the first of the series and reflects both on transdisciplinary practice itself, and on social environments and urban space. The editorial board, a pool of artists, scientists and theorists, established the theme of each volume which will be edited by a rotating team of editors. The proposed themes are listed below:

Transdiscourse:

Book #1: *Mediated Environments* -this volume is focused on urbanization, disconnection, climate change chaos, energy conservation as well as the civic city motilities of ghettos and of content in domes.

Book #2: *Turbulence* will highlight issues of change in our society, movement, mass displacement, Diaspora, migration, borders (cultural, social, political), disturbances, and activism.

Book #3: *Progress* will be concerned with a critical analysis of modelling, economy, visualization, surveillance, technology and ubiquity.

Book #4: *Participation* will be about connection to the community, networks, social networks, shapes/shaping (i.e. democracy), constructs that shape territory, enabling technology, collaboration and co-authorship.

Book #5: *Sharing* will collect research about the sharing of resources, equality / inequality, land-grab, waste disposal, water, species extinction, sustainability, time and energy.

Within the educational institutions of art and science, we are still very confined to focused disciplines, which tend to develop separately from each other, a strategy which inhibits holistic problem solving. The book series is therefore dedicated to a thematic approach to the discourses of transdisciplinary education. Our audience may be educational facilitators who are engaged in similar projects, or who are interested in the problems and methodologies of teaching across disciplines. The series is also for students who wish to explore not only the current debates, but also to investigate the catalyzing potentials of the arts in relation to science and society.

INTRODUCTION TO MEDIATED ENVIRONMENTS

Andrea Gleiniger, Angelika Hilbeck, Jill Scott

Outline

Mediated Environments addresses the problem that today society interprets our environment through the very conditioned and constructed representations of mainstream media and not in a transdisciplinary way with the help of artists, architects, filmmakers, cultural theorists and scientists. Inside most urban centres of the developed world, these fabricators and discoverers know that our lives are also mediated by the technologies that surround our everyday existence and affect our environments. In fact our very bodies are being shifted by different analogue, digital and artificial discoveries, and scientific translations of social and ethical realities that surround us. The writers in this book all are attempting to cross-correlate media from different disciplines and reconstruct it in relation to urban technology, sociology and scientific method. They see forms of film, activist and performance documentary as a key to a high level of reflective criticism, one that uses media as a new form of empowerment and communication about the pressing issues of urban life.

Main Aims

Our main aims were to focus on the potentials of media, art and architecture to address both socio-poetical issues in an environment that includes scientific information, sustainability in relation to physical urban development and the raising of comparative awareness in society. New approaches are not to be found in the popular mainstream of television and the daily newspapers, but in the observation, re-design and cultural meaning of representation by more creative and artistic strategies. As editors, we were interested in how the medium can be used as part of the message to work with community groups or transdisciplinary art and science teams so that the accessibility to expression can be shifted and new discourses found. In *Mediated Environments*, authors and researchers strive to encourage local people to find and hold onto their political and social voice. These authors were chosen because they all express this potential from the backbone of three basic sub-categories. These are: Mediated Architecture, ECO Art and Land Works and Art and Science correlations.

Mediated Architecture:

In relation to history of architecture, media has been incorporated as a potential voice for the urban crisis. For example, media information was seen as part of the initial Bauhaus Movement, and focused on the care of the social relations in dwellings. Today, this concept has now evolved and media technologies are integrated into architecture not only as actual materials, but also as transmissions about time and reflections on the surrounding space. The problems of social engagement have become an important link to address the problems of increasing urbanization, which is jeopardizing our continued existence and questioning our sustainability. Media can also help designers and architects to construct more than visions and utopias of a civic city environment, because many problems can only be solved with transdisciplinary solutions.

For example, in her essay *Emergency Design – New Semiotic Orders of Urban Survival*, Yana Milev describes various orders of "emergency design" and how these have been applied to strategies of urban survival and living. She suggests that new design strategies which actually cater for spontaneous social engagement, have to be considered. This need influences how the qualities of time-based media itself can be readily integrated into our local environmental planning.

Indeed, how to deal with the emergency of the overproduction of waste materials in urban centres has already become a problem in many dense urban environments. The architect Denise Scott Brown examines the potentials of recycling waste in these centres and makes an analogy within the context of the natural biological cycle of life. She correlates the urban decline in some western cities to an increase in art made from waste, and compares this scenario to the re-appropriation of waste in developing countries. Using examples ranging from the neon signs of Las Vegas, to the art-from-trash objects made for tourists in South Africa, she discusses (European and U.S.) class attitudes to waste, versus (African) views of it, and how the use of the everyday environment can become a cultural and artistic resource.

As an illustration of the fact that the urban landscape can inspire literary expression, Theresa Steffen elucidates on South African urban space as 'Mediated' Environment by providing a comprehensive review of Ivan's Portrait with Keys: the city of Johannesburg unlocked. In this essay Steffen "seeks to analyze the prolific creative processes" in Vladislavić's literary texts, which use various examples of South African urbanity not only as a context for creativity but also for mediality.

In all cases the growth of urbanity is seen as an enormous problem but also as a process in which the more challenging sets of materials and structures are available for the creative mind to grapple with. If media fits, then a summary of local histories and materials found along the pathways can become an inspiration about the space and place of experience. Thus, the emergence of new technologies of connectivity, network, communication and information can empower social equality by involving civic culture. Here the designer, the writer, and the architect, all build into 'their mediated cities' a certain level of narrative portraiture, that is as braided, fractal, and involuted, as the people who inhabit it.

ECO Artists and Local Living Conditions

Media Art can be seen as a label, which began to be applied in the early 90s, to the many artists who were interested in extending, criticising and accessing technology, even to the point of subverting its use in popular culture. Today the question is not so focused on which types of media or level of interaction is being used by the artist, but on how interactive media can play a role as interface for artists and art groups to raise public awareness about the environment. By taking on this interpretative and responsible role and combining it with more universal poetic metaphors for change, public oriented projects can affect human stewardship and help us understand the environment. This requires awareness on a more local environmental level as some of the examples in this section prove. Maya Kuzmanovic and Nik Gaffney are directors of FoAM, a group in Brussels, who work in media activism. They write about how group dynamics can help communities to organize and shift their collective focus onto a more local level. FoAM's objectives are to create discourses, contacts and propositions that look 'beyond and beneath' conservation and sustainability. They believe in small changes and that working in synergy with each other can help to share strategies such as permaculture and local food cultivation. Through their workshops and meetings, based on 'guild gathering', non-hierarchical participatory situations, open space technology, learning and sharing workshops and the construction of DIY tutorials, they have a record of causing discussions about needs of society rather than their wants. To this end they incorporate creative art practices, which they hope can help in these discussions.

In her essay, *Heat, Art, People and Climate Change*, Australian performance artist, Jill Orr describes her work with Indigenous Cultures and the new performative roles of artists to create a type of socio-poetic catalyst. By working with, and including local people and awareness of regional environmental problems she takes an inclusive approach to cultural construction. This approach can explore cross-cultural relations and address the blockages that manifest from historical long-standing issues like racism, poverty and genocide. She claims that an acknowledgement of difficult historical truths can contribute to an open debate, and artists must affect change together with others, rather than take any power over others in a creative process. In her essay, *Beyond Eco Art, 21st Century visualizations*, Tiffany Holmes makes a comparison of Land Art approaches with visualization projects that use dynamic feedback to trigger energy-responsible behaviour in the home or workplace. She cites a number of artists, and designers who are attempting to prove that dynamic feedback can produce a reflective response from viewers about their energy consumption patterns. She argues why certain strategies have helped consumers and cites some examples from her own abstracted 'Ecovisualizations' of how real time with local energy conservations can provide more effective encouragement than public data transmission. The challenge to shift behaviours is also addressed by Jill Scott a media artist who addresses the value of immersion in the dome format with 3D graphics as a catalyst to raise awareness and bring molecular behaviour based on scientifically robust interpretations about climate science into the public realm. By using planetariums as educational platforms linked to blogs in the home, representations can help to expand the potentials of understanding of 'the fear of the scale of the problem' and the level of community exchange. All the essays by the above artists discuss the formations of critical transdisciplinary spaces, where combined scientific and artistic approaches to environmental issues call for embodied practical, as well as theoretical solutions.

Art and Science correlations

This section provides a platform for writers who are concerned with the relations between art and science, and how collaborations might 'mediate' understanding, spreading content and help communities. How can new approaches to media help us understand the problems of agriculture and the landscape and the relevance of environmental scientific research? How is media shedding light on the problems in our environment? In her essay, Angelika Hilbeck, a scientist, critically reflects on why modern day agriculture and food production systems have failed to produce healthy food. This failure has led to the degradation of both human health and the environment. Today this form of production has generated social injustice while being economically very successful, and it has led to publicly funded research agendas to become complicit and complacent with the interests of private profit. She comments on the resultant disconnection and profound confusion for the general public and how the media was responsible for bringing this shift in science and technology development from public to private interest. However, the author suggests that media and art in the form of new investigative documentary films are today key in helping the public to reveal the disconnections and reconnect the dots. Thus democratic decisions can be made about societal choices for change in food, health and environment policies that can once again serve the public interest. Andrea Polli is an artist, who writes about her work in the context of air pollution and the commercialization of basic and essential resources such as water and air. By using examples from art and activist projects, she argues that these critical responses to controversies, new mechanisms for communicating problems relate to the environment in general, and climate change in particular. For example, some of these artistic works have served as catalyst that could turn consumers into decentralized producers, and in one of her own works *Hello Weather* she has helped citizens generate science by 'giving them' weather recording stations to record and monitor local air quality. She proves that art and artists have an important role to promote social movements and activism and empower them as the citizens of the earth.

Zvjezdana Cimerman, an artist and scientist, reflects in her essay on the polarity between science as the process of generating knowledge and the arts as the process of making, and puts this comparison into a historical perspective. She postulates that this polarity is now obsolete, as the ethical horizon has shifted from an altruistic quest for truth to a socio-political responsibility. Consequently, artists increasingly feel the need to focus on society and the burning issues that threaten our collective existence. Therefore she addresses the roles of contemporary scientists and artists. She also re-enforces and substantiates the shift in science towards applied techno-science only, driven by the urgent need for instant gratification in form of financially lucrative applications. With no room for an old fashioned division into basic and applied research fields, current scientific research projects are only started when there is a clear product in mind at its onset. She describes how two diverging scientific propositions for future agriculture and food production – agro-biotechnologies and organic farming – have generated different genres of artistic expressions and roles of artists and technologies in the ensuing democratic global trans-discourse of the future. Finally, the ideas presented in this part of the book are formulated and discussed in an interview-type essay with two founders of the eco- and activist art movement in the 1960s and 70s, Helen and Newton Harrison. The interviewer is Brandon Ballengée, an artist and biologist, who allows us to have a deeper insight into their perspective on art and science as a process of sharing creativity. While much of their work is being seen as eco-art and art activism, they do not think of themselves as activists but as 'responsible people responding to a circumstance'. They deplore that artists and also art critics are often afraid of sciences and eco-systemic thinking and are often basically ecologically illiterate and, in many ways, scientifically indifferent. They contend that the divide between artists and scientists needs to be removed in order to come up with large real world solutions. Recognizing today's shift in science towards serving private interests rather than public interests, in their relationship with scientists they often act as 'a stalking horse', saying a lot of the things scientists cannot say without taking serious risks of being ostracized by the scientific community, vested interest groups or being cut off from funding.

Conclusion

The above views from these three trajectories correlate to address the issues of 'mediated environments'. Although these authors have very different backgrounds from each other, spanning media art, architecture, urban planning, environmental science, social science, biology and cultural studies, the whole makes up a kind of 'transdiscourse' about the challenging task of working together on solutions to some global problems and to invent strategies for the raising of public awareness. For example, in 2007, for the first time in our human history, the number of people living in cities has exceeded the number living in rural environments. Of the planet's 6 billion people, more than 3 billion now live in urban environments where resources are running at maximum levels, food and water supplies are diminishing and urban slums are growing. As more financial crisis looms ahead perhaps this situation will reverse, and people may return to their barren lands to grow their own food? These migrations could be a factor that may jeopardize our continued existence. By gathering transdisciplinary solutions and thoughts about subjects like this, we feel that creative teams could change our way of thinking and, consequently, way of living.

In this light *Mediated Environments* could be a contribution to the discourse about a higher level of human stewardship toward 'sustainability'. By working with media, instead of against it, we all can create simple meaningful tasks and guide a new representational approach that could in turn encourage more local understanding of factual evidence. Certainly the role of mediated information should graduate from pure description and theatrical effect into the potential of communal liberty and citizen science, one that encompasses activist art making and a shared exploration of the impact of media on our society and on our environment. We feel that the projects documented in the book will also help the public broaden the discourse about urban environmental issues and re-define the impact of 'progress and development' on our education. The writers in this book are artists and scientists and see themselves as open-minded professionals in academia. We believe that only by thinking outside of our narrow disciplines, and changing the slope of our learning curves can we change our collective thought.

MEDIATING AND DESIGNING ENVIRONMENTS – ART AND NATURAL SCIENCE

Zvjezdana Cimerman

A crucial change is taking place today in the ancient difference between art and the natural sciences: the polarity between science as process of generating knowledge and art as process of making has become largely obsolete. Science is seen not so much in terms of the knowledge it creates as in terms of its impact on the global and human environment. Its ethical horizon has shifted accordingly from an altruistic quest for truth to a burdensome socio-political responsibility. Conversely, art has shifted its ground from the individually creative to the theoretical: in a climate of wide-spread anaesthesia brought about by techno-economics and the media, artists increasingly feel the need to focus on society and its issues.

'What is really uncanny, however, is not that the world is becoming thoroughly technologized, but that mankind is unprepared for this transformation – that we are still incapable of coming mentally to terms with what is dawning in our age.' (Martin Heidegger)

Art and science today[1] – a contrastive view

From Classical Antiquity through the Middle Ages to the Renaissance the boundaries between arts and sciences were not distinct. They were allies: the arts were conceived as poetic (from the Greek *poiesis* = making) the sciences as theoretical (from the Greek *theoria* = contemplation, overview). Since that ancient time, when arts and sciences were separated basically by the polarity between an epistemological and poetic moment, new differences arose. Consequently, a considerable distance between art and science has evolved.

The analytical approach, the fragmentation into many specialist disciplines and sub-disciplines are characteristics of science, whereas art opts rather for the synthetic view[2]. Science is governed by methodological rules, art is not; science aims for conceptual abstraction, art for concrete sensation. Science seeks to understand what it observed in nature and the laboratory and thus to ascertain and formulate the laws of the experienced world; art focuses on the world of experience not only in its outer reality but also in its subjectivity: on the inner condition of the observer as individual and as the subject of social change.

More recently, however, the polarity that derived from the concept of science as knowing and art as making has become largely obsolete. Under the impact of the shift from theory to technology, the poetic character becomes more and more important in science. Conditioned by the parameters of economic and industrial development, science has become techno-science. While exploring the possibilities for developing, science increasingly approximates invention, poiesis and the traditional role of art. And, seen no longer in terms of the knowledge it creates but of its impact on the global and human environment, its ethical horizon has shifted from an altruistic quest for truth to a burdensome social and political responsibility. Conversely, the driving force of art has become theoretical rather than creative. Since the 1960s, when Joseph Beuys set out to revitalize its social function, the epistemological claims of art have become more strident. Infused with theory, it has entered the social arena and demands a voice in political and ethical discussion. The German philosopher and art historian Wolfgang Welsch asserted in the 1980s that the era of domination by the sciences was over: 'Art is no longer the handmaid of science, seeking to imitate the manners and compensate the failings of its master. Now it is art that defines the patterns of science' (Welsch 1986). And the artist Marina Abramović observed in the 1990s that 'Artists are companions and guides in the quest for a new order' (Abramović cited in von Drahten 1993, p. 220).

Environmental footprints of art and science

What, then, are the deficits of today's order and what features should be looked for in the new? One way to answer these questions is to examine the characteristics of the environment, as well as the positioning of art and science in and in face of the environment – the term environment being taken in the broad sense as referring not only to ecological systems but to the whole socio-economic milieu in which we live.

Science as applied science

The current environmental order can be exemplified in terms of a dominant techno-economy and its consequences. As the French scientist Jean-Marc Lévy-Leblond put it in an interview:

> 'The problem is that fundamental research is becoming increasingly ambivalent. Until a few decades ago, one could still entertain the idea that research was motivated by curiosity, detached from any thought of its applications. But since the mid 20th century that distinction has become untenable. A single historical event of global significance (in both the literal and figurative sense) proved it so: the atom bomb. It was developed by theoretical physicists, who occupied themselves, purely by the desire to know, with the most fundamental question: how an atomic nucleus functioned. The bomb was developed by the scientists themselves. There was not knowledge transfer. From this moment on, pure and applied science have melded into each other; today they are scarcely separable.' (Lévy-Leblond 2004)

The original distinction between pure and applied research has already, in fact, vanished in certain disciplines, for the simple reason that fundamental research already embraces the objectives of applied research. No more being undertaken purely for the sake of knowledge, scientific research is directed *ab initio* to the attainment of practical, for the most part commercial goals. Consistently with this, knowledge and technology transfer between the university and industry plays an important role from the beginning.

Genetic engineering, for instance, has no room for a division into pure and applied. The traditional pattern of research coming before product development is even reversed, for in many cases researchers must have the product in view before they start – their very funding depends on their ability to present their case in this light. Indeed, biotechnological research frequently begins only after the product has been created. Genetically modified seed, for instance, must first be produced on a scale large enough for it to be agriculturally sown; only then, under 'natural' conditions, can long-term study of its processes begin. Similarly with cloning, which can only be studied once the clones themselves have been produced. Moreover, the distinction between pure and applied research tends to obscure the interests of those who stand to gain from it – the more so, the shorter the path to economically remunerative technology, as the biomedical sciences so effectively demonstrate.

The confluence of interests has engendered growing criticism of science: once the judge, it is now arraigned for its side-effects, from nuclear radiation through genetic damage to new ecological threats. In all these respects science is becoming aware of its limitations. Lévy-Leblond goes on to say:

> 'As a scientist I have the impression that all is not well with science. Increasingly it is encountering difficulties and contradictions, and it seems to me that these can only be overcome by having recourse to the experience gathered over the centuries by writers, artists and philosophers: to the cultural tradition from which it stayed aloof for so long.' (Lévy-Leblond 2004)

And he expresses his gratitude to the artists who have helped him find the critical distance required by contemporary developments in science and technology. For, ruled by economics, the technosciences and their products stand today at the head of a long chain impacting, deforming and intentionally aestheticizing (but at the same time anaesthetizing) the environments in which we live.

An anaesthetized world

Theoreticians of aesthetics have observed that aesthetics has moved from the sphere of arts to the daily life: 'More and more elements of everyday life are aesthetically exaggerated and everyday life itself is increasingly perceived as an aesthetic construct' (Welsch 1993, p. 13). Terms such as *mise en scène*, sensationalism, simulation, dominance of the artificial, generalized mimesis, hedonism and narcissism paraphrase the process of aestheticism (Lyotard 1993, p. 418). Urban spaces are beautified and adorned with elegant centres of consumerism, temples of innovation in design, materials and technology. The natural environment is presented as an arena of experience and leisure, replete with entertainment and events. The body is perfected; and to the industries of fitness, beauty, cosmetic surgery and pharmaceuticals we shall soon be adding a range of biotechnologies. The psyche is styled, aesthetic competence optimized.

In all these dimensions the traditional qualities of art are transferred to life; indeed reality itself is treated as a work of art – not, however, in Beuys's sense, but as a program of single-minded devotion to kitsch. And this in the overt interests of global economics, a battlefield on which the sciences through their applied disciplines are strategic players, for the beautification of reality is big business, and its strategies are business strategies. To gain and hold one's place in this aesthetic world one must at all times consume. Aesthetic objects are short-lived for the simple reason that the fashions that dictate them are short-lived. So business economics and advertising take on the task of ensuring that our aesthetic dreams and ambitions do not lack for sustenance. *Homo aestheticus* has an insatiable hunger for the euphoria of the new, but that is all he feels; in every other respect he is desensitized. Aestheticism has, as Welsch puts it (1995), become its own anaesthetic.

Art itself is subject to the laws of this market: in the global art industry the value of the work itself and its monetary price have become confused. The art world overlaps with the capitalist market – or, as Andy Warhol said, 'Good business is the best art', and being part of the global market, art runs the risk of being reduced to an aspect of lifestyle and entertainment, subject to the stereotypes of marketing, and presented for mass consumption in a multitude of easily digestible forms.

Aestheticism extends further, however, to the perception of reality itself. The perception is increasingly manipulated by mass media, and consequently dramatically exposed to aesthetic processes. The mediated world is an envisioned world, modelled and manipulated along aesthetic lines, a lightweight world, light-hearted and inconsequential; that it should be serious and logically convincing is secondary and ultimately dispensable. Available electronically at the tap of a button or click of a mouse, such a reality can be entered and left, deleted and repeated at will. By the same token it has relinquished the sphere of the real: it has been de-realized. Its correlative is the virtual world of 3D simulation and animation, chat-room communication and Google Earth, where one can travel as one will, scrutinize the topography of the remotest township, and make virtual friends 24/7.

The eidetic quality of this media-world harbours a vast desensitizing (or anaesthetic) potential, as Welsch explains in the following terms:

> 'In its rise to the status of an all-comprehending reality the media world of images fosters – if only because of its ease of access and universal availability – the gradual transformation of the consumer into a monad, in the sense of an individual filled with images but lacking any window [on the outside world].' (Welsch 1995, p. 15)

These and other footprints have been so stamped into our environments as to condition our lives at an existential level. Their unmitigated impact and destructive potential call for communication and discussion at all levels.

Communicating environmental issues

In the climate of widespread anaesthesia brought about by techno-economics and the media, artists increasingly feel the need to focus on society and its issues. They react to their environment by dedicating themselves to its critical mediation, not just reflecting the visible, but revealing its hidden implications, sensitizing a comatose society. As environmental conservationists and whistle-blowers they are effective when their language is powerful and original, when mood is crafted into a finely modulated message. But this requires a distance that is not always evident, especially where technology is concerned; and in such cases the language of art can easily be instrumentalised.

Scientists, too, necessarily seek contact with society. The more they assume the role of maker (*poietes*), the more crucial does their communicative function become, for the success of their products is built on social acceptance. But behind this newfound openness the hand (however veiled) of industry is all too easy to discern.

Science as communicator: the example of agriculture

Contemporary science has opened discussion on its topics to society, seeking to communicate the inherent fascination of its solutions to a wider public, and depending for its justification on society's perception of its role. As Wolfgang Welsch already put it in the 1980s:

> 'Science today is no longer taken as the single unquestioned benchmark of truth but as a means, useful and dangerous in equal measure, of shaping the world around us one means among many, possessing no monopoly.' (Welsch 1986, p. 128)

Scientists thus feel a duty towards the environment that includes the correction of earlier mistakes. But there is an inevitable ambivalence here: because of their interdependence with technology, scientists run the risk to cause further, long-term, possibly irreversible environmental changes. Agriculture demonstrates this par excellence.

The two basic positions of modern agricultural planning, agro-technology and organic farming, stand in diametrical opposition. Both have the backing of science, advertised not only in specialist publications but in politics and the media at all levels. Persuasive arguments and emotive proclamations invite the belief and commitment of society to one or other of these competing perspectives. Agricultural giants like Monsanto declare: 'We apply innovation and technology to help farmers around the world produce more while conserving more', and Syngenta's strategic goal of 'bringing plant potential to life' has the same impeccably ethical ring about it. Both companies cite leading scientists like Norman Ernest Borlaug, the initiator of the so-called 'green revolution' in the developing countries, who was awarded the Nobel Peace Prize in 1970 for his work on improving third-world agriculture. Today Borlaug sees agro-genetic technology as the most appropriate instrument for raising agricultural yields and fighting malnutrition. Organic farming, for him, is no solution: 'Mother Nature is a genetic engineer – merely one who has taken thousands of years for her crossbreeding' (Borlaug cited in Miersch, 2007). After ten years commercial planting of genetically modified seed there has not been a single proven case of damage – an astonishing safety record, especially for a new technology. Asked about the environmental risks of such procedures, Borlaug's comment was 'More paranoia, more searching for a perfect, risk-free world – absolute nonsense' (ibid.). The potential of agrotechnology, on the other hand, was immense:

> 'The next generation of genetically modified plants will have improved nutritive value, for example less cholesterol, more minerals and vitamins. These plants are on the verge of commercial application.

> Next will come plants that cope better with climatic stress, including global warming. That means resistance to heat and cold, salinity and drought. [...] If we manage to develop types like that, it will be a massive breakthrough, certainly a huge success.' (ibid.)

The 2008 *International Assessment of Agricultural Knowledge, Science and Technology for Development* (IAASTD) tells a very different story. Whilst it agrees that agricultural production must be stepped up and sustained at higher levels, its critique of industrial farming – and with it of agro-genetic technology – is devastating. The received model of high chemicals and energy inputs is no longer viable. It must be replaced with local, indigenous knowledge, high diversity, and a research focus on the small farmer and organic methods. More clearly than ever before the report emphasizes that agriculture is not a production system like any other, but one whose functions are equally important for nature and society. Which of these two scenarios will win? According to Mahler, '[t]he winner in international competition will be the one who can obtain informed public consent without delaying its industrial development plans' (Mahler cited in Dickson, 1987).

Art as communicator: the fascination of the techno-artefact

Two factors disturb the resonance of scientific messages to society: the abstract quality of scientific language and content, as well as an ingrained distrust of technological practice. These obstacles can be overcome by art. Derrick de Kerckhove, for instance, sees an important function of art as bridging the divide between technology and psychology: 'By lifting our perceptions to new levels [art] prepares us for the encounter with the new situations created by our own technological development' (1993, p. 137). Seen through the mirror of art, science takes on a more convincing human dimension, becomes more readily accessible, and can make its entrée into other areas of culture[3]. The motives for scientists in cooperating with artists lie, therefore, not only in the enhanced communicative potential but also in the legitimation art lends to their research. A prominent example is genetic technology, which has nourished the movements of biotech art, bio-art and transgenic art.

In 1999 the journal *Nature Biotechnology* carried an unsigned review of Ars Electronica, which in that year was devoted to the life sciences. Under the heading 'A Green Light for Debate' the writer argued that

> 'Art enters the debate as a third party. It is neither a moderator, nor an arbitrator, but a provider of a fresh perspective. It is capable of presenting with clarity that which entrenched parties find difficult to articulate.' (*Nature Biotechnology*, 1999)

It is, then, no coincidence that biotech art came on the scene precisely when genetic technology was being hotly discussed in social and ecological contexts and corporate money was available to fund its exhibitions[4] – among them Ars Electronica 1999, sponsored by Novartis, the Swiss pharmaceuticals provider. Some exponents of biotech art are Joe Davis (one of its founders), Stelarc, the Critical Art Ensemble, Eduardo Kac, and the Tissue Culture & Art Project (TC&A) run by Ionat Zurr and Oron Catts, who manipulate the growth of cell tissue, both animal and human[5], with a view to creatively disrupting received concepts of life and attitudes to its wealth of forms:

> 'As artists, we believe that our role is to reveal inconsistencies in regard to our current attitudes to life and to focus attention on the discrepancies between our western cultural perceptions and the new technoscientific understandings about life. This analysis cannot be separated from the current socio-economic and ideological contexts that govern western society.' (Zurr & Catts, p. 200)

The Brazilian Eduardo Kac[6] attracted a great deal of attention with his controversial *GFP Bunny*, a transgenic artwork involving a rabbit implanted with the GFP (green fluorescent protein) gene of a jellyfish, which fluoresced when exposed to blue light. Kac intended to return his rabbit 'Alba' to normal social life, in order to determine how genetically modified and natural creatures interact. Further actions of his include *The Eighth Day*, in which he investigated the ecological interface of GFP-treated plants, amoebae, fish and mice and a so-called biobot, a robot with an inbuilt biological element. Most recently his *Natural History of the Enigma* involves the production of a new hybrid plant, a cross between himself and a petunia. Called Edunia, it contains a gene that in its original setting is responsible for the identification of foreign bodies.

As these examples show, biotechnology has become an inexhaustible playing-field for artistic fantasy. The positions taken by artists are various: whilst TC&A maintains critical distance, Kac's empathy with genetic engineering is manifest. And even if most of the artists involved are somehow critical, their decision to use biotech processes demonstrates a certain affinity with the subject. The hybrid video tracks, curators of Berlin's 2005 *put on your blue genes* exhibition about biotech art, write in the foreword of the catalogue:

> '[...] for criticism, too, often functions at the same time as a call to accept the results of genetic research and to discuss the possible dangers of some new bio-regime, in which human biographies might be determined by genetic analysis, until the spectre has lost its power to threaten.' (NGBK 2005, p. 7).

In technology and products biotech artists are drawn closely into the Orbit of molecular biology and biotechnology, and their artistic goal of fostering a change of consciousness serves to communicate the nature and purposes of those sciences. But – possibly unintentionally – they build a bridge of societal acceptance in areas where technology is acutely disputed. Like the scientists who inspire them, biotech artists are liable at times to neglect considerations of safety and even ethics in the name (in their case) of artistic freedom.

In an ironic comment on the fruits of artistic and scientific freedom the Belgian artist Wim Delvoye created an installation with the Latin name *Cloaca* (= sewer). A machine that converted food into 'human' excrement, *Cloaca* was conceived for optical, acoustic and olfactory perception – in which latter dimension it is reported to have been most convincing:

> 'The installation's comment on the faith in technical feasibility displayed in media art, in bio-engineering, and in so-called biotech art, is as caustic as it is olfactory. At the same time, the installation is plausible in its technically meticulous implementation.' (Arns 2008, p. 42)

Thus Inke Arns, commenting on Delvoye's work.

Art liberated to explore and communicate the environment

What Delvoye targets in *Cloaca* is comprehensively laid bare in other works. From surface to deep structure, environments of every sort are analyzed and communicated – so much so that one can speak of a veritable research boom in art, paralleling that of science, for the space in which an artist can act is large and artistic perceptions correspondingly multifarious. The most interesting results are in areas of fuzzy focus where thought and reflection are stimulated not only to retrieve what has been lost in the (anaesthetic) encroachments of social aestheticism, but also to reveal the contradictions inherent in our culture. The following examples illustrate attitudes ranging from irony to serious commitment:

> 'The Mexican artist Santiago Sierra expresses the global predicament of low-paid labourers under neo-liberal regimes. His 1999 performance *24 Concrete Blocks moved continuously during one working period by ten remunerated workers* presents the harsh reality of exploitation in contrast to the aesthetically cushioned experience of its first world viewers. Two-ton blocks of concrete were moved from one room to another of the Ace Gallery in Los Angeles by labourers of Central American descent during the course of a whole working day, at the end of which the artist paid them an extremely low wage.' (Schneider, 2004).

Tavares Strachan from the Bahamas cut a four-and-a-half ton block of ice from a frozen Arctic river and transported it in a special container to Nassau, where he exhibited it in an open-air glass case cooled by solar energy. The transformation of water from a fluid to a solid state was intended to symbolize the impact of globalizing technology on the autochthonous culture of the Bahamas. Brought from a distant clime, the ice-block had to be artificially sustained in its subtropical location if it was not to revert instantly to water (Shenken 2009, p. 76).

Assuming the role of the field researcher, the Austrian Gerald Nestler has been invading the viral systems of the global economy like an antiviral agent since the 1990s and reporting his findings in art:

> 'I enter the structure in order to see from the inside how it functions on the outside, how one can act in this system, what one can start from there. A viral sequencing, so to speak. [...] I'd suggest the word "econociety" for the situation in which society, politics and the individual are subjected to the paradigm of economic parameters.' (Nestler cited in Buchhart 2009, p. 297)

Mark Dion questions the authoritarian role of science in society and uses his art to argue that 'nature is one of the most sophisticated arenas for the production of ideology' (Dion cited in Kwon 1997, p. 9). In his *A Yard of Jungle*, presented to coincide with the 1992 Earth Summit in Rio de Janeiro, he slipped into the role of the eco-politician, transporting a piece of Amazonian rain forest into the art gallery and analyzing it in one of the exhibition rooms in order to reveal its invisible micro-fauna. The point of the performance was to demonstrate the need to protect nature as a whole, including its unseen elements. The Canadian photographer Edward Burtynsky focuses on the impact of industry on nature (see Colour plate ii, Fig. A):

> 'These images are meant as metaphors to the dilemma of our modern existence; they search for a dialogue

> between attraction and repulsion, seduction and fear. We are drawn by desire – a chance at good living, yet we are consciously or unconsciously aware that the world is suffering for our success. Our dependence on nature to provide the materials for our consumption and our concern for the health of our planet sets us into an uneasy contradiction. For me, these images function as reflecting pools of our times.' (Burtynsky 2009)

Hermann Josef Hack, a pupil of Joseph Beuys sees the ozone hole as a global sculpture on which we are all working (Althöfer 2000). For the Swiss artist George Steinmann the question of the responsibility of art for society and the environment is of central importance. He sees 'art as a form of knowing on a par with the natural sciences and the economy', and argues that it represents 'a chance [to attain] a culture of sustainability' (Steinmann cited in Fiedler 2006, 46). Over some of his drawings and photographs he places a wash of bilberry juice as a metaphor for a holistic, differentiated vision. The bilberry is a traditional therapeutic plant whose berries contain myrtillin, a colouring agent that enhances visual clarity (see Colour plate ii, Fig. B).

The 'landscape artist' Robert Smithson employed an ecological rhetoric to communicate environments. His 1970 sketch *Floating Island to Travel Around Manhattan Island*[7] depicts a barge bearing the indigenous rocks, trees and paths of Manhattan being tugged down the Hudson River as if on a sightseeing tour round its original habitat – a tiny relic of a once-natural landscape set off against the skyscrapers of New York City (see Colour plate iii, Fig. C).

Climate change: the world as laboratory or as studio?

Our own habitat, even when extended through virtual worlds, is not infinite and its path is not arbitrarily variable. In at least two directions, the socio-economic and the ecological, its growth is bounded. In 2003 the French sociologist of science Bruno Latour ironically remarked that we have left the epoch of science behind and entered that of the global experiment, generating a world wide lab. But whilst we know how to conduct an experiment in the controlled conditions of a laboratory, we are entirely ignorant about what might happen when the experiment becomes a collective cultural action on a global scale. Today we are certain of one thing only: the world-wide-lab is threatened from without by imminent climatic change. Latour describes this in the following terms:

> 'Of course, nothing is more 'global' than global warming, which seems to be eroding the very planet from the outside. The key question of global warming demonstrates the fact that experiments are now taking place on a life size scale and in real time. To be sure, many simulations and complex models are being tried out on huge computers, but the real experiment is happening to us, through the action of each of us, with all the oceans, high atmosphere and even the Gulf stream – as some oceanographers argue – participating. The only way to find out if global warming is indeed due to anthropic activity is to see what happens if we try to eliminate noxious emissions. This is indeed an experiment in which we are all involved'. (Latour 2003, p. 32)

Whether we are a key factor in the global climatic experiment or not, the experiment goes on, affecting and challenging us all, whether scientists or artists, national societies, global society, or just individuals. Scientists seek sustainable solutions, climate researchers collect data and construct models, environmental politicians push through measures to protect the planet, whilst artists are eager to express political and scientific issues in the language of art. Art is independent of rules and norms and can simplify complex contexts, emphasizing certain aspects for the sake of impact and employing the emotions to heighten perception. The harnessing of art as translator of political and scientific ideas has undoubtedly contributed to the shift of environmental and climatic concern from a narrowly ecological to a societal forum[8]. Artists feel both able and obligated to be among the leaders in the move towards a sustainable society.

The art spectrum ranges from work with a clear didactic intention, through dangerously oversimplified popularizations of science, to subtle multi-faceted expressions of mood and response. Some artists take up political positions[9], carefully researching and provocatively revealing the economic interests and forces behind climatic issues, with the aim of stimulating their viewers into action. Others see their role in the transfer and communication of scientific research: whilst their 'studio' is the lab, their methods and solutions are their own[10].

Art has a unique ability to shape moods into a form that works powerfully on human perceptions. The Danish-Icelandic artist Olafur Eliasson has shown this in his explorations and interpretations of familiar situations and objects (see Colour plate iii, Fig. D). Eliasson sees art as a language that is

> '[...] not exclusive and [...] not only usable within a closed art sphere. In itself, the artistic language doesn't say much, but as soon as it is deployed in a specific context, it has the potential to become very important. Basically, the quality of the language depends on what you want to say. For this reason, art can easily engage in a dialogue with car design and environmental issues, with science or with fashion, to name but a few. As such, there is no area with which art can not interact. And in this interaction, it can contribute with new ideas and questions.' (Eliasson 2007)

Moving between art, science and design, Eliasson has demonstrated his ability to use his chosen language in many different contexts, including that of climate change. His installation *Your mobile expectations – BMW H2R project* was calculated to incite astonishment. Eliasson had been offered a BMW hydrogen-cell racing car (which had just broken the speed record for such vehicles) in the run-up to the 16th BMW Art Car Project in 2007. Removing the streamlined silver laminated carbon fibre bodywork and replacing this with a delicate coat of steel mesh garnished with small metal plates, he laid bare the technical world of the vehicle's interior. He then inundated the whole construct over a period of several days with 985 litres of water and chilled it to form a network of ice. The result was a profound and expressive transformation of one of society's most cherished objects, the automobile. Eliasson created an aesthetically charged mood inviting reflection at many levels, one of which, for him, was intimately concerned with responsibility:

> 'Just as we need to transform our idea of the car, we also need to transform the language that we use to talk about cars. As unstable object, the car always echoes other situations, other uses, expectations and memories. A friend of mine has suggested the term "echo object". Looking at the car as an echo object, we can see and think and hear it resonating

> with ideas that come from design, economy and the development of our society; from environmental movements, politics and discussions of how to act responsibly; from our urban everyday situations. The car is a complex echo object in the midst of all these networks of questions. When we view it as such, it gives us much more than if we consider it merely as an object within a particular discipline.'

From which he concludes:

> 'What I find so interesting in this research on movement and environmentally sustainable energy is the fact that it enhances our sense of responsibility regarding how we navigate as individuals in our shared, complex and polyphonic world.' (Eliasson 2007)

The German artist Hermann Josef Hack has recently claimed that '[o]nly art will stop climate change' (Hack 2009). The awareness of responsibility alone is not enough: the artist must create an environment in which each individual will awaken from the condition of anaesthesia, where the senses are activated and people finally realize that sensibility and creativity must replace consumerism.

When this is reached, then we may begin to move out of the epoch of experiment into that of art. The climate experiment will have become a work of art.

Transdiscourse towards a future environment

Traditional science has brought us an ever more sophisticated techno-world, but one in which homo sapiens has collectively considered its tools to set it above the environment. Rather than inhabiting it as an integral and subordinate part, it has corrected and adapted the environment to its purposes; and the environment, in return, has became ever more obtrusive and confined. Only recently have we begun to suffer acutely from the destructive results of our actions and attitudes. But the task is now clear enough: it is a matter, as Gernot Böhme put it in 1989, of 'men and women coming to terms with themselves in [their] environments' (Sich-Befinden des Menschen in Umgebungen). Yet the inertia of established behaviour is hard to break.

Scientists are well aware of the little room to manoeuvre that still remains, and they make every effort to revise their concepts and strategies to cope with this situation. It is not a matter of dispensing with technology – for there can be no way back to an inviolate nature – but of embedding technology within the concept of a sustainable society, and developing new ideas and designs for a human habitat on this planet. On its own, however, science cannot break free from the complex network of received and established structures and thought patterns. The crises of the present are interlinked. The ecological crisis is neither conceptually nor politically separable from that of humankind as a whole, and cannot be solved in isolation. Without cooperation with the humanities and the social sciences, all the inventions, innovations and sustainable concepts of science and engineering will be incapable of overcoming the crisis.

Nor can art be left out of the equation. After a long period of indifference and isolation its growing commitment to the actual human predicament is manifest. Art explores and expresses the world in its myriad environments. But to what extent can it serve as a pattern for science? To what extent can it have a constructive effect on the world? Is art not also lost in the maelstrom of a techno-economic society? Can art show modern women and men an alternative way?

Such questions must still be answered. Gernot Böhme sees art as the place where the senses are returned to humanity (Böhme 1989/1995). And he doesn't mean the senses merely as faculties of perception geared to gathering data in a material world, but as the sum of the affective, emotional.

Notes

1 The following observations are concerned with the natural sciences and the fine arts.

2 Whether or not there was real progress in either art or science during this period is a matter of dispute. Already at the end of the 19th century the Viennese art historian Alois Riegl (1927) had ruled out the idea of progress in art: styles change, but art does not progress in any quantitative sense. Paul Feyerabend (1984) saw the sciences as comparable with the arts in this respect; here, too, there was no objectively ascertainable progress.

3 Art and science are everywhere approximating: studios are turning into laboratories, art is drawing on science for its themes. Examples can be found in biotechnology, artificial intelligence, robotics and the neurosciences.

4 For example: Ars Electronica 1999-2001 in Linz; Paradise Now, Picturing the Genetic Revolution 2000 in New York; Gene(sis), Contemporary Art Explores Human Genomics 2001 in Seattle; the European Media Art Festival 2003 in Osnabrück; put on your blue genes in Berlin.

5 See artists' website at <http://www.tca.uwa.edu.au>, accessed June 30, 2009.

6 See artist's website at <http://www.ekac.org>, accessed June 30, 2009.

7 Smithson's project was only realized in 2005: see <http://www.haberarts.com/smithson>.

8 For example, the film *An inconvenient truth*, numerous exhibitions, and projects such as *Canary Project* <http://www.canary-project.org> or *Cape Farewell* <http://www.capefarewell.com>. Launched in 2001 by the British artist David Buckland, *Cape Farewell* has taken artists, educationalists and media people together with scientists on 7 different expeditions to the Arctic between 2003 and the present. The project aims to convey climate issues at emotional and educational as well as scientific levels. Art originating from the experience has been exhibited widely in Europe, North America and Japan. In 2005 a 60-minute film on the project was made with the BBC, and in 2006 a book was published containing essays and statements by scientists and artists.

9 For example, Mitch Epstein with his photographic series *American Power* <http://www.mitchepstein.net/>, or Amy Balkin with *Public smog* <http://www.publicsmog.org>.

10 For example, Peter Fend, *Ocean Earth*, 1994; Andrea Polli <http://www.andreapolli.com/>.

References

Althöfer, H 2000, *Kunst und Umwelt – Umwelt und Kunst*, Peter Lang, Frankfurt/M.

Arns, I 2008, 'On contemporaneity: The media arts in the age of their postmedium condition', in *Media Arts Zurich: 13 Positions from the New Media Program, Yearbook 3*, Zurich University of the Arts, Scheidegger & Spiess, Zurich, pp. 41–61.

Böhme, G 1989, *Für eine ökologische Naturästhetik*, Suhrkamp, Frankfurt/M.

Böhme, G 1995, Atmosphäre: *Essays zur neuen Ästhetik*, Suhrkamp, Frankfurt/M.

Burtynsky, E, *Edward Burtynsky: Photographic works*, website, accessed 30 June 2009, <http://www.edwardburtynsky.com/>.

de Kerckhove, D 1993, 'Touch versus vision: Ästhetik neuer Technologien', in W Welsch (ed.), *Die Aktualität des Ästhetischen*, Fink, Munich, pp. 137–168.

Dickson, D 1987, 'Europe splits over gene regulation', *Science*, vol. 238, no. 4823, pp. 18–19.

Dion, M 1997, 'Miwon Kwon in conversation with Mark Dion', in LG Corrin, M Kwon, & N Bryson, *Mark Dion*, Phaidon, London, pp. 7–33.

Eliasson, O 2008, *Your mobile expectations: BMW H_2R project*, Lars Müller, Baden.

Feyerabend, P 1984, *Wissenschaft als Kunst*, Suhrkamp, Frankfurt/M.

Hack, HJ, *Hermann Josef Hack*, website, accessed 30 June 2009, <http://www.hermann-josef-hack.de>.

Hodgson, J 1999, 'A green light for debate', *Nature Biotechnology*, vol. 17, no. 10, p. 933.

IAASTD 2008, *Summary for decision makers of the global report*, accessed 30 June 2009, <http://www.agassessment.org>.

Latour, B 2003, 'Atmosphère, atmosphère', in S May (ed.), *Olafur Eliasson: The weather project*, Tate Publishing, London, pp. 29–41.

Lévy-Leblond, J-M 2004, 'Die Wissenschaft und die Welt, die Kunst und ich', *FTE Info: Magazin über Europäische Forschung* (special issue), accessed 30 June 2009, <http://ec.europa.eu/research/rtdinfo/special_as/article_811_de.html>.

Lyotard, J-F 1993, 'Anima Minima', in W Welsch (ed.), *Die Aktualität des Ästhetischen*, Fink, Munich, pp. 417–427.

Miersch, M 2009, 'Agrarwissenschaftler Norman Borlaug: Mutter Natur ist Gentechnikerin', *Weltwoche*, no. 41, 10 October, accessed 30 June 2009, <http://www.weltwoche.ch/ausgaben/2007-41/artikel-2007-41-mutter-natur-ist-gentechnikerin.html>.

Nestler, G 2009, 'Der Mensch als Derivat', interview with Gerald Nestler, by Dieter Buchhart, *Kunstforum*, no. 197, pp. 296-309,

Put on your blue genes: BioTech-Kunst und die Verheissungen der Biotechnologie, 2005, (exhib. cat.), Neue Gesellschaft für bildende Kunst (NGBK), Berlin.

Riegl, A 1973, *Spätrömische Kunstindustrie*. 2nd ed., Austrian State Printing Office, Vienna.

Schneider, E (ed.) 2004, *Santiago Sierra: 300 tons and previous works*, (exhib. cat.), Kunsthaus Bregenz, Walther König, Cologne.

Shanken, E A (ed.) 2009 *Art and electronic media*, Phaidon Press, London.

Steinmann, G 2006, 'Kunst als gesellschaftsbezogene Praxis'. Interview with George Steinmann, by Andreas Fiedler. In: *Prix Meret Oppenheim 2001–2002*: Interviews, Bundesamt für Kultur, Bern, pp. 35–71.

von Drahten, D 1993, 'Welteinheit: Traum oder Wirklichkeit: eine Überlebungsfrage', in F Meschede, (ed.), *Marina Abramović*, Edition Cantz, Ostfildern-Ruit, pp. 205–224.

Welsch, W 1986, 'Kunst und Wissenschaft', *Kunstforum*, no. 185, pp. 124–129.

Welsch, W 1993, 'Das Ästhetische: eine Schlüsselkategorie unserer Zeit?', in W Welsch, (ed.), *Die Aktualität des Ästhetischen*, Fink, Munich, pp. 13–47.

Welsch, W 1995, *Ästhetisches Denken*, 4th ed. Reclam, Stuttgart, p. 15.

Zurr, I & Catts, O 2003-2004, 'The ethical claims of bioart: killing the other or self-cannibalism?', *Australian and New Zealand Journal of Art: Art & Ethics* vol. 4, no. 2, and vol. 5, no. 1, pp. 167–188, accessed 30 June 2009, <http://www.tca.uwa.edu.au/atGlance/pubMainFrames.html>.

BEYOND ECO-ART: 21ST CENTURY ECO-VISUALISATION

Tiffany Holmes

Eco-visualisations – artworks that translate ecological data into easy-to-understand images and sound – expand the trajectory of the environmental art arena. Eco-visualisation artwork promotes sustainability through a shared experience of a real time 'happening' that is controlled by a computer or associated electronic technology – as opposed to organic materials like liverworts that filter water in Jackie Brookner's recent biosculptures. Much of this eco-visualisation work is quite new – and so far there are very few examples. Due to technical complexities, some installations remain permanently in the prototyping stage. Conceptually, the work is quite strong due to the innovative exploration of new educational strategies made possible by increasingly accessible media forms such as computer algorithms and large publicly accessible databases. Overall, the eco-visualisation projects incorporate a message of positive environmental stewardship as a primary focus – often through display in a public place to facilitate community dialogue. But do the viewers receive and process the message? This is a point to debate.

Overview: From Eco-art to Eco-visualisation

Land art, earthworks, and environmental art made prior to 2005 constitute an impressive lineage of creative activity that provided evidence that artistic interventions, particularly when made in public space, can have a beneficial societal effect and also raise public awareness about ecological issues. Art historians like Grant Kester have suggested that artists – as opposed to engineers or scientists – might possess unique abilities to visualise and halt the effects of environmental degradation (Kester, 2004, p.66).

This paper concerns itself with this primary question in terms of how it relates to contemporary art and design: Can visualisation projects that use dynamic feedback trigger ecologically responsible behaviour such as energy conservation? To consider this question, new works from several artists and designers who visually translate energy data via dynamic feedback for the purpose of promoting stewardship will be assessed using the following criteria:

- Did the artwork increase conservation behaviour in the viewing population? How was this accomplished, and for how long?
- What forms of visualisation are most effective to aiding conservation of resources?
- What are the aesthetics of 21st century *eco-visualisation*? Do particular kinds of aesthetics inspire greater amounts of conservation action or knowledge?

Contemporary art and design that integrate dynamic feedback related to electricity usage will be the focus in the sections to follow. To reiterate, the selected creative endeavours break new ground conceptually and also in their material execution. These projects have not been critiqued in academic journals, nor in art magazines, much less published in books. It is the combination of innovative concepts, state-of-the-art technology, and contemporary visualisation aesthetics that make all of these projects target environmental problems in a completely novel way. These projects extend the history of eco-art into the 21st century, so there is a strong connection to the past. However, the contemporary works like HeHe's *Nuage vert* (2008) offer new knowledge about how public art can impact a community's ability to engage in site-based learning (Goal 1), conserve resources (Goal 2), or establish new dialogues about resource conservation (Goal 3). In addition, hybrid art-design project like STATIC's 'smart' household decor, DIY Kyoto's *Wattson*, and Ambient Devices' *Energy Orb* offer local citizens and organizations the opportunity to personally regulate and control their own resource consumption. STATIC, DIY Kyoto, and Ambient Devices focus on introducing custom objects into the home or work space that offer dynamic information feedback at a glance. All of the projects described here do not presume to offer a universal solution to the problem of over-consumption, but rather, to explore art and design as a means of promoting varied forms of environmental stewardship.

Nuage vert: The cloud that counted kilowatts

Nuage vert was a city-scale light installation produced by the collaborative HeHe composed of artists Helen Evans and Heiko Hansen and Pixelache. (see Colour plate iv, Fig. A). Every night from the 22nd to the 29th of February 2008, the vapour emissions from the Salmisaari coal burning power plant were illuminated with a high power green laser animation. The animation drawn with the laser corresponded in real time to how much electricity was being used by the city residents. If the green cloud shape was very large, the energy consumption citywide was reduced. If the green cloud was small in area the electricity loads in Ruoholahti were presumably quite high (see Colour plate v, Fig. B). Viewers were expected to work collectively to unplug devices in their homes to increase the size and scope of the green cloud hovering above the smokestack.

How effective was the *Nuage vert* project, and how many people got to see it or be influenced by it? The project got an enormous amount of media coverage: all the local newspapers, the citywide press, national radio and regional TV news featured the project prominently (Evans 2008). For roughly 574,000 residents of Helsinki, this media coverage must have been significant. The Ruoholahti district is located in the south-western part of the central city area of Helsinki, close to the Lauttasaari Island, and it functions as the principal connection between the Helsinki city centre and the city of Espoo to the west. In an effort to mediate messages for *Nuage vert*, the artists developed a communications platform that employed an iconic language designed by Devalence, a Parisian design group. Working with local cultural management students, slogans were created for flyers and posters, such as: 'Aurora borealis in Helsinki?' With Dodo, a Finnish environmental activist group, *Nuage vert* was presented and discussed with 240 local school children, between the ages of seven and sixteen. Local community groups distributed posters. A custom-designed sticker for electrical outlets asking people to *Unplug!* was distributed to 4000 households. Although the above-described communication strategy focused on activating Ruoholahti residents, the greening of the cloud was visible beyond the boundary of the neighbourhood, over 10 km away (Evans 2008).

In addition to the masses of Helsinki residents who saw the public work, there was a body of people who normally were not connected with the art world who were perhaps overwhelmingly affected by the piece. The glowing cloud was the product of a four-year intensive collaboration that began in France. Initially HeHe tried to orchestrate the piece in Paris but met resistance. The artist duo patiently initiated and ultimately negotiated the right to exhibit the public artwork in Ruoholahti with support from the following organizations: the laser physics department at Helsinki Technical University, the computer science department at the University of Illinois, as well as a medical laser manufacturer, and the power plant itself, Helsinki Energy. The sheer number of co-sponsoring organizations outside of the traditional art world was impressive and given the technical challenge, the support of each was vital to the project's success. Also, these diverse groups from culture, science, industry, communication and ecology would not ordinarily work together – the artists were the linking factor. Given the number of persons involved, the project most likely deeply impacted each of the collaborators and facilitators and their families. Although not quantifiable, this opportunity to work on a community project with high visibility must have influenced each team member's opinions about electricity conservation and the ability of public art to bring these conservation issues to 'light', literally.

Overall, the *Nuage vert* project is the most exciting public art project to date that utilized dynamic feedback to inspire a local population to conserve electricity. As mentioned previously, *Nuage vert* most likely influenced a great number of persons who live in the Helsinki area because of the extensive media platform and the spectacle of the green cloud viewable from ten kilometres away. The project thus can boast positive influence more in the category of awareness raising via a visual spectacle than in measurable effectiveness in lowering power consumption. In addition, *Nuage vert* has won a number of prestigious art prizes:

the Ars Electronica Golden Nica (Austria) and the 01SJ Green Prix for Environmental Art (USA). In a sense, these awards are a direct indication of the project's immense influence and esteemed quality but the awards do not convey any information about the cloud's effectiveness, or the ability to encourage and foster greater energy conservation. Perhaps more significantly, the power plant, Helsingin Energia and a local artist's collective, Pixelache are collaborating to produce future artworks related to collective energy consumption in Helsinki area (Pixelache 2010) following the success and positive reception of *Nuage vert*. The fact that the power plant and Finnish artist would be willing to work together to create open-ended creative projects that highlight energy consumption is confirmation that art can indeed shape public opinion about conservation issues. Yet because the green cloud was directly linked to the output of the power plant, there is some real quantitative proof that this public art has a proven record of encouraging energy conservation. As described previously in conjunction with the marketing platform, HeHe facilitated an 'unplug' event in Helsinki, on the evening of Friday the 29th of February. Between 7 and 8pm Finnish time, 4000 local residents reduced their energy consumption by 800 kilovolt-amperes (kVA) (Evans 2008). This is roughly the equivalent of the power generated by one windmill running for one hour. This collective attempt to conserve – admittedly for a very short period of time – represents the great potential of *eco-visualisation* to help the general public conserve and witness the collective power usage dynamically by watching the green cloud grow as power demand decreased.

The *Nuage vert* project marks the very first time that an invisible digital infrastructure measuring local electricity consumption had been made public and visible via an *eco-visualisation* for a radius of ten kilometres. Incredibly, despite the current energy crisis and the ever-increasing demand, energy flows freely. Electricity is monitored in most countries on an individual basis via a meter locked up in a boiler room or basement. The encouraging outcome of HeHe's 'unplug' event speaks to the myriad future possibilities for urban planners and private business interests to make ecologically relevant data and networked information available in a public forum – perhaps through *eco-visualisation*. Giving a literal green outline to the relationships between power companies and those that consume their services could lead to the creation of a new form of pro-active citizenry and the aesthetic and potentially moral transformation of an urban community.

The green laser performance must have been dramatic for the residents of Ruoholahti all of whom were accustomed to viewing the white steam pouring from the power plant's smokestack. The aesthetic choices here could not be more specific and targeted, though the visual paradigms could confuse those who were not immediately on the scene. *Nuage vert*, translated from the Finnish means 'Green Cloud'. The laser drew an outline of the moving cloud onto the cloud itself, enshrouding the usual white vapour in a vivid green hue (Figure 2). Promotional material distributed by HeHe encouraged residents to 'feed' the green cloud and make it larger by turning off lights and generally not using electricity. In this sense, the larger green cloud was imagined as a potent and benevolent symbol of collective conservation. On the other hand, the acidic green of the larger cloud could make one consider imagery of poisonous, possibly radioactive sorts of noxious vapours, and thus this presumed symbol of sustainability could also be interpreted as a malevolent orb hovering over a guilty populace. In other words, HeHe set up an open ended visualization rubric using real-time data from the power plant. Some viewers might think the larger green cloud was 'good', others might perceive it as 'bad'. The artists stated that they fully intended for both aesthetic readings of the cloud to take place.

> 'As a transmitting architecture, *Nuage vert* conveys multiple ideas: could this green cloud be a toxic cloud or an emblem for the collective effort of the local community? The meaning is left open for each and all to decide, and will depend upon the level of engagement...*Nuage vert* is ambiguous, as it doesn't offer a simple moralistic message, but rather tries to confront the city dweller with an evocative and aesthetic spectacle, which is open to interpretation and challenges ordinary perception.' (Evans 2008)

Perhaps the larger question here is whether it is indeed appropriate for an artist's group to fully aestheticize a power plant without being direct about the message. In other words, does information visualization as art have any potentially negative consequences? The design works to be discussed shortly by DIY Kyoto and Ambient Devices have far more literal interpretations of the data stream. Perhaps HeHe should have worked harder to document the effectiveness of the piece and clarify the meaning conveyed by the green cloud. Helen Evans disagrees 'Must we say the power plant is bad or that it is good? The point is that everyone projects his or her own meanings onto a cloud, no matter what. *Nuage vert* is an art work – it is there to provoke questions, to make people look again and rethink what they are seeing.' HeHe desired an open-ended, non-didactic piece but made a striking spectacle of the power plant, drawing all eyes to its daily production of energy. It was simultaneously gorgeous and shocking. The acidic quality of the light might have subtly communicated an ill feeling, but the majority of the effect was perhaps overly celebratory of the laser display. On the other hand, perhaps the real hidden horror of the piece is in the futility of the practice of conserving energy on specific days with no real duration or sustained conservation effort. Why is energy conservation for an event like HeHe's 'Unplug' potentially meaningful in the short term as a site-based learning event and potentially futile in the long term? Since vast amounts of energy cannot be stored, producers across large geographical regions have to produce precisely the amount of energy that is being consumed, within micro-seconds. In Finland, the energy grid is linked to Norway, Sweden and Denmark, which means that if people in Ruoholahti consume less for a day, there will be no less coal burned at the Salmisaari power plant. However, there would ultimately be less coal burned somewhere within the Nordic Pool at that moment. This is the hopeful point, yet the reality is that the *Nuage vert* installation lasted only a week for a variety of reasons most of which involved acquiring security for the lasers, which were quite energy efficient, requiring only 8 watts of power to illuminate the cloud. It is quite likely that consumption levels went back to normal after the green cloud left the sky. The key point here is that a group of artists collaborated with a rather unlikely entity, a Finnish power plant, to encourage the corporation to make collective energy demand data visible and accessible. Often such aggregated data is viewed as proprietary and held internally with some secrecy. The artists confirm that the power plant 'continues to make this data public, so the experience of *Nuage vert* had a lasting impact on the behaviour of a large public utility.' In the next section, the efforts of three design groups – STATIC, DIY Kyoto, and Ambient Devices – to visually communicate energy usage creatively using colour, image and/or light will be discussed. The products that these design groups are creating are far more gadget-oriented than the more open-ended production of the ever-changing green cloud. Despite the differences between HeHe's art-oriented response to electricity data visualization and the more literal design strategies, it is important to consider all approaches to using easily accessible visual communication strategies as a novel and emerging conservation strategy for the future.

'Power' of the gaze: Smart objects promote energy conservation

STATIC's 'smart' household decor, DIY Kyoto's *Wattson*, and Ambient Device's *Energy Orb* are smart objects with embedded data-harvesting technologies that explore design as a means of promoting increased awareness and to provoke responses and dialogue about environmental issues. Most importantly, all of these objects attempt to communicate data about real time energy consumption to their users in one instant via a simple glance. In most cases, the information is reduced to a memorable colour key. According to David Lewis, psychologist and advisor in aircraft cockpit design, such smart objects can allow humans, already suffering from information overload, to comprehend data quickly and accurately: 'Filtering information in this way makes sense, since trying to process too much information is a source of stress and can lead to mistakes' (Background Illumination 2004). Next, some of the smart objects that visualize energy usage via image and/or colour will be investigated and their effectiveness compared.

STATIC (Sweden)

STATIC is a design research program led by the Interactive Institute in collaboration with Front, and the program was funded by the Swedish Energy Agency 2004-2005. STATIC created a palette of sample prototypes to illustrate the possibilities offered by household objects that deliver dynamic energy feedback. The research approach in the STATIC group has two primary focuses: (1) the idea that the collaborative might work with energy monitoring not only from a technical but also from an aesthetic point of view, and (2) the notion that the prototypes need not only be about utility and ease of use, but also about inspiring critical conversation in the context of use (Backlund et al. 2006). The collaborative makes clear its aim to completely rethink the look and feel of every energy-consuming device in the home:

> 'Consider, for instance, how the "design problem" of providing artificial light using lamps is split between the shaping of things like lampshades and fixtures on one hand and the systems for producing and distributing power on the other. If we do not want to hide energy consumption under "discreet and pleasant surfaces", but instead expose issues such as sustainability as an integral part of an object, we somehow need to make energy itself more present in the design of the thing itself and the design of interacting and living with such things.' (Backlund et al. 2006, pp. 3)

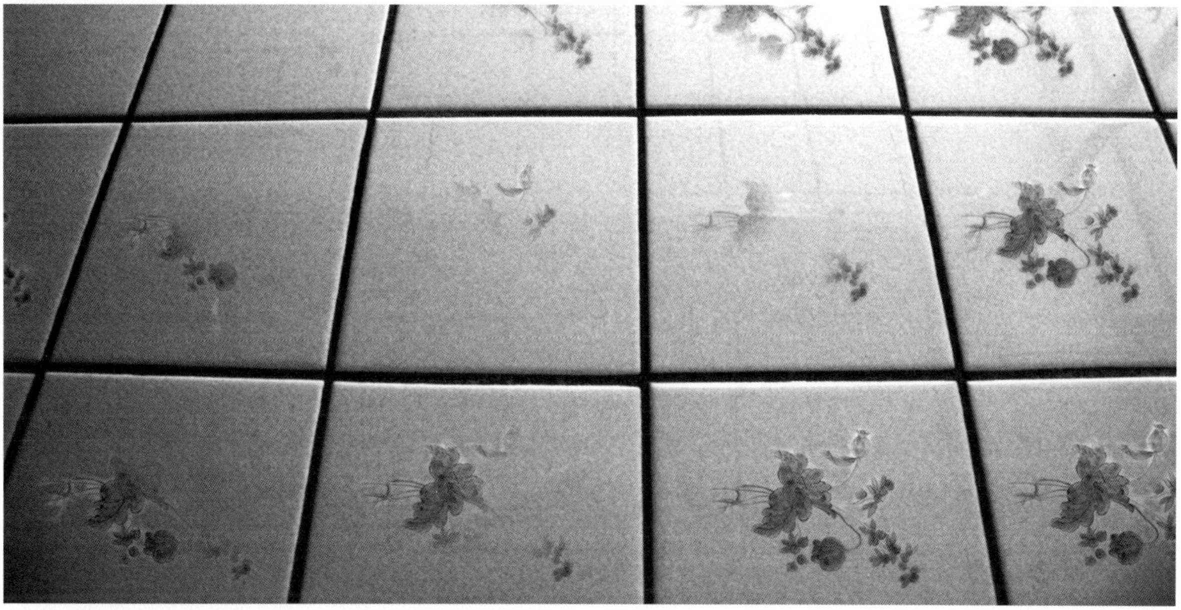

Fig. 1: STATIC, Disappearing Pattern Tiles, prototype, By Front and Interactive Institute. Project Team: Sofia Lagerkvist, Charlotte von der Lancken, Anna Lindgren, Katja Sävström, Photo: Front, 2005

While there are many scientific studies that describe how real time energy monitoring can alter habits of electricity usage via numeric feedback, there are very few precedents for electronic art or design works that give dynamic feedback for energy usage. The capacity of such art works to alter habits of consumption have not been adequately measured and documented. The closest examples of objects that have been designed, but not tested, are STATIC's *Flower Lamp, Disappearing Pattern Tiles*, and the *Power Aware Cord*.

Household light fixtures typically have very basic functionality with respect to energy usage; a lamp is either switched on or off. In the *Flower Lamp* example [see Colour plate vi, Fig D], it is not just the light of the lamp, but its very form that reflects the amount of energy used in the household. The experimental lamp does not show how the precise number of watts are being consumed in real time. Rather, the light fixture displays the overall trends in home energy consumption. If the household decreases its energy usage, the *Flower Lamp* rewards by slowly opening up to 'bloom'. If, on the other hand, energy loads increase over time, the lamp closes shut. Thus the lamp, in both light and form, is reflecting the cycles of local energy use in a subtle and poetic way that makes smaller sacrifices of heat and warm water potentially worthwhile. Thus, a change of behaviour is required if residents are going to see the lamp bloom while present in the home. One might perceive the chosen aesthetics here to be a bit counter-intuitive. The greatest reward, the lamp in full bloom, can occur when no one is at home consuming power.

In terms of basic functionality and unique aesthetics, STATIC's prototype for *Disappearing Pattern Tiles* is by far the most sophisticated and accomplished, and thus perhaps most usable piece.

The project team decorated basic white bathroom tiles with patterns drawn with thermo-chromic ink. This ink reacts to heat, fading away to reflect splashes and various intensities of hot water use (Figure 1). So, the longer a resident lingers in a warm shower the less decoration there is on the wall. The dynamic architectural surface acts as a subtle reminder of personal energy use over time, reflecting the duration and waste of heat energy during a lengthy shower. Unlike the *Flower Lamp*, where positive feedback is an 'estimation' of the reduction of household energy use, the tiles offer direct and consistent feedback with a unique aesthetic: vanishing surface adornment.

STATIC's newly patented *Power Aware Cord* (2005) (see Colour plate vi, Fig. C) is an award-winning prototype of a smart power strip. Power strips are used in nearly every home as a means of safely transporting energy to multiple electronic appliances with basic surge protection. STATIC has retooled the humble power strip and given it a transparent cord made from electroluminescent wire. This wire contains a phosphor layer that glows with an intense blue-green light when an alternating current is introduced. The *Power Aware Cord* also has a cable that glows red if loads increase on the line. Due to the colour of the phosphor, the wire appears to be white when unpowered, a feature that greatly reduces the appearance of the device when no energy is used. It should be noted that one critique of the *Power Aware Cord* is that the device itself consumes electricity in order to create the varied colours. Like HeHe, the STATIC team focuses their efforts on using colour, or non-numerical forms of communication to depict real time energy flows. The creators of the *Power Aware Cord* are presently experimenting with other types of data mapping in addition to colour, specifically pulsing light signals to indicate periods of high power use. Because electrical current is such an abstract concept in and of itself, the team believes that hue and pulsation rates would be good aesthetic metaphors to imagine power usage. The project team states:

> 'Our aim is also that users might perceive the light patterns as the actual electricity in the cord, if not on a direct level then at least on an intuitive and metaphoric level. By this, we mean that people might talk about and refer to the light just as if it would be the electricity itself, even if they on a logical level would realize that it is just a representation.' (Gyllensward & Gustafsson 2005, pp. 1424)

Unfortunately, this product has not been widely tested, only in a study that involved interviews with six households (Löfström 2007) and one earlier analysis. The 2007 investigation concluded that the cord worked to raise awareness and visibility of energy flows but recommendations were made that the cord be used in conjunction with other methods of information distribution to actually increase household conservation. The prototype was not working fully when the 2005 user testing was conducted so the users merely observed different 'states' of the *Power Aware Cord* and the users' ability to interpret the different power levels via hue and pulsation was recorded. No other prototypes have been evaluated at this point. People felt that the static hue with subtle colour shifts was very pleasing to the senses, however most thought the pulsing lights were more informative. The pulsing light at high energy levels were often seen as irritating to the eyes although some felt transfixed by the blinking: 'One person remarked that he felt something being transported when the cord was pulsating compared to when it was shining in a constant level of intensity' (Gyllensward & Gustafsson 2005, pp. 1424). Despite the negative aspect of the pulsing lights, overall, the *Power Aware Cords* with static colours only were considered less informative than those with hue shifts and pulsing flashes – more frequent pulses meant more energy was being used by the cable.

The STATIC group has made real strides in terms of designing prototypes that deliver poetic, yet dynamic aesthetic feedback in the home with regard to how much energy is being used at any given moment – yet there is a real need for further evaluation. Of all of the STATIC projects, *Flower Lamp*, *Disappearing Pattern Tiles*, and the *Power Aware Cord* do this the best. However, the group has not performed comprehensive user testing so it is not possible to quantify precisely how much electricity has been conserved or how many persons have been impacted by the project. Rather, the STATIC group's best contribution to this discussion about the potentials of introducing 'smart' objects into the home is their tremendous creativity in considering how familiar objects such as lamps, tiles, and cords can actually 'talk' about sometimes bothersome numbers, like kilowatts, in an aesthetically appealing and abstract manner.

Wattson/Holmes by DIY Kyoto (UK)

Conceived by Royal College of Art design students, *Wattson* is a portable wireless unit that allows real time reading of electricity use anywhere in the home. The device is sold in the UK via a company aptly titled DIY Kyoto. The interactive device is primarily used in the UK although there is a small user population in Scandinavia. The book-sized console unit is moulded to sit on a table in an upside down 'U' form. (see Colour plate vi, Fig. E) The *Wattson* has an accompanying sensor clip which attaches to either of the main electricity cables leading from the meter box to the fuse box. This cable is also plugged into a transmitter that sends information to the wireless unit. *Wattson* uses light as the primary mode of information transfer. However, there is an LED digital display that additionally shows exactly how much electricity is being consumed in watts or pounds. The aesthetic presentation is as follows. *Wattson* features an ambient light display (also LED) on the underside of the console. When the lights glow blue, energy use is below average. When *Wattson* emits a purple glow, usage levels are approximately average for the household. When the lights are red, more electricity than usual is being used.

Of all of the various objects that have been examined in this chapter, only the *Wattson* has been manufactured with general sustainable design principles in place. The product is constructed without adhesives for easy disassembly and recycling. The white outer and inner casing is constructed from polycarbonate, although polycarbonate may leach bisphenol A (Carwile et al. 2009). The LED display is mounted on the printed circuit board that controls *Wattson's* operation. The product is manufactured locally in Margate, Kent although some components are produced in China. The *Wattson's* packaging is made from lightweight recycled card, and uses inks with minimal environmental impact. The latest version of *Wattson*, *Wattson 01*, uses up to 4W of energy – costing only £4 per year to run. Together with companion software *Holmes*, which offers more detailed analysis of energy use and opportunities for savings, *Wattson 01* can help reduce a typical household electricity bill. *Holmes* offers more densely detailed energy usage maps, while *Wattson* offers the information at a glance that is the topic of this particular section.

DIY Kyoto founders Richard Woods, Greta Corke, and Jon Sawdon Smith claim their customers can save up to 25% on their energy costs. At the moment, there is not any evidence supporting this claim, although the user community is expanding. By making energy-usage information engaging and enjoyable, consumers who paid approximately £149 are generally pleased with the results. User Wendy reports her family's experience with the *Wattson*:

> 'Shortly after getting it we uncovered a fault with a pump which serves a well in the garden – it had become faulty and was constantly on making for extremely high electricity bills. We also stay in quite a large house so it is useful to look at *Wattson* before going out to make sure the children haven't left anything on – I think after a while you get to know what a "normal" reading is for a particular time of the day.' (DIY Kyoto 2009)

The *Wattson* has inspired an entire community of people to compare their energy usage. This is hugely significant. Because the *Wattson* is a household object, the comparisons could go on indefinitely, while projects like HeHe's *Nuage vert* only allowed the community access to energy data for one week. As of January 29, 2009, 301 *Wattson's* were connected and broadcasting live data to the website *Wattson Village*. An average daily usage of 12,817 kilowatt hours (kWH) was reported (DIY Kyoto 2009). Having access to this data additionally enables the 'green-conscious' consumer to see how one's household data stacks up against the reported average. One potential issue with these comparisons is that the household size is not a variable taken into consideration – at some point in the future it would be useful to include this baseline data. As demonstrated by the literature in Chapter 2, social commitment was proved to be very effective in increasing a population's ability to conserve energy. Although *Wattson Village* is comparatively new, as it launched in December of 2008, the potential to inspire a whole group of users to conserve over a longer period of time is enormous, especially if the capacity to compare energy usage among homes of similar size is incorporated.

What might inspire an individual to actually want to compare energy data in a virtual community? Watson Village is part of an enormous wave of social networking software that enables individuals to keep in touch about a whole host of issues. Residents of the *Wattson Village* join perhaps wanting to be a part of a fashionable do-gooder community, and also wanting to compare their household's energy consumption with others. The new online community has much room for improvement based on what exists already in the numerous Web 2.0 communities online:

> 'At this point the *Wattson* ...would benefit from more customization features. The main way users can clearly customize their pages is through the notes section, which is basically a list of comments below the user's energy data. (For example, one user tries to justify his high energy bill by explaining that his house in Finland is freezing and needs to be heated a lot.) The company says it has implemented a tagging feature so that users can point out where they're

> saving money, but I didn't see a lot of people using those features. [...] At this point all of the users have the same white (but cute) anime-style *Wattson* logo; light customization could enable hardcore users to stand out and make the community more sticky.' (Fehrenbacher 2008)

The *Wattson* community is emerging and certainly many more features could make the *Wattson Village* site more enticing: Facebook compatibility, a greater number of users, and some way of not only tracking conservation of energy over time, but also comparing select households' consumption data. DIY Kyoto's *Wattson* has been shown to have great potential to attract a community of long-term conservers, but there is simply not enough evidence at this time to evaluate its effectiveness. The next smart object to be profiled, the *Ambient Energy Orb*, has garnered substantially larger user communities, and also proven to increase levels of energy conservation, perhaps due to its hackable, more open format interface.

Ambient Energy Orb by Pacific Gas and Electric Company (USA)

Ambient Devices, a Cambridge, Massachusetts start-up firm staffed mainly with MIT graduates, introduced the *Energy Orb* as a saleable object in 2004. The *Orb* proved popular out of the box; Ambient sold 20,000 in 2004 (Felberbaum 2004). The web-connected glass balls were programmed to glow different colours based on the performance of the US stock market. If the Dow average was up for the day, the *Orb* glowed green. On a down day, the *Orb* reddened. The colours' intensity reflected the extent of the swing; yellow meant that the stock market was stable. Not surprisingly, a number of *Orb* users wanted to track data other than the stock market via the classy glass balls on their desks. Ambient users have programmed *Orbs* for a remarkable array of tasks: tracking job openings in Atlanta, measuring the flow of visitors to a Boston-based interactive design agency's Web site, gauging energy use in a New York City apartment, tracking eBay auctions, notifying someone when a certain number of e-mails have arrived, and monitoring the amount of electricity used in high demand cycles in California. The idea behind the *Orb* itself came out of the Massachusetts Institute of Technology's Media Lab, where 'Tangible Media' research led by Professor Hiroshi Ishii who promised to replace computers' graphical user interface with tangible representations of the data they produce – giving physical form to information. Ishii and other members of the Tangible Media Group at MIT believed that information gathered in one glance from a visual image can be more memorable than numeric data garnered from a computer screen (Ishii and Ullmer 1997).

In 2006, the *Energy Orb* was released for free to a limited audience: companies that used tremendous amounts of electricity. The goal was to get previously identified 'energy hog' customers to conserve power during high demand cycles. Southern California Edison power station manager Mark Martinez was looking for an innovative way to get these customers to use less energy, and prior attempts using automated text messages, emails and phone calls had no effect whatsoever. So Martinez bought an Ambient *Orb* and the hacking began. Martinez realized he could use the *Orbs* to signal changes in electrical rates, programming them to glow green when the grid was underused – and, thus, electricity cheaper – and red during peak hours when customers were paying more for power. He bought 120 *Orbs*, retrofitted them to glow based on the dynamic California electrical grid, then handed them out for free to his biggest energy consumers, and awaited the results (Thompson 2007).

In about a month, the *Orb* users reduced their peak-period energy use by 40 percent (Thompson 2007). Why? Because, Martinez explains, the glowing sphere was less annoying and more persistent than a text alert. 'It's nonintrusive', he says, 'It has a relatively benign effect. But when you suddenly see your ball flashing red, you notice' (cited in Thompson 2007). Martinez discovered, via the *Orb*, an excellent way to broadcast key environmental information: *eco-visualisation*, or dynamic feedback coupled in this case with a monetary reward, cash rebates. The *Energy Orb* had an easy to read interface that was abstract enough not to require more than a millisecond to comprehend. The PG&E consumers responded well because dynamic feedback can aid conservation efforts, generally because of the ease of receiving the data. 'Cognitive psychologists call this pre-attentive processing', said Ambient Devices President David Rose, 'because it uses a part of your brain that happens before your conscious mind attends. Think of it as pure peripheral vision; you receive the information without perceiving it as being taxing' (cited in Walker 2004). The reward component was fairly substantial, and will next be illustrated through one company's particular experience with the *Orb*.

The Buck Institute is an example of an energy-consuming customer who received a free *Orb* from PG&E. The *Orb* sits on the desk belonging to Ralph O'Rear, vice president of facilities and planning for the Novato Age Research Institute. On days when the region's demand for electricity threatens to outstrip supply, O'Rear's *Orb* will change colour, from blue to yellow (see Colour plate vii, Fig F and Fig G). When the yellow *Orb* event occurs, Buck Institute managers will contact PG&E and let the company know how much the Institute can reduce its use of electricity. The Buck Institute will receive a payment based on that amount. Because it has its own generator, the institute can even sell a portion of its power to PG&E in some situations. O'Rear is thrilled with the reward arrangement for conservation of energy:

> 'Every dollar we can save on electricity is a dollar we can spend on science [...] The Institute spends between $550,000 and $600,000 a year on energy... If we could save 30 percent of the money we spend on energy each year, that could allow us to hire one more investigator, or add one more person to a research team.' (cited in Rogers 2006)

As the *Orb* continues to change from yellow to red, Buck Institute managers will transfer some of the building's most important functions to its own generator, and reduce power consumption in the rest of the building. How does the Institute actually conserve power? O'Rear continues to explain:

> 'Parts of the building will shut down, and our heating, ventilation and air conditioning will be reduced to the lowest comfortable standard...We'll be turning as many of our lights off as we can, and switching to emergency power.' (cited in Rogers 2006)

That kind of voluntary conservation could help the region avoid the kind of blackouts and brownouts that plagued California during the electricity crisis of 2000-2001, according to PG&E representatives. PG&E believes that the *Orbs* can help reduce power consumption by 600 megawatts – enough power to supply 450,000 homes - in critical situations.

> 'Up until the early 1980s, California was one of the paramount states for energy conservation', said Lloyd Coker, a PG&E spokesman. 'We seem to have gotten away from that. But with the recent concern over energy, we're hoping to be able to rectify that.' (cited in Rogers 2006)

Other California utility companies have experimented in similar ways with the *Energy Orb* and generated record energy savings. In 2004, Southern California Edison, one of the state's three utilities, launched a pilot program to test dynamic pricing. Half of the customers in the project were given an *Orb*, programmed to track electricity costs. It glowed blue during off-peak hours and green when the price of electricity was at its peak. 'The customers with the *Orbs* conserved twice as much electricity as the customers in the control group', says Mark Martinez, the project manager who conceived and implemented the program (cited in Scanlon 2005). The *Energy Orb* project has since been expanded to all three California utilities, and 15,000 to 18,000 *Orbs* were distributed in 2005 alone.

The *Energy Orbs* are an incredibly significant development in the landscape of *eco-visualisation*. As discussed previously, the *Orbs* deliver 'at a glance' visual feedback about electricity loads on the California grid in real time. Enormous amounts of electricity were conserved as reported by Southern California Edison, and in the case of the Buck Institute, large quantities of money were received as a reward for conservation. The *Orb* and the *Wattson* both represent two of the only examples of *eco-visualisation* that have been tested on a large scale on a long-term basis (i.e. longer than a few months). Unlike DIY Kyoto, the Ambient Devices firm is not particularly concerned with marketing the *Orbs* with sustainable design principles in mind; the *Orbs* are made in China via standard manufacturing. So the *Orb* is perhaps not as green as it could be although the glass could be recycled. On the positive side possibly due to the volume in sales and versatility, the *Orbs* are more cost-effective to use. In 2004, they were priced at $300; today they retail for around $100. The *Orb* is infinitely more configurable than a device like STATIC's *Flower Lamp* or DIY Kyoto's *Wattson*. Ambient operates a server that pushes all sorts of data to *Orbs* that are set up in various ways. Any *Orb* consumer can bring an idea forward, like the innovative project manager Mark Martinez did who helped distribute the *Energy Orb* to 18,000 utilities customers. Of all the smart objects discussed in this section that offer easy to read data at a glance, the *Orb* is by far the most effective in assisting individuals to conserve electricity on a large scale despite the lack of attention to green design principles in its construction.

Conclusions about Eco-visualisation for resource conservation

Dynamic feedback – when delivered in a visual 'at a glance' form – works to reduce energy consumption. *Nuage vert*, *Flower Lamp*, *Disappearing Pattern Tiles*, *Power-Aware Cord*, *Wattson*, and the *Energy Orb* all share the same aim: to use creative imaging – *eco-visualisation* – to encourage a local population to cut back their energy usage. More traditional curtailment strategies using numeric feedback on standard LCD screens could be doomed to fail especially in light of more innovative imaging data communication solutions. The question is, will gadgets like the *Orb* and the *Wattson* retain their effectiveness over the long term? Or will they be consigned to the landfill with the rest of our handheld electronics? And are relatively short-term but large scale visualization projects like *Nuage vert* useful, and to what degree, given the limited time frame? While devices like the *Flower Lamp* and the *Wattson* offered interesting ways for home users to monitor their levels of energy consumption, the truly pioneering projects were the ones that integrated creative visualisation directly with the data from the local utility company. The *Nuage vert* public installation and the *Energy Orb* project both enabled local energy consumers to actually see and be connected with the load usage statistics of the nearby power plants in real time. *Nuage vert* required extensive cooperation from the power company, and in the case of the *Energy Orb*, the project was initiated by the utility and required widespread cooperation from the resident users. Both creative endeavours should be held up as exemplary efforts from both the public and private sector as modes of initiating periods of curtailment of consumption as both worked quite magically though in very different ways. *Nuage vert* due to the complexity of the security involved with the lasers was restricted to a very short exhibition period, although the project had a lasting impact in that the power plant made aggregated usage data available online to Helsinki residents; this is not a common practice in the industry. Conversely, the *Energy Orb* allowed a whole population of consumers to save vast amounts of money on energy by equipping willing companies with a glass ball that changed from blue to yellow to show periods of lower energy pricing. Artists and designers hoping to expand on the legacy of HeHe and Ambient Devices should emulate both projects in the future, and tweak them to be even more effective and provocative to retain audience participation and interest. Despite the gloomy outlook on the advanced state of global warming, creative thinkers, artists, and designers are clearly making great strides in introducing new ideas to the planet to promote energy conservation.

References

Background illumination 2004, *Economist*, June 10, accessed online at Ambient Devices's website 1 April 2010, <http://www.ambientdevices.com/cat/news.html>.

Backlund, S, Gustafsson, A, Gyllenswärd, M, Ilstedt-Hjelm, S, Mazé, R & Redström, J 2006, '*Static! The Aesthetics of Energy in Everyday Things*', in Friedman, K, Love, T & Corte-Real, E (eds), Wonderground: Proceedings of the 2006 Design Research Society International Conference, 1-4 November, Lissabon.

Carwile, JL, Luu, HT, Bassett, LS, Driscoll, DA, Yuan, C, Chang, JY, Ye, X, Calafat, AM & Michels, KB 2009, 'Polycarbonate bottle use and urinary bisphenol A concentrations', *Environmental Health Perspectives*, vol. 117, no. 9, pp. 1368-72.

DIY Kyoto 2009, *Wattson* product sales website, accessed 1 April 2010, <http://www.diykyoto.com/uk>, and user testimonials accessed 1 April 2010, <http://www.diykyoto.com/uk/casestudies>, *Wattson Village*, accessed 29 January 2009, <http://community.diykyoto.com/members>.

Evans, H 2008, '*Nuage vert*', *Cluster Magazine*: Transmitting Architecture, no. 7, May, Torino, accessed 27 January 2009, <http://www.cluster.eu/v2/editions/evans>.

Fehrenbacher, K 2008, '*Wattson* Your Holiday Gift List?' *Earth2Tech* December 23, 2008, accessed 1 April 2010, <http://earth2tech.com/2008/12/23/*Wattson*-your-holiday-gift-list>.

Felberbaum, M 2004, 'New technology relies on human visual system: Ambient Orb changes colour to reflect trends in information', *MSNBC: Technology & science/ Tech and gadgets*, April 16, accessed 1 April 2010, <http://www.msnbc.msn.com/id/4758931/>.

Gyllensward, M & Gustafsson, A 2005, '*The Power-Aware Cord: Energy Awareness through Ambient Information Display*', in Proceedings of Computer Human Interaction, ACM, New York, pp. 1423-1426.

HeHe 2009, *Nuage vert*, accessed 1 April 2010, <http://hehe.org.>free.fr>.

Ishii, H & Ullmer, B 1997, '*Tangible Bits: Towards Seamless Interfaces between People, Bits and Atoms', Conference on Human Factors in Computing Systems*, Tangible Media Group, MIT, Cambridge/MA, accessed 1 April 2010, <http://tangible.media.mit.edu/projects>.

Kester, G 2004, *Conversation Pieces: Community and Communication in Modern Art*, University of California Press, Berkeley.

Löfström, E 2007 *Visualizing energy in households: the power aware cord as a means to create energy awareness*. European Network for Housing Research International Conference, Sustainable Urban Areas, Rotterdam.

Rogers, R 2006, '*Buck Institute works to avoid summer blackouts*', Marin Independent Journal, May 18, accessed 29 January 2009, <http://www.marinij.com/ci_3836909>.

Scanlon, J 2005, 'An Orb with a Galaxy of Uses', *Business Week*, July 21, accessed 29 January 2009, <http://www.businessweek.com/innovate/content/jul2005/di20050721_708133.htm>.

Thompson, C 2007, 'Desktop Orb Could Reform Energy Hogs', *Wired Magazine*, July 24, accessed 29 January 2009, <http://www.wired.com/techbiz/people/magazine/15-08/st_thompson>.

Walker, L 2004, 'Start-Up Builds Less Demanding Machines', *Washington Post*, October 14, accessed 29 January 2009, <http://www.ambientdevices.com/cat/press/WashingtonPostA29127-2004Oct13.html>.

HELEN AND NEWTON HARRISON IN CONVERSATION WITH BRANDON BALLENGÉE

Helen & Newton Harrison, edited by Juanita Schläpfer-Miller

Pioneers of the eco-art movement, the collaborative team of Newton and Helen Mayer Harrison have worked for almost forty years initiating transdiscourse between scientists, architects, urban planners and other artists. What follows, is a conversation they had with Brandon Ballengée, an artist who is known for his exploration of the boundaries of art, science and activism.

Brandon Ballengée (BB): Could you talk about your early projects with technology? Did you work with NASA?

Newton Harrison (NH): In retrospect, in 1968 or '69, I was working and thinking in a rudimentary way in three disciplines. They were; oceanography, plasma physics and biology. In oceanography, I did a work based on a wave-action ocean pump, invented by one of the directors of the Scripps Institute of Oceanography, John Isaacs. It won the E.A.T. prize for California works by an artist for technological work that was outside of the normal Art domain. John Isaacs was worried that any reviews we got might make him look silly since the idea of a scientist helping to engender a work of art seemed so odd to him. I asked a second year class of mine if they could imagine hanging colour in space, think Rothko. A very bright physics student laughed and suggested I get a bell jar, a vacuum pump, an anode and cathode and a 12-15,000 volt, 1/3rd amp fluorescent light transformer and he would kindly hang some colour in space for me. Out of this experience, I developed an artificial aurora with five, 10 foot tall, 18" diameter vacuum chambers, a rare gas injection system, different for each gas and programmable. With it I created a sort of collective artificial aurora. It was exhibited at the American Pavilion in Expo 1970 and thereafter, in the Art and Technology exhibition for the LA County Museum of Art. For the LA County museum work, I proposed in addition the acquisition of a Nike Apache missile to be shot off at Point Mugu, south of Los Angeles, in order to generate an artificial aurora from the release of appropriate rare gasses from Los Angeles to San Francisco. On the way up, the rocket was intended to make releases of atmospheric coloured gasses, so meteorologists could begin to understand the wind patterns that operate in our upper atmosphere. Thus, Science would be served one way and Art another. The museum work was done in Jet Propulsion Laboratories. Richard Feynman was the advisor for the project. We became friends. He didn't much care about plasma physics, but he was interested in Art and the processes of Art making. Meanwhile, Secretary of Defence Laird, refused permission to fire off the Nike Apache as 'he didn't want to give an artist that much power'. Years later, NASA invited us to do just that.

Helen Harrison (HH): However, when we first wanted to make the missile shot, the innovation would have been a lot more of an act for science. In fact, the way that releases would have reacted to the winds in the lower atmosphere in San Bernardino California would allow meteorologists to understand more fully the way the winds worked. Therefore, the missile release would have been a scientific experiment at the same time as making a beautiful Aurora as a work of Art. But by the time NASA wanted to do this with us, the meteorological experiments had already been done, so from our perspective, there was no point in sending up a missile just to make a work of Art with negligible scientific outcome, while at the same time leaving a bunch more debris in space! So, we did the unimaginable. We turned him down. However, most amusing was that spaceship companies had begun to write to us explaining that their rockets, for instance, the Astro B, were much cheaper than Nike Apache and would do almost the same job.

BB: That's interesting to see that NASA has continued with Art programs, since the late 60-70's. They also have an art collection and commission artists to do works for their permanent collection. I created a work for them last year. Also, they sometimes have an Artist in Residence program, with people such as Laurie Anderson who did a residency with them a while ago. With organizations like NASA, I've always wondered what happened exactly with the late 60's art-science and technology movement.

NH: Well first of all, it's a big non-understanding, people didn't realize the difference between science and technology. The only person doing science in the whole art-technology show was me. Every body else was using scientific phenomena, mostly electronically driven, to create visual phenomena. For instance, when we got to do the *Brine Shrimp Piece* at the LA County Museum, we were doing it in a sort of ad hoc way, an experiment that, surprisingly, even had outcomes for space. For instance, the productivity in one of our 10ft X 20ft X 8" deep ponds if scaled up, would produce about 16,000 pounds per acre/ per year, that is if the algae were fed with Save-on liquid plant food and the water temperature during the days at over 85 degrees and the nights, at roughly 70 degrees. But the Billy Klüver sensibility held sway in those days and biological considerations were almost viewed by that group with contempt. (Johan Wilhelm (Billy) Klüver (1927-2004) was an electrical engineer at Bell Telephone Laboratories who founded Experiments in Art and Technology (E.A.T.) with Robert Rauschenberg and others). Also, when I was working at the Jet Propulsion Laboratory, people saw what I was doing as a sort of scientific experiment possibly interesting for other reasons. You see, it's when you share creativity in this context the creativity bifurcates at one point toward Science and at another point toward Art. But the core creativity is that you have that insight and act on it. Concretely speaking, I'm one kind of a being and the scientist is one kind of a being and he wants A and I want B; but each in collaboration with, and never to the exclusion of the other.

BB: Absolutely, I fully agree with you. I think there is a potential energy sharing in creativity, especially in collaborative art and science projects. There is no differentiation in terms of the creative dynamic. In certain relationships, that I have developed for a decade or more with biologists, we have this sharing energy at a level creative platform. There is no hierarchy. We talk and brainstorm collaboratively, thinking and debating ideas, also inspiring each other and there is no distinct role in this part of the process. Then we do the projects. The biggest difference, I think, is in the outcome whether or not it will be publicly revealed in a scientific journal or in an Art museum, sometimes both. Goals and expectations can also be another distinction, but often they are not clearly defined when we start the projects, there is an openness.

BB: Is the *Brine Shrimp Piece* the precursor to the *Survival Series*? (see Colour plate x, Fig. E - I)

NH: Not exactly. It's the second one. The first one was called *Hog Pasture* shown at the Boston Museum of Art in a show called '*Earth, Air, Fire and Water*'. It was our first meadow, right before Helen and I began actively collaborating. (see Colour plate viii, Fig. A)

HH: This was the first pasture and grasslands piece. Pastures and Grasslands have been a theme in our work. For instance, in the restoration in Art Park, with the meadowlands, forests and pastures in former Yugoslavia and the *Endangered Meadows of Europe* among many others.

NH: But *Hog Pasture* was the beginning! Do you know who Bob Kushner is?

BB: No, please tell me!

NH: Well, Bob was a student of mine in 1970. Actually, now he is a well-known decorative painter. One day, I told him: 'Bob, go look at these seed catalogues! I'm going to get some groceries. Select for me the three most amazing names!' So I took a sort of Duchampian or John Cage view. The idea was to make a chance selection, which is where somebody else seems to make the decision. And what came up was 'R. Shumway Seedsmen's Annual Hog Pasture Mix'. Who could ask for more? That's how the first Survival Piece began. By the time I did it I understood I had made a meadow and I had already made Earth and Helen had planted the indoor pastures. By the way, I don't know if you know our making Earth pieces, they can be seen on the website.

BB: I have read about them. They were among your first 'ecological' investigations.

NH: Back to what I was saying, that is actually when The Survival works really began. And we took a decision. Try to imagine... Earth is being wrecked globally, we are in 1968 or 69: What's Earth? It's where everything grows. But I wanted to see for myself. So, I got all kinds of shit, leaves, mulch, sewage and some other stuff and started to shovel them. They smelled awful. But after a few months of shovelling and watering, the 'earth' smelled so good that you could smell it and taste it as the farmers do! That's when we started to think like farmers and grow the plants.

HH: And we explored other ideas about using viable earth, later even such as making bio-fuels.

NH: That's true! But in the beginning, I didn't think viable earth. I thought smell good, taste ok, would be viable. But you know lots of stuff came after the fact. I wouldn't want to make the argument that we preconceived things. A lot of creativity is what comes out of your mouth and on the fly.

BB: Exactly! There is a commonality here, humans are experiential animals, and our understanding comes first from the senses, later we analyze. Inspiration in this case comes first from the senses. Likewise, the work of art can come to being this way. At first, it seems that the idea is loose but the potential is there; even if the outcome is not yet mentally framed and by exploring over and over again, somewhere along the way, the ideas get shaped and the project sculpted.

BB: Could you explain this work here at the gallery to me (*Greenhouse Britain*)?

NH: We were working with the effects of global warming on Britain and seeing land shrink, so we began to think about the concept of the upward movement of people and we posed a question. How much land do you need to sequester enough carbon to equal the local carbon footprint of about 9000 people? It turns out to be, after working with a really smart team, about 42 square miles or 27,000 acres. But the other question is: how do you find the land? We found the land in the Pennines. It was open and impoverished. It had about 4000 people living on 27,000 acres and therefore, in our plan, you could add about another 5000. The idea was to invent a system of housing in which you don't violate the eco-system you are in. There are about 18 mini-watersheds in the area and if you locate them correctly the watersheds tell you where the meadows and the forests should be, think about it as 2/3 meadow (about 18,000 acres), and 1/3 forest (about 9000 acres). They will collectively sequester 36,000 tons of carbon. And research tells you what species will live on the meadows and thus a new system is invented for farming which is post-monocultural. All this information is in the text. However, the implications are interesting because in this miniature universe that we argued for, monoculture is virtually impossible because people will have to collect edible plants and animals from the whole environment, rather than grow a whole lot in one place and the monocultural economic system therefore can't work in this new system.

HH: Now the other thing is that you have to train people to understand that all harvesting has to preserve the system rather than destroy it, which is much more like what nature does. So the next question would be about the size. You need to understand that the external shape of the 27,000 acre site is a permeable membrane and if a group at the edge wants to join... Well, if they have 100 people they need to contribute 300 acres, because it takes 3 acres per person to sequester carbon, which is the design parameter. But there is enough redundancy built in, that, if 10% of the people or even 15% could tell you to get lost, they could live there anyway. Now we are actually working with a team of scientists who can deal with the relationships of meadow to forest to what species are harvestable, wilding and other ideas about the animal population. Actually, this is a complex system we are attempting to put on the ground and it obeys the rules of what a complex system is in nature, because it will recreate itself by taking energy into itself and expel energy from itself, because it has creature-like properties with both constancy and non-constancy built in. We will use this and that building (pointing to architectural model) as a double essay on complex systems, this work-study we will put as an essay in the Journal of Structure and Dynamics, as we did for *Peninsula Europe*.

BB: That's a really interesting point. Do you integrate, as a part of your practice, a differentiation in the way you view this process?

NH: The first question we pose is: how big is here? Once we discover a here, there are boundaries. So you have a kind of field of play that sets up a field of thought. Then, as an ethical and knowing being, you can observe and say: 'Look at all that is happening and what am I going to do about it?' And you set off to do something about it. Personally, we don't think about activism at all. We think of ourselves as responsible people responding to a circumstance. So, I think we need to de-label. I know I'm an artist because I've done that since I was a little boy.

BB: Some of my earlier projects dealt with declines in marine fisheries. Surveying seafood markets here in NYC with a small team I put together. We just did it. The project titled *The Ever Changing Tide* took place between 2000-2002, here we catalogued over 400 species and presented the results at the Queens Museum of Art as well as participating seafood markets. With much of your work, I really got a sense that this dynamic is what you would call I guess a 'do it yourself' attitude and method. In fact, it is a problem solving approach. It is what I gather looking at the way you solve localised problems, even if there are larger ramifications. Do you address the problem first?

HH: That happens afterwards. The first thing that happens is a narrative. You tell yourself a story. We all build narratives in the mind, willy-nilly, whether we like it or not, or sometimes, whether we know it or not. That's why (pointing to artwork) I took you over here because every place tells the story of its own becoming.

BB: That's something that has been a part of your working process throughout. Do you consider it as a form of poetic discourse?

HH: Well, it's poetic discourse ... it's a language, I guess. Poetry is to Literature, which deals with connotation as well as denotation, as math is to science. It's a language of condensation. If you try to unpack these poems you would open about a thousand pages. So we use the poetic form as a form of compression.

BB: And the kind of narrative that arise, are they in a sense site specific? Are they reactions to a site?

NH: No, no, they are recreations of what one might call a cultural landscape, operating within the construct of our basic question: how big is here. The cultural landscape because the dominant culture of the place determines it. How do they determine it? They tell stories to each other. 'A dam here, a town site there, we will make money here, we will kill the native culture there, then we will do whatever we wish to do.' All this takes a narrative form, at first, speculative. So what Helen and I want to do is get to the core and find the narrative thread in order, if possible and if desirable to the common good as we see it, to veer it in another direction.

BB: So the narrative comes first...

NH: Yeah...

BB: Existing narratives?

NH: No... you don't know what it is. You tell yourself a story. You see other people tell other people stories, etc.

BB: Do you think that the working environment in Western Europe is more favourable for projects such as yours than in the USA?

NH: In many ways yes, precisely because art there has reinvented itself so many times as well as culture.

BB: For what I know, in Switzerland, it looks like they don't make a strict difference between applied art, art for community and fine art. I also think that with Clement Greenberg and out of modernism particularly, in North America a major change happened: the big divide that art should be separated from society, and I don't think we have really recovered from that.

NH: Exactly!

HH: Well, if you look at the idea of the starving hero or heroine living in the attic you have begun separating artists from society. By the end of the 18th and 19th century, you have those kind of images going on. But artists were part of the society historically in Europe because there was a whole point where they wanted to be in guilds. In the Renaissance, the artists wanted to be in this guild because that was the only way they could get funded. You have the artists as a working part of society.

NH: That's very true! Also art critics are afraid of sciences. They are afraid of eco-systemic thinking too. They don't say so but you can tell that the fear exists because they don't want to do any research on it. They don't inform themselves so they are basically ecologically illiterate and, in many ways, scientifically indifferent.

BB: Is it because we have such a strong division here in North America between sciences and the humanities? We took C.P. Snow's essay *The Two Cultures* as a manifesto. This fuelled an unnecessary divide between disciplines, which has severely limited communication and cooperation. Luckily there have been attempts towards reconciliation, but still we face real barriers.

NH: I don't know, I just know that Helen and I are rare birds because of it. We were so fortunate to come into the university when it was formed. The University of California at San Diego is one of the top thirty universities in the world now and I was the second hire of the art department before Dave Antin, Eleanor Antin and Allan Kaprow. Back then, the scientists really thought we were a kick! The physicists would invite us to their parties and we would have them to our parties. They would say: 'Who is this person making an aurora borealis, fish farms and portable orchards or stuff of that sort?'

BB: That's one of the things I get reading about the art-science and technology movement of the 1960s, there was just a real openness on the part of Bell Labs and others....

NH: That's right! MIT and many places....

BB: When I was reading Georgy Kepes, he came up with this whole idea, what a visionary!... My understanding is he started as a painter. He introduced the notion of civic art and the fact that art could actually function and help society. Also the role between artists, scientists and technicians needed to be removed by thinking in a group dynamic in order to come up with large real world solutions.

NH: Georgy Kepes discovered me in 1969, I was a tech-artist at the time and I was thrilled. He invited me to be in the '69 Sao Paulo Biennale, what I did was work with liquid crystals. In a 50-foot tall room, I created a 60 foot long thermometer, 1 foot wide! It was 5 feet on the ground, 50 feet up and 5 feet on the ceiling and would change colours very slowly. Every increment of colour change represented increasing temperature because it got hotter and hotter toward the ceiling. Then I got a call at the Jet Propulsion Laboratories while working on the glow discharge tubes and Kepes said: 'we are not going to go because Brazil has become a fascist country and we need to protest.' And I got in a big argument with them and said: 'What you want is the wildest art possible to go there as an act of contra-distinction to the repression, you don't want to remove yourself and let repression take up the space you left.' But he said no and he, with the consent of the majority, cancelled the exhibition.

BB: You were a part of one of the art-science technology groups on the West Coast?

NH: Firstly, from 1948 to 1958, I was a figurative sculptor and by 1955 to 1957, I had lots of commissions. That leads us into 1958, when I won a fellowship in Florence. During that time, the Sputnik went up. And I said to myself: 'I understand that the Sputnik is not a scientific thing at all, in fact, it's an act of technology.' Then I thought: 'It is a global performance that is bigger than the globe. What am I doing making sculptures, trying to recapitulate these old masters?' So I turned down my sculpture commissions and buried them. After this radical decision, I became a field painter and practiced it in New York during the early 60's. Around the mid 60's and late 60's, I turned into a tech-artist. In fact, I took the decision to refuse any work that did not benefit the eco-system without quite knowing what an ecosystem was.

BB: When you decided to focus on work dealing with eco-system problem solving, were there any influences such as Rachel Carson?

HH: Oh! Rachel Carson just blew my mind! I could remember when the sky was black with Canadian geese coming down to migrate for the winter and you could hear their wings, the sounds were an enormous pageant. Fifteen years later, when I went to the beaches - we were living in Old Saybrook - and was stupefied by what I saw: there weren't many shells anymore! I mean, as a child, the beaches used to be covered with shells! Then I thought I have to do something about all this. I didn't know what, but I wanted to do something.
So I continued with the things I was working on. I was getting a PhD in Psychology and I had a Masters in educational psychology and I had done an undergraduate work in psychology and anthropology and also I'd graduated as a Chaucer's scholar, originally, but then, I wanted something else.

NH: So, when we took this decision to work together, Helen was the head of educational program at the university extension in line to be

Director of the Extension and the first women vice-chancellor in the whole university system.

HH: I came from more of an activist background than Newton and I was the first New York Coordinator of Women's Strike for Peace, back in 1961. We also ran a Peace Center out of our house, the Thompkins Square Peace Center and collaborated with the Greenwich Village Peace Center, the War Resistors League, the American Friends Service Committee, the Living Theater group, Dorothy Day and the Catholic Worker and Dave Dellenger's group from Glen Gardner in many peace demonstrations. Our political position at the time was close to the pacifist/anarchists.

BB: I think it helps to show where you are coming from. It actually enroots your practice.

HH: Yes, absolutely.

BB: I'm trying to sort out where my different influence and inspiration could come from. I've been reading and following up this process as part of my PhD research about art-science and technology. Through that, I realised that series of amazing events happened in the 60s and 70s continuing in the 80s or the 90s...

NH: Obviously, we were mostly a part of them. But let me take you into another direction. In 1970-71, Smithson was alive and Haacke was still doing ecological stuff, Helen and I were part of E.A.T. and also Sonfist was doing interesting stuff. That was enough of a core to have made a big movement. But...Haacke gets pissed off because of the Guggenheim scandal and thereafter only does political work, Sonfist trivialized his ecological work with his own ambition, Smithson died in an air crash, which left Helen and I carrying this thing that we hoped would be the Art and Ecology movement. So we just did what we did and continued! But for the possibility of a movement, we had to wait pretty close to forty years. Then it happened over the past decade with guys like you and many others, emerging and coalescing.

BB: And what about Joseph Beuys? What role did he play during that time?

NH: Practically zero. After Feldman started the gallery in New York in 1974, he brought in Helen and I, Joseph Beuys and Bucky Fuller, all in one week! The month before he had cornered the Duchamp market...

HH: About Beuys, he clearly invented social sculpture but it's a term, it doesn't unpack very well. Beuys does *7000 Oaks* in 1987, we were at Documenta at the time while he was doing it, we were doing another piece there in the orangery. I was thinking: 'This guy is nuts! Oaks don't belong in beech country! There is a beech forest all over the place, why are they talking about this Beuys in terms of ecology?' In fact, it was about symbolism. And it had to do with mythic as a part of the mythos of the region. The Oak tree has profound significance in Germany.

NH: Right, but if I call a piece of art 'ecological', I want to know about its niche. I want to know: what are the eco-transformations that are going on; which energy is coming in, which energy is coming out; the social function if there is one; and so on and so forth. But none of that applies to Beuys. However, he, with a small group of people, did the

Green Party and all is forgiven.

BB: Beuys said himself that the *7000 Oaks* was supposed to work in biospheric terms. It was an active social sculpture to get people planting. So it was more of a symbolic act like in the free university. A lot of the works were symbolic actions such as the Bog action.

NH: You see, I have no objection to that. I think it's terrific! But I won't accept that these are ecological works! If someone uses the term ecology with me, I want to know something about how the system works. If he is using 'mythic work' that's fine, if he is using 'social work' that's fine or if he is into 'social systems', I agree. That he has invented what I consider the basis for the Green Party and about 10 to 15 other people make the claim, that's fine. But, Brandon, you work in biology. For instance, if we were able to do our Ocean piece where we talked about the world ocean, systems thinking at a perturbatory's condition and what that will take, then we are talking about system thinking at a large scale: partially social system, partially eco-system.

BB: You've been talking a lot about systems. I'm wondering whether at the beginning of your practice, you were familiar with Jack Burnham's writings.

NH: Jack Burnham! Read *The Western Salt Works* where he begins with Smithson and ends with us. The author claims that we are in a process of creating an ecologically based art or nature based art at a very high level of utilitarianism. So he makes that claim for us after the early 70's.

BB: I read *Beyond Modern Sculpture* where he talks about the necessity to go ahead and challenge the sculptural aesthetic standards and suggests moving for a system's approach. The sculpture could not be reduced to an artefact status, depending on the context (museum, market value, etc) but would become an element of an environment or even the environment itself! Today, the lack of theoreticians or others to give a solid philosophical analysis for the Eco-arts movement makes it difficult. Critics are writing about it but there are no thinkers like Jack Burnham really pushing, standing out with an analytical system, at least from what I am aware. Attempts are being made in Europe to give theoretical grounding to current bioart practices, but there is a long way to go.

NH: Are there any critics trained well enough to do it? You need somebody who is systems trained, ecologically trained. The problem with the training of theoretician is their imprisonment into postmodern theory. For example, Lyotard, God help us! Spare me postmodernism, it's already done, you've to get out of that! It's a kind of endless, intellectual, self-gratifying feed-back loop; we have to go beyond that.

BB: I've given a lot of thought to it and I think we should re-question the boundaries between eco-art practice and postmodernism or even modernism! I think there might have been a separate trajectory from where these works stem pretty much since the Renaissance. The relationship between artists and scientists already existed, often in the same individual. They were looking for practical solutions to problems, leading to the work presented in public, varying in the forms: either poetic or visual, sculpture or painting... The relation seems to have appeared more specifically during the birth of popular science. Maybe, there is a parallel creative process that we don't even realise or haven't taken the time to really map.

NH: Hmm, it could be... But if you look at what happened to modernist science: reductionism in nature, and by being reductionist in nature, the process becomes self-framed; in self-framing, it doesn't invite other influences. It's seriously risk adverse. Why? Because they want the answer beforehand to assure the grant!

BB: Which is one of the dangers now with current primary research science, so driven by the market! It's very problematic, a lot of the biologists I worked with, have had trouble funding their amphibian research. There is such a push for molecular biology and product driven science that field and eco-system studies are very overshadowed.

NH: Even if they get grants, they can't get other grants to follow it up...

HH: That's our relationship with a lot of scientists where we can act as a stalking horse saying a lot of the things they can't! Because we can say a lot of things as artists and they can show artworks and espouse certain positions without taking a fiscal risk...

HH: For example there is a piece out there showing us as the stalking horse; *The Mountain in the Green House 2001*. We raised the issue of how far ahead can you predict. It appears that 90% of researchers are afraid to go beyond a moderate certainty! That's true... they are also afraid to take the chance, so we, as artists, made the predictions. The scientist we were working with, Dr. Georg Grabherr, was able to show this artwork to his students and others making the point without risk.

BB: That's something I've also experienced when I first approached scientists in 1995: their interest in getting me into the labs and be involved in fieldtrips and research. It can be explained by the following statement: The scientific community has become so insulated that reaching the public is barely possible. And if you attempt, then you are pointed by the criticism of socio-biology or you are 'watering down the sciences' only because of interacting with the public. Bringing a message to the public was always a part of your intention.
Could you explain a little bit about the *Lagoon Cycle*? Did you travel as part of your research?

HH: In '78, we travelled to Sri Lanka. Metromedia had just begun funding the *Lagoon Cycle*, so we were well-funded. The Japanese and Russians had been fishing out the lagoons and this was visible from the small fishing village we stayed at. Everywhere we went people were fishing even at the hotel they were fishing! At the fish farm we had done in London, we discovered that the catfish didn't travel well in the air, even if they travelled well in the water. But our friend from Sri Lanka, Ranil Senanayake, an amazing young ecologist, said that the crabs from Ngumbo did travel well and he had his mother send crabs from the marketplace to us, with pegs in their claws packed in wet banana leaves and more than half of them lived. And, unlike the catfish, the crabs did mate in small places. So we researched this hardy creature that could live under museum conditions (Ranil had suggested this type of crab because it was the last to die when the tidal ponds dried up). Later, I'll show you in the *Lagoon Cycle* book and you will see how they breed and live.

And we had to get a permit, from the Scripps Institute of Oceanography, to bring an exotic creature into the country, which they kindly gave us. We spent two almost three years studying those crabs. We had the tanks in a little building we got on campus and we would bring ocean water and fresh water to keep and study them. John Isaacs, the head of Scripps, became a good friend and was amazed that we had decoded the mating behaviour of these crabs. Actually it was quite simple, one had to drop the specific gravity of the water 20% and toss in a lot of food, while keeping the temperature in the 70s. And at some point, Ranil sent us from Sri Lanka mangrove seeds and a couple of fish that lived in the ponds. This was in 1974, four years before, we took the trip to Sri Lanka and visited with crab-fishermen in order to visit the actual ponds. And we realised that the ponds that we made in America which were 4 paces by 5 paces and waist high, matched up with the smaller places that the crabs lived and bred in. And thereafter, we decoded their cannibalism behaviour and found that cannibalism stopped when they were provided with about 7 different hiding places per crab in different sizes and configurations in our tanks. We discovered much more, but never codified it. It turns out that crabs, when confined in a tank, develop very particular kinds of social behaviour and have very individual characteristics. Altogether this experience, where we actually did experimental science and oddly even, I must say by accident, we out-competed the lobster project. This experience was a very formative one for us and became in some ways the 'background noise' in many other works. I know this is a rather long rant, but the whole *Lagoon Cycle* was the outcome from this experience.

BB: With the *Lagoon Cycle* series or piece, you develop the technique to breed this crab in captivity. In a sense, it's primarily research biology inside the context of artistic practices. Did you publish this work scientifically?

NH: We didn't realise it at the time, we were simply trying to make it easy for ourselves. But we were debating much experimental science belief. We did the experiment and then took issue with the science. We called it dubious science on the grounds that scientists think that they can control more than they do. And so, this was our first whole system approach. We called it *Sea Grant: The Second Lagoon*. In it you can see the science underpin the art while literally retaining its identity as Science.

HH: Yes. Where we go very simply is: the tank is not a lagoon nor is it a tidal pond neither does the mixing of fresh and salt water make it an estuary. Filters are not the cleansing of the tides, water from the hoses is not a monsoon, lights and heaters are not the sun and crabs in the tank do not make a life web. We argued back and forth over this. (Reading from the *Lagoon Cycle* book) 'Remember, the Witness character says: An experiment is a fragile system and anything may go wrong. The electricity may fail, the tanks may break and disease may enter; something necessary may be missing, trace elements may not balance'. The Lagoon Maker reads: 'Remember, a metaphor can be a powerful instrument, if we believe it and we enact it, it develops a life on its own. A metaphor can be a fragile idea, an improvisation born of discourse and observation and anyone may change it or reinterpret it for any reason.' Back and forth they go. Yet, the metaphor for nature is a strong metaphor, that draws attention away from the destruction of habitats, a valuable metaphor that will lead to the regeneration of habitats but it's only a tank. The crabs don't know it's only a tank, yet when we feed them, they look up so already they behave differently.

BB: So the intention here was to create a sustainable human food source with the *Survival Series*? (see Colour plate viii-ix, Fig. B - D)

NH: No, we did not have single intentions. We had many intentions.

1. The Japanese and Russian fishing fleets were fishing out this crab, so saving gravid females and returning them back to the lagoons to reinhabit was really important.
2. We wanted to make an exhibition where something survived.
3. We wanted to add to the body of scientific knowledge.
4. We wanted to tell a story.
5. In the process we understood that most experimental science that attempted to separate the part from the whole was probably systemically wrong and likely to lead to unfortunate, unexpected consequences while appearing to be valid!

HH: These many concerns basically began our understanding of complex systems.

NH: The Sea Grant people called us and said: 'We want to give you a big grant. We want you to grow crabs in little cages and we want you to do what the Lobster people are not doing well.' So that's when we said: 'No, we won't do that.' We thought it was a bad idea. But that is when we thought of the Salton Sea and started to invent larger systems.

HH: Yes, we got very angry at caging the little creatures into separate little prisons, which bore no relationship to their natural environment!

BB: Yes, I was always under the assumption that your goal from the beginning was to find a sustainable food source. In fact you were fundamentally interested in the crab's welfare first and foremost. This intention completely reverses the anthropocentric reading of the work, in reality it was much closer to an early animal rights artwork.

NH: For the first three years of this project, the crabs were our teachers, much better teachers than anybody else. So we respected our crabs.

HH: And the crab fishermen were also our teachers. They told us what helped the crabs to survive.

NH: Once they got over the idea that we wanted to look at the crabs mating and we weren't just some weird Americans! But you see where it comes from. Look to most scientific works that is experimental in nature and seeks outcomes. It always simplifies. We don't. We complicate, we accept complexity as it bubbles up. And that's, I think, the key difference between us, per say, and most others.

BB: As mentioned earlier, another problem appearing is the isolation of the biological researchers. They are often pigeon-holed within the scientific peer review community. This can be very limiting in many ways. They often lack the time and means to bring their findings to the public arena. As a result, even as an undergraduate art student contacting biologists, many welcomed me to their labs and on the field-surveys. They saw the potential that art has to reach the public. Additionally, being an artist and later 'free-lance' biologist has given me the flexibility to conduct research in diverse localities (cross-nationally) without a predetermined outcome, this type of investigation is very difficult for most biologists to secure funding for.

HH: That's why we were invited to give keynote presentations at three different large biodiversity conferences. The scientists wanted to know how we could work at the scale we do in projects. For instance, how we were able to do Holland. Of course, it has to do with systems thinking and the key question: 'How big is here?' What are we seeing and experiencing? The next thing is to follow fearlessly what is discovered...

HH: And the main thing is caring about what you are doing and knowing well the systems you are dealing with.

NH: And also moving any self-interest to the far perimeter of your field of thought.

BB: And we should be aware that: when a work involves living systems, ethics have to be addressed some way. That's a huge problem. Artists, working with animals and eco-systems, are not always so conscious about this. Are you familiar with a recent project by an artist who let a dog starve to death in a gallery? (<http://www.euroweeklynews.com/2008031747782/news/costa-del-sol/artist-guillermo-vargas-habacuc.html>) It was horrible and apparently no one intervened - it is unimaginable to me. Why, in the West, does art exist fundamentally as a non-truth? Did visitors believe the dog was really not suffering? Our practices are the antithesis of this mindset and the concept of ethics has to be explored whenever artists are dealing with life forms. And it's relevant to hear your perspective on it. For my work *Species Reclamation*, I've raised amphibians in museums and galleries but also refused to do it if the conditions were not adapted to the animals. It's coming from a different place of working. Now, it seems to be an emerging trend with artists showing Bioart and living systems inside of galleries. Ethics has to be part of the discussion. Were you ever interested in Peter Singer's writings or any of the animal liberation people or rights writers, like Tom Regan?

Both: Yes, Regan, definitely.

BB: Currently, I'm working on a book focusing on the long-term amphibian research project. This investigation, *Malamp*, seeks the origin of developmental deformities in wild populations of frogs, toads, salamanders and newts. It is both art and science. The UK version was commissioned by the Arts Catalyst and funding from the Arts Council of England proved difficult.

NH: Yes the *Fish Farm* was also misunderstood in London. They thought I was a mad American electrocuting catfish! I thought I was behaving humanely because according to the Laws of American Fish Farming that say you have to electrocute catfish!

BB: I read that the animal rights community had a problem with that piece. The activists had stepped in to say they had issues with the fish electrocution. Electro-shocking is still a standard procedure when doing field collection of some species of fish, like some species of eels. It is actually considered one of the most-humane ways of culling fish.

NH: To be a fish farmer, I went to the fish farms at Brawley and trained there. So I became a worker in their field. They could skin a catfish in 55 seconds. I became accepted when I could skin one in 1minute and 10 seconds. Then I was tolerated. They showed me how to do all that stuff; so I simply behaved as they behaved for the exhibition, that's the whole story.

BB: When conducting primarily biology research, I bring the public each step of the way, by setting up Bioart laboratories, by doing experiential fieldtrips and in a sense creating publishable science done with a group dynamic. It is transdisciplinary; art, science and ecological awakening. There is a real push towards environmental education and trying to inspire people to enact change while asking real world questions and seeking answers to complex questions.

HH: Strangely we have found that the improvisation and risks that we took early on with the cell, the crab, meadow, global warming and, in the mid-70s, watersheds, reclamation at small scale as in Art Park, all became interwoven themes in our work in the context of ever-enlarging scale as our understanding of the issues involved became more and more lucid and now, *The Force Majeure* (see Colour plate xi, Fig. J & K), which is our way of understanding the global impact of planetary warming.

14th January 2009 at the Ronald Feldman Gallery, New York.

THE INVISIBLE PRESENT: ART AND SCIENCE PROJECTS FOR MEDIATED DOME FORMATS

Jill Scott

The Invisible Present – 'In the absence of long-term research, serious misjudgements can occur in attempts to manage the environment.'
(John J. Magnuson 1990)

Introduction

This paper outlines some of the representational issues related to the anthropogenic effects on climate change and the various approaches of artists and scientists to deal with the scale of this problem. Through discussions and a case-study proposal I recommend a set of guidelines for the formations of transdisciplinary teams where discussions about producing film projects for existing immersive educational environments like the Planetarium Dome and half-dome technology can help to raise awareness levels and help educate the general public about the responsibilities of climate change. Anthropogenic effects are problems derived from human activities, as opposed to processes that occur in the natural environment without human influences. Although some examples of media already exist that address this issue, there is a genuine need to work with art and science teams to help audiences gain a deeper understanding about climate research and the sustainable roles they can play in the future.

As Lloyd Anderson, director of science at the National Endowment for Science, Technology and Art (NESTA) in the UK[1], has suggested, art and science teams could become 'agora's' or real meeting places where substantial levels of time and space can foster ethical discussions and ideas can flow more easily, The ecological necessity of building 'green corridors' around urban spaces could be used as a metaphor here. In ecology, these corridors are not isolated biotopes, but communities, which can promote bio-diversity and allow animals to exchange habitats. Since 2003, I have co-directed the Swiss based artists-in-labs program[2] with Irène Hediger and we have attempted to create such 'green corridors' between art and science researchers, by placing many artists into the laboratories of science for residencies. Here the aim has been to utilize applied 'hands on' contexts so that cultural exchange can occur based on public themes of social and ethical relevance. We are currently engaged in workshop proposals to also train scientists in visual communication and art production process. In one instance, David Copeland invited a combined team from both fields on a field trip to Greenland to examine ice damage. The results were shown in an exhibition at the Natural History Museum in London[3]. In all the above examples, artists have learnt about what scientists do on field trips and in their labs, and the scientists have gained some information about the semiotics of communication and contemporary art. In our artists-in-labs documentation (Scott ed. 2006) the exposure of artists to more specific research contexts in the fields of physics, biology and technology has also shifted their inspiration and directly affected the outcome of what they produce. These artworks were certainly more scientifically robust! If more scientists were involved in collaborations of media and art production they could learn about the benefits of more interactive tools of communication and explore the virtual potentials of 'science to public' projects. This know-how transfer between disciplines is sure to promote a better public understanding of science, as art can become a viable interpretative catalyst for scientific debate.

However, building exchange communities like these require long-term goals, and because of the need to 'sustain' more swiftly, I propose to address four questions, which may help to make the present more visible. Firstly, how can more local anthropogenic effects of climate change be translated into an immersive technology and through this interpretation turn into effective global metaphors? Would these results be different than other approaches to the problems of climate change? Secondly, how can these transdisciplinary teams deal with the scale of public denial or the need to create more public social support for the issues at hand? In relation to representation, why could interpretative film and surround sound installations in planetariums or virtual theatres make any difference to the dissemination of scientific knowledge for the general public? Finally, in what ways can approaches by transdisciplinarity shift our perception of the problem of climate change? In other words, how can our local and global atmospheric conditions be interpreted and edited into viable chunks of digestible knowledge?

The Value of Local compared to Global Approaches

Scientific research has proven that the extremes typical of climate change can only be accurately measured on local levels and the effects of warming on a global level are difficult to predict or model. My approach is to not only to compare the resistance and resilience of ecosystems in more local environments with each other but also to use planetary metaphors to create links for the viewer between these stories. For example, if similar local facts from two different sources would be compared, like the rate of ice melt of the Tschierva Glacier in Switzerland with the retreat of the ice in the Urals, these locations could be associated together by using similar comments from recorded interviews with old people who have lived their whole lives at these respective locations. The aim is to encourage viewers to identify with how people's lives are actually affected rather than to simply rely on 'before and after shots' of disastrous situations. When local scenarios are depicted, associated audio information is often not included (i.e. the 'sonification' from satellite weather data) and this exclusion tends to dampen a larger biotope view.

Some reflection on ecological theories from recent history may also be an important factor to include in any film script. As early as 1979 the environmental scientist, James Lovelock (1988), suggested that our atmosphere was our only biotope or in his own words 'our very own species life support system'. Poetic visual and sound metaphors could transfer this message of reliance across to the public in a different way. Although one can find a number of educational projects, activities, literature and web links[4], which are currently being produced in this area, many approaches and interpretations do not discuss the long time it is taking for the Western public to respond at all! This is why cloud-biologist and author Tim Flannery (2005) fears that this low level of public response might result in lack of coordination and therefore the goals of carbon reduction that has been set be scientists and governments at Kyoto will not by reached without the effort of millions. Humanity would have to act promptly on an individual, national and corporate level to decarbonise the electricity grids by 2030 and the transport system by 2050. Companies and industries are also expected to avoid out-right disasters by reducing emissions, a reduction which might only produce some recovery over a long period of time. Many Green advocates and artists[5], prefer the humble approach, with each individual taking energy consumption seriously, in order to reduce local levels (i.e. click green power options on your energy bill). Perhaps the only real equitable way to reduce emissions may be to grant every individual an equal and limited 'right to pollute' locally with greenhouse gas and fine those who exceed their limits. On a planetary level Flannery posits that the formation of a major organization called The Earth Commission for Thermostatic Control may be necessary to monitor global consumption and also control an economy based on carbon emissions trading. These solutions would take an immense level of organization and monitoring, and a 70 percent reduction of CO_2 emissions by 2050 constitutes a very 'tall order'.

Thus, the sheer scale of the phenomena of climate change cannot be underestimated! Should we then focus on particular measurable scales of the desecration process that started almost 100 years ago or invent new metaphors for the sheer scale and magnitude of our anthropogenic effects? Scare tactics seem to be as useless as learning from history. Instead visual and sound metaphors that transform real data into digestible chunks of knowledge need to be encouraged, especially for the young voters of the future. For example, regarding CO_2 secretion, these metaphors could depict carbon emissions above the cities they actually live in or compare emissions from brown coal in the air as abstract swarms of pixels, which behave differently in each atmospheric layer[6]. Scientific graphs that depict the total planetary level of brown coal emissions are useless for most people, but an animated close-up of the dark wings of a battered moth might be more poignant. Or what about animating how the reflection of UV Rays on concrete causes more heat in the athmosphere?

Through suggestions like these, transdisciplinary teams may not only develop new visual metaphors, but also share methodologies and discuss how to educate the public about the challenges ahead. For example, one of the largest challenges is about how to break the cycles of avoidance and denial that the majority of the public are experiencing as a reaction to climate change today. If climate change is always depicted in mass media as a global dystopia, then the topic tends to suffer from a high level of conjectural disbelief and cognitive illusion. These reactions can prevent people from seriously accepting the necessary changes. If one compares the few popular media films on the subject of climate change, which have been produced, the filmmakers have often over-laced them with scare tactics (*Day after Tomorrow*)[7], or they have been directed specifically at the children's market and over simplified (*SOS*)[8]. Instead, the renowned documentary, *An inconvenient truth*[9] was aimed at an audience of adults. Directed by Davis Guggenheim and produced by Laurie David and Lawrence Bender, the film incorporated aspects from the life history of Al Gore with animated graphs and photographic evidence in the form of 'before and after' comparisons. Although the film did serve as a wake up call for the public about climate change by accurately depicting climate change effects and the dangerous outcomes if humanity does not react, it failed to deliver an understanding of atmospheric particles, or present local, real peoples' stories that can verify these changes. Instead, it is dominated by Al Gore as the main character, with whom the audience identifies as a 'would have been' president. This dominance tends to dampen the content. But I think the biggest problem of the film is the omission of any direct comments from scientific researchers and their dedicated work. In a transdisciplinary team the scientists would have to represent an accurate scientific approach while the media artists would focus on young urban voters and their reactions to environmental knowledge as well as a combined engagement with these communities online and offline.

Confronting the Psychology

It seems that the theories of causes and effects of climate change have been proposed and rebutted for decades inside scientific circles, so it is no wonder that from the public viewpoint no scientific theory, regardless of supposed 'consensus' (itself often a political, not a scientific, concept) is ever beyond scepticism and debate. The current consensus exists simply because it is the argument that has won out. This has been helped by fairly recent substantial evidence in science, like those of James Hansen and his colleagues, who revealed that our planet is now absorbing more energy and emitting an extra 0.85 watts per square meter into our atmosphere (Hansen et al. 2005). This fact means little to the general public, because a diagram of this process only informs people about the density but basically not about the implications. These are problematic factors to consider when one needs to convince any audiences to respond and act. People rarely believe something they cannot see and therefore may often imagine false implications. The atomic, molecular and cellular behaviours of the atmosphere may need to be somehow 'experienced'. Otherwise climate change seems to be outside their control, and besides rallying on the street or donating to Greenpeace, they cannot imagine how to help. While visualization and audification may solve some of these problems by offering more facts, narratives about how others have achieved sustainability in their home seems to help people think they can also personally act. Additionally, if scientific information is converted into dramatic visual and sound scripts it would also help. For example, in Dendrochronology, voices from widely spaced rings in tree trucks could speak about warm and bountiful growing seasons, when the sun shone and rain fell at the right time, compressed rings record little growth in the tree and tell of adversity, when long hard winters or drought blighted summers tested life to the limits. Another problem is encouraging people to go and see such productions, because avoidance still seems to be the major hurdle. This may be because, as programme leader for forest and climate change Norbert Kräuchi posits (2007), humans are trapped inside Magnuson's *invisible present* or living for an era of the moment, and long-term research results are not often revealed to the public. This may not just be an attitude per se; it may be a grave fault in the human species. Instead of providing a sensible generational contract where the legacy of one generation effects the management of future generations, the human species prefers to live entirely in the present where cause and effect are temporarily disconnected. This attitude renders the uncertainty of future climate prediction as an intolerable concept. Another theory of public denial toward climate change is related to 'progress'. 'The human species', as Flannery suggests, 'have come such a long way in such a short time that our imaginations are irretrievably mired in the past 100 years of progress' and furthermore, 'these ideals of progress are deeply instilled in future trajectories producing a 'myth of limitless growth' (Flannery 2005 p. 296). Both of the above reactions are also worth considering when attempting to construct content for the mediated stage. Of course, other reasons why people step back when confronted with global turmoil, could be that they associate natural disasters with religion or with nature's backlash against humanity!

However, in relation to being engaged in climate literacy, the sheer scale of addressing the solutions to global warming is also a rejection factor. Just count the number of cars, houses or factories where so many people would need to change their behaviour in order to create any effect! Add to the above variation and reaction to prediction, the three most disastrous scenarios scientists are suggesting might happen if emissions are not curtailed: the slowing or collapse of the Gulf Stream, which would cause a drastic decrease in European temperatures; the demise of the Amazon rainforests, which could deprive us of high oxygen levels; and finally, the release of gas hydrates from the sea floor or methane from melting permafrost that are normally prevented from escaping by ice encapsulation. All these predictions are certain to add 'fuel' to the warming atmospheric fire as well as increase more humid water vapour evaporation. Somehow people have to be given hope that they can actually shift these calamities through collective action and simple meaningful tasks and here the study of psychology may help to guide our representational approach in any art and science collaboration.

According to psychologist Stanley Cohen (2001), the capacity to avoid a given level of awareness is the normal state of affairs for people in an information-saturated society. Firstly, he argues, 'far from being pushed into accepting reality, people have to be dragged out of reality'. According to Cohen's definition, avoidance involves a fundamental paradox – that in order to step away from something it is necessary at some level to recognise its existence and its moral implications. This, he says, is a state of simultaneous 'knowing and not-knowing'. People find it extremely hard to accept their responsibility for a crime of such enormity like climate change. Furthermore, the language of 'climate change', 'global warming', 'human impacts', and 'adaptation' are themselves scientific euphemisms that suggest that climate change originates in immutable natural forces rather than in a direct causal relationship with moral implications for the perpetrator. Psychoanalytic theory contains valuable pointers to the ways that people may try to resolve internal conflicts like angrily denying the problem outright (psychotic denial), seeking scapegoats (acting out), indulging in deliberately wasteful behaviour (reaction formation), projecting their anxiety onto some unrelated but containable problem (displacement), or trying to shut out all information (suppression). As the impacts of climate change intensify we can therefore anticipate that people will continue to construct mechanisms of avoidance along these lines. Consequently, transdisciplinary teams should be prepared to brainstorm about an educational advocacy for the public, which considers these psychological reactions. This requires appropriate studies of how an audience identifies with certain stories, because we all remember that past social movements have been built through identification with others who care enough to share their collective concerns.

The majority of the viewing public is tele-visually literate; this has to be taken into account. New digital films could actually deal with the problem that there has been an increase in the knowledge about climate change but not about climate science literacy. On this level, there now seem to be various levels of interest in climate change: denial, uninterested, unaware, interested, attentive and engaged. While the public understanding of global warming is on the increase, members of the public who become attentive or engaged is not really increasing. Climate science literacy should help the public understand the research processes that scientists are involved in. For example, climate scientists assume that the climate system is understandable and therefore predictable, that climatology is cumulative and still evolving and that empirical evidence can be reproduced and validated through peer review. Effective stories about scientists must be woven together with other characters and an emphasis should be place on informing and guiding non-scientists in how to think scientifically and not in telling them 'what' to think. I think that this problem of climate science literacy is far too great for any one discipline to tackle alone so transdisciplinary collaboration can only increase climate literacy. In documentary film, negative connotations such as dislocation, displacement, loss of work, species depletion, agricultural effort and disease are already using these narrative tactics. Spaces like Virtual Theatres and Planetariums are very appropriate venues to increase this awareness, also simply because the sheer scale of them can provide production teams with more potential to turn these delicate approaches from the spectrum of public denial to public engagement.

Planetariums and the Dissemination of Knowledge

It is time that older planetariums shift their emphasis away from simply explaining the universe and become more experimental places where issues like climate change can be played out. People already go to these venues to experience an unimaginable sense of 'scale' in relation to the human body. Just the curved and impressive interior space of a dome and the actual relational scale of the viewer to the screen highlighted by surround sound can produce automatic feelings of human insignifi-

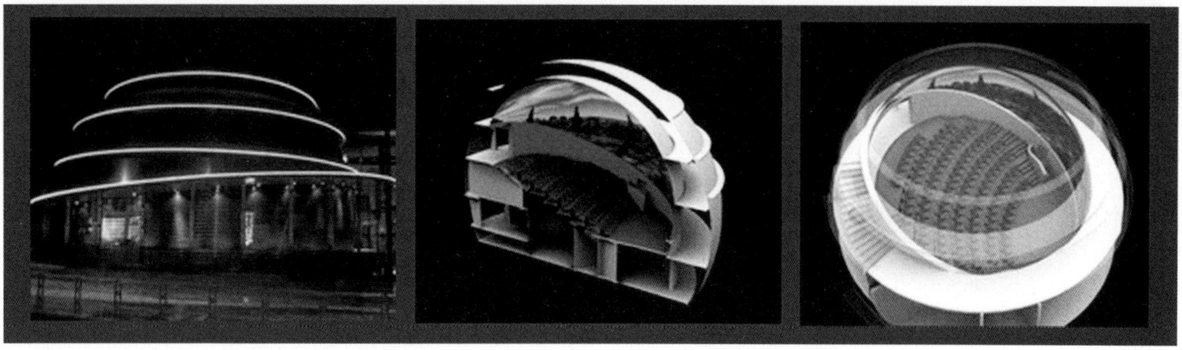

Fig 1. Designs for the Tholos virtual reality theatre in the Foundation of the Hellenic World, Athens. Architects: George Andreakis, Natalia Efraimoglou and Ioannis Tsiomis. 2003.

cance and planetary fragility! For 15 years, digital domes with their Skyscan[10] technologies and 3D graphics, allowed 6x high definition screens to be patched together seamlessly into one visual system. This structure already allowed for productions to be added to the starry potentials of old central mobile Zeiss projectors. However, today, newer domes and half domes are virtual theatres where interactivity with the educational narratives can be constructed. Affectionately called SDPs or Small Digital Planetariums[11] or Virtual Theatres, these platforms offer individual interactivity that can even permit each participant to control his or her own processes of discovery and influence parts of the narrative or storyline. (See Fig. 1)

By carefully utilizing this sense of scale and immersion in the story projected on the spherical screen, inherent dynamics of both a local and a planetary nature can be not only awe-inspiring but also further enhanced by 'zooms' and 'fly-through' pathways. Furthermore, sections of immersive experience can highlight the debates about scale in relation to being 'in charge of your own destiny' and perhaps transfer a sense of responsibility about sustainability to the viewer. Certainly, by allowing the audience to shift the focus or agree to add changes, deeper cognitive associations can be attained than in flat film projections. For example, with interaction from the seats, simulated models could place the audience at the top of carbon levels and from there would all have to work collectively to clean the air or make relative comparisons between clusters of information. By mixing pre-recorded sections of a narrative with real stories or accurate scientific segments, a powerful underlying narrative could be built and combined and the results could have a positive impact on improving climate literacy. As Ka Chun Yu[12] once suggested, digital video full-dome planetariums have much more potential to bridge the comprehension gap than film, because the very use of 3D virtual simulations in immersive environments enhances learning. Other educational theorists have proved interaction and immersion can increase student engagement. An ability to view 3D models from multiple frames of reference can give additional insights into any phenomenon that occurs in a 3D physical space (Raja 2004). These experiences can be augmented by an 8x channel surround system for audio and 'sonification' of related visual data sets, an aspect that can enhance the cognitive impact of the experience because sound cues are an essential part of retaining information.

However, in the past, other approaches to the Dome format by art and science teams have shown that all members of the team need to proceed with some caution. For example in 2001, when commenting on a dome production called 'Grey Matters: The Brain Movie', Roger Dannenberg and Rob Fisher from Carnegie Mellon University (Dannenberg 2001) complained that while the artists in the team 'were not permitted to be neuroscientists and acknowledged the need for scientific accuracy, some of the scientist assumed the roles of artists and began to override all our decisions'. They conclude that mutual respect for each others disciplines, expertise and roles must remain clear from the beginning. In such teams the role of the media artist will always be to question, transform and challenge the technologies that they use, as our AIL team discovered in 2004 from the experience of placing two artists-in-residence (Clea Waite, Andrew Quinn) at the Planetarium in the Museum of Transport in Lucerne. Furthermore, time restraints and technological constraints can often be problematic during the testing phase as Planetarium staff often prefer linear narratives rather than montage scripts favoured by today's filmmakers (Scott 2006).

Nevertheless, Planetariums and other experimental virtual theatres, which have grown up in the last years, can pave the way for new art and science proposals because the potential effect of the dome formats to create a sense of 'telepresence' for the audience is amazing. The word 'telepresence' was originally coined by Marvin Minsky twenty-five years ago (Minsky 1980), and it is defined as the sense of 'being there', a state when a viewer responds psychologically to a mediated environment as if that environment was real, not remote or virtual. By using various visual metaphors of 'telepresence', researchers have shown[13] an increase in attention will occur not only in the persuasiveness of the mediated message, but also in improvements in memory and retention and in enhancements to task performance. Therefore, I want to suggest that any increase in 'telepresence' will increase the effectiveness of specialized content about climate change and raise the levels of audience literacy. Furthermore, because anthropogenic effects on climate change require complex spatial understanding of climate science reality in the atmosphere, the audience is sure to gain from visualization software running in such venues.

Art and Science Dome Narratives

As I have already emphasized in this paper, experimental teams of artists and scientists can construct narratives for the public realm based on common goals and a sharing of knowledge. However, this will not take place without a further weaving of more comprehensive science narratives with enthusiasm, fiction and curiosity and an influence on more art narratives with robust fact and essence of climate science. It seems that most people are unaware about the day-to-day scientific research narratives that are taking place within the study of climate change. Mainstream media not only misrepresents scientific processes or stories, but also evidence-based depth is often over-shadowed by the 'dumbing down of science' or by the fact that journalists prefer 'breaking news'. Generally, environmental science does not move ahead in great leaps and bounds or with sudden breakthroughs, instead discovery moves in small increments, which are constantly revised. Themes emerge from a great deal of collected evidence on many levels, and the narratives found in the mainstream mediums of television, radio and daily newspapers often misrepresent this process. Unlike journalists who are trained to balance their reports with both sides of the debate, art and science teams should attempt to dispel the idea that there is not so much debate in climate science anymore. Our young educated public are not only ready for more in-depth updated knowledge about science, but they can understand that evidence about climate science does not just 'pop out of nowhere', it is a painstakingly systematic process, derived from what is measured, and how, what and why it is being researched in the first place. Therefore the reasons and revisions of climate science needs to be included in the narrative structure and 'real characters from science' or scientific messengers need to speak in order to dispel cognitive illusions or misinformed associations for the public.

Art narratives can often be full of cognitive illusions and sometimes artists could include some more factual evidence in order to reach outside of the art-world's own informed and fashionable audience. In the last 20 years, media artists have become fascinated in non-linear narrative, because today we live in an age in which the stories from mass media and the internet heavily influence the public. Therefore, it is imperative that media artists explore issues which can increase the audience's perception, by allowing them to navigate through the information in their own time and space. This has already spawned much collaboration between artists and scientific engineers or programmers, but the relations between natural scientists and the media artists are still fairly underdeveloped. Experimental media artists no longer see industrial partnerships as advantageous for artists seeking to exploit new technologies, rather many are now interested in the potentials of media to deal with real world issues and further contribute to the aesthetics and the design of the future.

These ideals are far from new in the design world. In the 70s, industrial designer Victor Papenek already confirmed that design must be revolutionary in the most radical and in the truest sense by thinking about the concepts of *bionic design* (Papenek 1985). '*Bionic design* never means to copy by using a visual analogue. Rather it means to search out the basic underlying organic principal and then finding an application.' He even further supported the concept of 'Re-design' which required the application of three functional principals, (1) use nature's principal of least effort or doing the most with the least, (2) consuming less, minimum diversity with minimum inventory and (3) using things longer or recycle. Thus 'human and bionic centred design' can be seen as a great starting point and in fact, Papenek's principals were recently used as one of the main ideas for a digital screen art project in the dome format.

Case Study: Atmosphere one

Atmosphere one was inspired by discussions with a group of artists and scientists[14] about the fact that many people may not really understand greenhouse physics or the behaviour of the atmosphere and that dome format could be used as a way to increase their climate science literacy. Atmospheric change is basically associated with the balance of molecules in four cycles: the water vapour cycle; the oxygen cycle; the carbon cycle; and the electrical energy cycle. The project combines art and

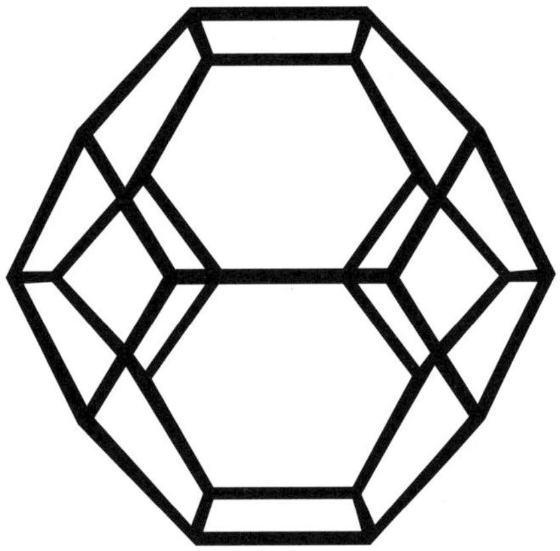

Fig. 2: Lord Kelvin's- Tetrakaidecahedron

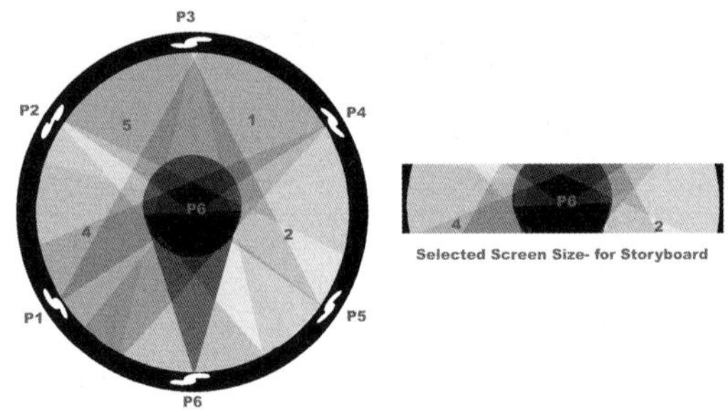

Fig. 3: Graphic Layout of the Dome Projection System

science displays to show how shifts in these cycles and imbalances can jeopardize our future. However, it used bionic and human centred design as a catalyst for this information and to offer some solutions, which may lead to a more 'sustainable atmosphere'. Thus the development process of *Atmosphere one* should help to discover new artistic metaphors and narratives in immersive mediated environments, ones that can help an audience understand the effects of climate change on different communities. Using three characters, a climate science researcher, a design fabricator and a learner, imbalances are measured and discussed from a scientific perspective. The results should encourage the development of new 'urban citizen ecologists' or 'environmental stewards' by teaching young adults how to think about and invent new ways to curb stress in the atmosphere by becoming more 'engaged' on the ground level to reduce energy usage. Perhaps then they can start to share the responsibility of environmental stewardship. Instead of these 'dos and don'ts' appearing as lists in books, *Atmosphere one* immerses the audience in several journeys through greenhouse gasses and their behaviours: the 'number one' priority for a sustainable balance. The project uses design and communication metaphors as well as artistic and sonic interpretations to create a better understanding of these interrelated cycles and how they can be sustained. Based on this synopsis we have already developed a first treatment, a stage that has been funded by the Swiss Ministry for Culture under their Sitemapping Awards-Digital Screen Section and some 3D sketches from further brainstorming by myself, Andrew Quinn and Marille Hahne have been included in this book.

In these sketches the Tetrakaidecahedra (Tetra (4) kai (and) deca (10) hedron) has been appropriated as the basic bionic metaphor for the strength of the individual, as a transportation vehicle and as a stage for the presentation of content. Based on Lord Kelvin's minimal space-dividing cell[15], the Tetrakaidecahedron shape can be found in many basic plant forms, algae and nuts. When many Tetrakaidecahedron are joined together they can form the strongest possible structure found in nature. (See Fig. 4)

Fig. 4: Multi Tetrakaidecahedra: Dome Storyboard Structure

As the full tilted dome planetarium is also made up of a six-sided projection, the points on the Tetrakaidecahedron can also coincide with either tilted dome technology or be re-adjusted for the half dome 4-point presentations. (See Fig. 3)

Also the 14 sides of the double Tetrakaideacahedra can be used for texture maps of real films or the whole shape can be used in a stereoscopic way, thus allowing the four natural cycles and their disturbances in *Atmosphere one* to be displayed in new ways. Furthermore various science-fiction films in the past have successfully affected the learning curve of young audiences by using the shrunken micro-method of travelling in the human body[16] like in *The fantastic voyage* (1966 USA) or through the molecular world *Innerspace* (1987). Therefore we have appropriated this immersive approach in order to encourage the audiences to identify with molecular and cellular levels of sustainable behaviour. (see Fig. 5)

The Tetra carries the 'two main protagonists' who make experiments and the 'learner' (who represent the young urban youth) who helps them. Thus, stories are revealed through discussion, flashbacks and flash-forwards and the myth of natural stability is dispelled. Issues like the suddenness with which climate can change, the runaway green house effect, the creation of oxygen, the roles of radiation, the effects of condensation and weather prediction must all be told through clever scripting with humour and drama. Interaction should give the audience clear choices and help them to reveal and identify the significance, evidence, and proof, found in scientific research. This part of *Atmosphere one* will focus on the need to take some responsibility for the preservation of the Earth as our exclusive and natural home, (see Colour plate xii-xv, Fig. A - H)

Fig. 5: Art Sci Discussion in a Tetra in *Atmosphere one*-Sample (2x16x9 ratio) 3D Image

As suggested by the Intergovernmental Panel of Climate Change-fourth assessment (IPCC 2007) it is important for the general public to understand that the atmospheric concentrates of carbon dioxide, methane and nitrous oxide have increased markedly as a result of human activities. Levels now exceed the pre-industrial values determined from ice cores, spanning many thousands of years. Specifically, increases in carbon dioxide are primarily due to the burning of fossil fuels and land use change, while those of methane and nitrous oxide are primarily due to agriculture. In this educational and worthwhile endeavour, science needs to solicit the help of artists and designers who are not only trained in the semiotics of communication, but are also interested in finding poetic visual metaphors about nature rather than duplicating journalistic facts. Therefore, the methods of extraction, filtering and abstraction can be used as interpretations to understand the underlying principals of climate science. This challenge is augmented by an acquired experience in constructing narratives with sound and visuals rather than text. Many media artists are already dealing with environmental themes. Some are designing projects for the extreme hostile atmosphere of micro-gravity (Kirsten Johansen) while others are sonifying data or translating scientific metrological data into sound (Andrea Polli) or designing *eco visualizations* to compare kilowatts used by certain communities (Tiffany Holmes). Therefore, issues like carbon emissions, the health of the lungs and our forests or the controversies around agro-fuels have become important factors for art researchers to consider.

Conclusion: Sustainable Futures

In this paper I have argued for the further development of transdisplinary art and science brainstorming to produce climate change literacy for the general public. Mediated dome environments and virtual theatres are relevant venues for these aims, because the actual scale of the problem requires it, and the content can immerse the audience for a deeper effect. The presentation of content by climate scientists is focused on the condition of the atmosphere and their conclusions are generated by collection, analysis and knowledge about local conditions. Results are either used to verify these conditions, or for prediction models. These scientists already believe in a responsibility to reach out to the public with their results. Artists on the other hand employ educational, metaphorical and communication skills to explore the borders between fact and fiction, and they are interested in raising awareness and redesigning attitudes of the public so that they feel empowered to invent some sustainable solutions of their own. However, there are certain requirements, which need to be agreed upon by both parties about how to share, gather, and weave, diverse scientific research results in order to generate dynamic attention amid our already overcrowded information binge. Rather than scare tactics or 'before and after' comparisons, a psychological approach based on the interpretation of knowledge or educational ecological advocacy is sorely needed in order to provide a more positive role for the viewer. Today's young urban youth for example, must begin to construct cultural mechanisms for social support and participatory communal experiences. So if these teams can treat the dome format as a 'blank canvas' for the audio and visual interpretations and education of climate change, and encourage an audience to feel more localized and engaged in relation to the scale of the problem, compared to feeling so remote from the problem, perhaps they will gain some scientifically robust knowledge in an exciting and awe-inspiring manner. Thus more serious misjudgements may be avoided to help manage the environment and take the role of mediated information past pure description and theatrical effect to a place where '*the invisible present*' becomes a more audible and a more visible future.

Notes

1 NESTA, Science, National Endowment for Science, Technology and Art, <http://www.nesta.org.uk>.

2 The Swiss based artists-in-labs program can be found at <http://www.artistsinlabs.ch>.>

3 *The Art of Climate Change* 2006, Natural History Museum, London, Curator: Birgit Arends. A document from the Art and science project: Cape Farewell, David Buckland, see <http://www.capefarewell.com>.

4 *Tiempo Climate Portal: Education*, accessed 15 March 2010, <http://www.tiempocyberclimate.org>/portal/education.htm>.

5 For artists and activist art on environmental issues see: The Green Museum at <http://www.greenmuseum.org>/> for a wide list of activist activities see <http://www.dmoz.org>/Society/Issues/Environment/Climate_Change/Activism>.

6 According to a report published by Hamilton in 2001, when oil (or compressed Plankton-single cells known as phytoplankton) is burnt it produces high levels of CO2 in the atmosphere, but by comparison the burning of brown coal (which is younger, more porous and more moist than black coal) produces 130 percent more CO2 than oil, and it is increasingly used for most of our energy requirements. Climate models are systems of differential equations based on the basic laws of physics, fluid motion, and chemistry. To "run" a model, scientists divide the planet into a 3-dimensional grid, apply the basic equations, and evaluate the results. Atmospheric models calculate winds, heat transfer, radiation, relative humidity, and surface hydrology within each grid and evaluate interactions with neighbouring points, the problem that all of these elements often behave in a chaotic way. For example highly variable solar and magnetosphere energy inputs can make Ionosphere models very chaotic see: 'Ionosphere Storms A Review' by MJ Buonsanto, vol. 88, no. 3-4, April, 1999, *Space Science Reviews*, pp. 563-601 Springerlink.

7 *The Day after Tomorrow* 2004, film directed by R Emmerich, accessed 11 March 2010, <http://www.imdb.com/title/tt0319262>. Unfortunately this film posits a completely desolate dystrophic relation to climate change in true Hollywood style, and uses completely inaccurate data.

8 *SOS Planet* 2003, IMAX film directed by B Stassen, narrated by W Cronkite, funded by WWF, accessed 11 March 2010, <http://www.travelvideostore.com/product_info.php?products_id=3702>. Supposed to focus on the issue of conservation for children – the greenhouse effect, marine conservation, and deforestation, but the themes 'earth first' message is delivered up in a very slapdash manner based more on cute characterization than information.

9 *An inconvenient truth* 2006, film directed by Davis Guggenheim and produced by L David and L Bender, accessed 11 March 2010, <http://www.calendarlive.com/movies/reviews/cl-et truth24may24,0,577270.story?coll=cl-mrevie>.

10 Skyscan Technologies, <http://www.skyskan.com/Products/index.html>, The Museum of Transport,

Lucerne (Verkehrshaus der Schweiz, Planetarium) uses both Zeiss and SKYSKAN technologies, including 6 stitched screens in HDTV, technical know-how and 8-channel surround sound see <http://www.skyskan.com/Products/index.html>.

11 A really fine example of a virtual dome theatre is the Tholos Virtual Theatre Athens, accessed 15 March 2010, <http://www.tholos254.gr/en>. Another is the Digitarium at <http://software.einnews.com/article.php?nid=22770>.

12 Yu, KC 2005, 'Digital Full-Domes: The future of virtual astronomy education', *Planetarian: Journal of the International Planetarium Society*, vol. 34, no. 3, pp. 6-11, accessed 15 March 2010, <http://www.ips-planetarium.org>/planetarian/articles/imagesand-docs/special_focus1.pdf>.

13 Two seminal references are pertinent to list here: Reeves, B & Nass, C 1986, *The Media Equation: How people treat computers, television and new media like real people and places*, Cambridge University Press. pp. 193-293; and Abbatantuono, B P 1995, Armand Spitz: Seller of Stars, *Planetarium, Journal of the International Planetarium Society*, vol. 24, no. 1, pp.14-22.

14 The initial group were the scientists: Space X Lab <http://www.space-x.ch>, WSL Centre <http://www.wsl.ch/forschung/forschungsprojekte/index_EN>, Paul Scherrer Institute, Villigen <http://www.psi.ch>, and the artists: Johannsen, K <http://www.kirstenjohannsen.de>, Polli, A <http://www.andreapolli.com>, Scott, J <http://www.jillscott.org>, *Holmes*, T <http://www.tiffanyholmes.com>, Hahne, M <http://ssl.einsnull.com/paymate/search.php?vid=2&peid=13>.

15 Tetrakaidecahedron was first described by mathematician Lord Kelvin in the *Proceedings of the Royal Society of London*, vol. 55, 1894, pp. 1, <http://zapatopi.net/kelvin/papers/on_homogeneous_division_of_space.html>. Computer simulators and designers have long been fascinated with the strength of the cell (January 17, 1894). He then suggested that 'the form of cell essentially consists of fourteen walls ... of which eight are hexagonal and six quadrilateral; and with thirty-six edges, generally curves, of meeting between the walls; and twenty-four corners where three walls meet. A cell answering this description must of course be called a Tetrakaidecahedron, unless we prefer to call it a fourteen-walled cell. Each wall is an interface between one cell and one of fourteen neighbours. Each of the thirty-six edges is a line common to three neighbours. Each of the twenty-four corners is a point common to four neighbours.'

16 *Fantastic Voyage* 1966, film directed by R Fleischer, accessed 12 March 2010, <http://www.imdb.com/title/tt0060397>.

References

Abbatantuono, BP 1995, 'Armand Spitz: seller of stars', *The Planetarium*, vol. 24, no. 1, pp. 14-22, accessed 12 March 2010, <http://www.ips-planetarium.org>/planetarian/articles/Armand.html>.

artists-in-labs (ail), program in Switzerland, Zurich University of the Arts (ZHdK), accessed 11 March 2010, <http://www.artistsinlabs.ch>.

Buckland D 2006, *The art of climate change*, A document from the art and science project: Cape Farewell, Curator: B Arends, Natural History Museum, London, accessed 11 March 2010, <http://www.capefarewell.com>.

Buonsanto, MJ 1999, 'Ionospheric storms: A review', *Space Science Reviews*, vol. 88, no. 3-4, April, pp. 563-601, Springerlink, accessed 11 March 2010, <http://www.springerlink.com/content/bu96nph2hg72/?p=c6223217756346279e1777156de65f02&pi=85>.

Cohen, S 2001, *States of denial: Knowing about atrocities and suffering*, Polity Press, Cambridge.

Dannenberg, R & Fisher, R 2001, 'An audience-interactive multimedia production on the brain', *Proceedings of the Connecticut college symposium on art and technology*, accessed 11 March 2010, <http://www.cs.cmu.edu/~rbd/papers/brainshow/brainshow.htm.

Digitarium, virtual dome digital planetarium theatre, accessed 11 March 2010, <http://software.einnews.com/article.php?nid=22770>.

Flannery, T 2005, *The weather makers: The history and future impact of climate change*, Text Publishing, Melbourne, reviews of this book accessed 11 March 2010, <http://www.theweathermakers.com/global-warming>.

Green Museum, online museum of environmental art, accessed 11 March 2010 <http://www.greenmuseum.org>.

Hahne, M, artist website of Marille Hahne, accessed 13 March 2010, <http://ssl.einsnull.com/paymate/search.php?vid=2&peid=13.

Hansen, J, Nazarenko, L, Ruedy, R, Sato, M, et al. 2005, 'Earth's energy imbalance: confirmation and implications', *Science Express*, vol. 308, no. 5727, pp. 1431-1435, also available in *Science*, accessed 11 March 2010, <http://www.sciencemag.org>/cgi/content/abstract/308/5727/1431>.

Holmes, T, artist website of Tiffany Holmes, accessed 12 March 2010, <http://www.tiffanyHolmes.com.

Innerspace 1987, film directed by J Dante, accessed 11 March 2010, <http://www.imdb.com/title/tt0093260>.

Intergovernmental panel on climate change: fourth climate change assessment, 2007, accessed 11 March 2010, <http://www.greenpeace.org>/raw/content/canada/en/documents-and-links/publications/greenpeace-briefing-on-the-ipc.pdf>.

Johannsen, K, artist website of Kirsten Johannsen, accessed 12 March 2010, <http://www.kirstenjohannsen.de>.

Kräuchi, N 2007, interviews with Norbert Kräuchi, by Jillian Scott, Swiss Centre for Forest Snow and Landscape Research (WSL), May, accessed 13 March 2010, <http://www.wsl.ch>/personal_homepages/kraeuchi/index_EN>.

Lord Kelvin, 1894, 'On homogeneous division of space', *Proceedings of the Royal Society of London*, vol. 55. 17 January, p. 1, accessed 12 March 2010, <http://zapatopi.net/kelvin/papers/on_homogeneous_division_of_space.html>.

Lovelock, J 1988, *The Age of GAIA: A Biography of our own living earth*, W.W. Norton, New York.

Magnuson, JJ 1990, 'Long-term ecological research and the *invisible present*: Uncovering the processes hidden because they occur slowly or because effects lag years behind causes', in *BioScience*, vol. 40, no. 7, pp. 495-501, accessed 11 March 2010, <http://limnology.wisc.edu/personnel/magnuson/articles/magnuson_biosci_v40-7-495.pdf>.

Marshall, G 2001, 'The psychology of denial: our failure to act against climate change', *The ecologist*, 22 September, accessed 11 March 2010, <http://www.ecoglobe.ch>/motivation/e/clim2922.htm>.

Minsky, M 1980, 'Telepresence' *Omni*, vol. 2. no. 9, pp. 45-52, accessed 15 March 2010, <http://web.media.mit.edu/~minsky/papers/Telepresence.html>.

National Endowment for Science Technology and the Arts (NESTA), accessed 11 March 2010, <http://www.nesta.org.uk>.

Open Directory Project, 'Environment: climate change: activism', accessed 11 March 2010 <http://www.dmoz.org>/Society/Issues/Environment/Climate_Change/Activism/>.

Papanek, V 1985, (1971), *Design for the real world: Human ecology and social change*, second ed. Thames and Hudson, London, p. 210.

Paul Scherrer Institute (PSI), Villigen Switzerland, accessed 13 March 2010, <http://www.psi.ch>.

Polli, A, artist website of Andrea Polli, accessed 12 March 2010, <http://www.andreapolli.com>.

Raja, D, Bowman, DA, Lucas, J & North, C 2004, 'Exploring the benefits of immersion in abstract information visualization', Proceedings of the Immersive Projection Technology Workshop. Siggraph <http://people.cs.vt.edu/~bowman/papers/ipt_dheva.pdf>.

Reeves, B and Nass, C 1986, *The Media Equation: How people treat computers, television and new media like real people and places*, Cambridge University Press, Cambridge/MA, pp. 193-293

Scott, J, artist website of Jill Scott, accessed 12 March 2010, <http://www.jillscott.org>

Scott, J (ed.) 2006, *Artists-in-labs: Processes of Inquiry*, Springer, Wien/New York, accessed 11 March 2010, <http://www.springer.com/springerwiennewyork/art/book/978-3-211-27957-1>.

Sky-Skan Technology, accessed 11 March 2010, <http://www.skyskan.com/Products/index.html.>

Space X, Space Exploration Institute, <http://www.space-x.ch>.

WSL, Swiss Centre for Forest Snow and Landscape Research, accessed 13 March 2010, <http://www.wsl.ch>/forschung/forschungsprojekte/index_EN>.

WHO OWNS THE AIR? EMISSIONS TRADING AND CONTEMPORARY MEDIA ART

Andrea Polli

The accelerating crisis in climate change and the realization that humans are the primary cause of this change has raised questions about ownership and responsibility. Who 'owns' the climate change crisis and who is responsible for mitigating and reversing it if possible? The overwhelming response to these questions by governments on an international level has been to propose a market solution, in essence, to sell the atmosphere. This chapter explores the idea of air for sale from an economic, political and cultural perspective. Contemporary art projects that attempt to address the politics of air will be discussed in the context of the author's experiences while curating the online Aer exhibition for the Green Museum in California.

The Buying and Selling of Greenhouse Gasses

Ecological economics provides both a mechanism for the valuation of environmental resources and an incentive for keeping within an established environmental 'budget'. In 1997, the US Congress described it in this way:

> 'From an economic perspective, pollution problems are caused by a lack of clearly defined and enforced property rights. Smokestack emissions, for example, are deposited into the air because the air is often treated as a common good, available for all to use as they please, even as a disposal site. Not surprisingly, this apparently free good is overused. A primary and appropriate role for government in supporting the market economy is the definition and enforcement of property rights. Defining rights for use of the atmosphere, lakes, and rivers is critical to prevent their overuse. Once legal entitlement has been established, markets can be employed to exchange these rights as a means of improving economic efficiency.' (US Congress, 1997)

Property rights to air, or the right to pollute the air, has been rising in popularity as a way to control emissions. What follows are several examples of contemporary trading systems with various goals and structures. The Kyoto Protocol required 35 industrialized countries and the EU to reduce greenhouse gas emissions by an average of 5% below 1990 levels by 2012 (The United Nations Framework Convention on Climate Change, 2007). The Kyoto protocol includes a global greenhouse gas emissions trading system that has now been in place in Europe for almost three years. This emissions trading system could also be called a 'cap and trade' system. In the first year, credits are generous and the total amount of emissions for each company is determined. Each company has to achieve no more than that amount. Then, each subsequent year, the amount of credits allotted to each company is reduced, allowing companies to slowly lower emissions. The design of this system can be compared to other models of trading systems.

Sulfur Dioxide Trading

In 1990, the US launched a cap-and-trade program in sulfur dioxide as an amendment to the Clean Air Act. An initial objective of the program was to reduce sulfur dioxide emissions from utilities by 8.5 million tons below 1980 levels. To accomplish this, electric utility plants above a certain size were given an initial allocation of emissions allowances based on historical patterns. The Act included stiff penalties for excess emissions, at a value more than 10 times that of reduction costs. The program achieved a very high degree of compliance and the US Congress considers the program a success. The current European greenhouse gas trading system is modelled after this system, but can it work in every situation? (US Congress, 1997).

CFC Trading

Another model is The Montreal Protocol on Substances That Deplete the Ozone Layer, an international treaty that entered into force on January 1, 1989 designed to protect the ozone layer by phasing out the production of a number of substances believed to be responsible for ozone depletion, in particular CFCs and halons. This Montreal Protocol created a system for the international trading of allowances. In the protocol, trading is combined with a tax, to offset any large profits from allowances that might discourage the reduction of CFCs. Since the Montreal Protocol came into effect, the atmospheric concentrations of the most important CFCs and related chlorinated hydrocarbons have either levelled off or decreased. Kofi Annan, Former Secretary General of the United Nations calls the protocol 'Perhaps the single most successful international agreement to date' (Natural Science, 2007). However, by 1997, smuggling of CFCs from developing nations, where they were still permitted, into the U.S. and other developed nations had become big business. In Miami in 1997 smuggling of CFCs was believed to be second only to cocaine. A market solution can be very susceptible to this kind of exploitation. The difference between a CO_2 market and both the CFC and sulfur dioxide markets is that technology exists to clean up CFC and SO_2 emissions and applies only to a relatively small number of companies with outdated technology, while the CO_2 system applies to thousands of companies and despite optimistic talk of 'clean coal' there is presently no existing technology to make coal burn more cleanly or sequester carbon emissions more safely on a large scale.

Rights of the Airwaves

Another model for distributing air rights that can be examined is the right of the airwaves, or broadcasting rights. The US Federal Communications Commission (FCC), which was created out of the Communications Act of 1934, regulates all non-government wire and wireless communications. The Act specified only that broadcasting be in the hands of American citizens, and left it up to the FCC to decide how to license broadcast rights. In the past, applicants were required to describe plans for programming to be judged on general usefulness to the public and on its practicality. In practice, this resulted in a combination of private and governmental control. However, in 1993 congress gave the FCC authority to use competitive bidding, and since 1994, the FCC has conducted auctions of licenses for the electromagnetic spectrum, open to any eligible company or individual that submits an application and an upfront payment. According to the FCC, the auctions more effectively assign licenses than previously used hearings or lotteries and has reduced the time from initial application to license grant substantially. In 1997 congress passed legislation that required the FCC to use auctions for all licensing unless exemptions apply, for example public safety, educational and public broadcasting. For a commercial broadcaster, purchasing through auction became the only way to gain rights to the airwaves (The Federal Communications Commission, 2007). This system created a broadcasting sphere widely dominated by the large commercial interests with the resources required to win this bidding war for the airwaves. In 1996, the system was changed to favour large corporate media even more. The FCC relaxed the rules that restricted broadcasters from owning several radio or television stations in one market, allowing broadcasters, for example, to own an unlimited number of radio stations. This move has created an increase in advertising prices and caused an unexpected outcry from communities who have found that the consolidation of the media within the hands of a few large corporations has resulted in a loss of quality local programming, with corporations instead polluting the airwaves with homogenized, computer controlled broadcasts. The lesson to be learned here that might also apply to a market in greenhouse gasses is that the de-regulation of the market, allowing the unrestricted purchasing of air rights, be it polluting or broadcasting, could well result in a disastrous reduction of the quality of air and the airwaves.

A fundamental aspect of the greenhouse gas emissions trading system is the granting of property rights to the air. The idea of ecological economics as illustrated in these models, came from the understanding that environmental resources are finite, and since these resources can be destroyed, there should be incentives for protecting them. The question of how these incentives should be created, however, whether through a trading system or through regulations or some other means, is a topic of great controversy. What follows are some of these conflicting viewpoints.

Air and Property rights

> 'Economic super-powers have been as successful today in their disproportionate occupation of the atmosphere with carbon emissions as they were in their military occupation of the terrestrial world in colonial times.' Andrew Simms, The New Economist Foundation (Simms, 2006).

Emissions trading systems have been criticized for a long time. At the 1992 Earth Summit in Rio, the NGO Global Forum emphasized avoiding pollution trading schemes that 'perpetuate or worsen inequities hidden behind the problem or have a negative impact'. Later, arguments escalated, calling trade in greenhouse gases a new form of colonialism. Arguments for and against this system range from concern about flaws and possible abuses of the system to criticism of its fundamental assumptions about ownership.

The biggest beneficiaries of a greenhouse gas emissions trading scheme can be found in the banking industry (in the US, this industry is currently lobbying heavily for the implementation of a carbon cap and trade system) and the nuclear power industry that stands to gain a loosening of restrictions on the production of new power plants. However, despite the support of banks, not all economic experts support the use of such a system. Many would rather see a carbon tax in place. In practice, a carbon tax functions very much like a trading system because polluting companies either pay a tax or pay for carbon credits for their emissions. Both systems will also raise consumer prices on fossil fuels. However, critics of the tax system say that it does not provide the incentive or 'race for the pot of gold' that the *carbon trading* system instils by financially rewarding companies that can substantially cut emissions (Solomon, 2007). There are critics of the trading system on both the political right and the left. From the right, Nicole Gelinas, a journalist of *The Wall Street Journal* argues against a trading system in the US by stating that the global competition created by the system will hurt US based corporations. If US energy companies cannot limit emissions, the international cap and trade system would require them to buy emissions credits from other countries. Interested in protecting the financial interests of these US corporations, she calls the trading system a 'direct subsidy to developing nations by paying for their power-plant upgrades'. She argues that a Federal carbon tax, an alternative to the international carbon cap and trade system, would provide revenue to the US government that could then be used to subsidize US power plant upgrades, while an international cap and trade system could put this revenue in the hands of other countries, particularly those that already have reduced emissions. Gelinas's views seem to be in line with those of the US government. In fact, one of the reasons the US has stated it is against the Kyoto Protocol is that it provides exceptions for developing countries, the countries that stand to benefit most from the protocol and lose the most from the consequences of global warming (Gelinas, 2007).

In *The weather makers*, Tim Flannery debates this position, stating that although developing nations were not bound by the Montreal Protocol, it was very successful. Flannery has mixed feelings about the subject of *carbon trading*. On the one hand, he observes that emissions trading is cost effective, and as a tool to reduce pollution, it has been successful in the past (for example in the case of sulfur dioxide trading). On the other hand, he talks about the case of eastern European countries whose economies have suffered ruin since the 90s and therefore are producing approx 25% less CO_2 than they were in 1990. Since the Kyoto trading system requires emissions only 8% less than 1990 levels, without doing anything to actively lower emissions, these countries end up with a surplus of carbon credits, known as 'hot air' to critics of the protocol. Flannery posits that creating a new global currency is too risky, since the foundation of any currency is based on trust - in this case trust that the seller will lower emissions, and so far he has not seen any guarantee that this will happen (Flannery, 2005 p. 225).

Arguing from the political left in *Carbon trading*, Larry Lohman quotes Flannery's work when outlining the potential effects of climate change, but he is much more pessimistic than Flannery, particularly in regard to the commercial markets. He focuses on the seriousness of the problem and predicts that many markets will eventually collapse. He uses the example of the insurance business, providing quotes from insurance specialists who estimate that chaotic climate change could increase insurance rates several times higher than that of world economic growth, creating a situation where the world economy will not be able to sustain the losses and will collapse. Lohman is critical of the hopeful attitude held by many industrialized countries about technological developments, which would allow continued use of fossil fuels such as carbon sequestration as the solution. He devotes a chapter on analyzing how these technological solutions are nothing but a smokescreen used to distract public attention away from the government's lack of necessary action. He calls this distraction the 'second strategy'. He calls the first strategy the public denial of the existence of anthropogenic climate change.

> 'The first strategy works to reshape or suppress understanding of the climate problem so that public reaction to it will present less of a political threat to corporations. The second strategy appeals to technological fixes as a way of bypassing the debate over fossil fuels while helping to spur innovations that can serve as new sources of profit. The third strategy appeals to a 'market fix' that secures the property rights of heavy Northern fossil fuel users over the world's carbon-absorbing capacity while creating new opportunities for corporate profit through trade.' (Lohman, 2006 p. 54)

In *Earth in the balance*, Al Gore embraces in part what Lohman critically calls the 'second strategy', proposing an SEI (Strategic Environment Initiative) which like the existing US SDI (Strategic Defense Initiative), would require a major national effort, but with a focus on the environment rather than the military. Although he does emphasize that any new technologies should be evaluated, his focus is primarily on developing new technologies to combat climate change (Gore, 2006).

Finally, Lohman is very critical of what he calls the third strategy, the 'market fix', primarily because of the property rights issue, the privatization of the air. Like Flannery, he is concerned that if a 'top down' creation of a greenhouse gas emissions market was created without public debate, it will result in a market filled with distrust, including a lack of faith in both the structure and the implementation of the market. The bottom line according to Lohman is that the current emissions trading structure allocates the most allowances to the biggest emitters, effectively giving a handout of billions of dollars to the most egregious polluters and providing incentives to them to keep polluting.

In *The great emissions rights give-away* (2006), Andrew Simms, policy director of the NEF (New Economics Foundation) and Feasta (The Foundation for the Economics of Stability), proposes an alternative structure for EU *carbon trading*. In his structure, the EU's emissions allowances would be divided into an equal per capita basis and distributed to every EU resident. Residents would then be able to sell these allowances to companies or keep them off the market, thus actually promoting cleaner air. Simms compares this approach to some other alternative approaches. For example, the Sky Trust in the US proposes a system where any money made from the sale of emissions credits are kept in a trust in order to insure that any financial gains are used to benefit the public. The proposals of both The Sky Trust and NEF/Feasta are based on the fundamental principle that the atmosphere belongs to all people equally and not to any governments or corporations (Simms, 2006).

Selling Air

One might think that the idea of 'air for sale' is absurd, however it is in place in the abstract arena of the market. After all, no one would actually pay for the air they breathe. Culturally, this may no longer be the case, as evidenced by the rising popularity of something called the oxygen bar and portable canned air. In both the cases, oxygen is touted as a cleansing medical 'therapy'. Advertisements focus on the healing power of air, using aromatherapy or 'oxygen therapy'. Advertisers promote the air as energizing for exercise, effective in combating cigarette smoke and curing a hangover. They sell air based on the idea of being pure, fresh and clean, and many promote it as an escape from the smog of city life. The oxygen bar started as a trend in the 1990's in Japan, Mexico and South America and quickly spread to nightclubs, spas, casinos and malls in Europe and the US (Rimbach, 2003). Portable canned air is becoming just as popular and widespread. In Japan, a recent large-scale commercial venture is O2supli, a portable can of oxygen. How could our global culture have gotten to a point where the absurd notion of buying and selling the air is acceptable on any level, corporate or individual? Perhaps the arts, specifically conceptual artworks, have played a role in making buying air a culturally acceptable activity?

Air for Sale in Contemporary Art

> '*When art becomes idea, idea becomes commodity.*' (Alberro 2006)

As creative works, art and architecture have value in society, not just cultural value (although they have that too), but monetary value. In the 50's and 60's, Yves Klein's concept of *Air architecture* challenged the definitions of art and architecture by building with ephemeral materials, but on a wider scale it may have contributed to the idea of commodifying the public resource of air. Klein was interested in the ways that humans can use science and technology to conquer the ephemeral, even to the point of turning even air and fire into building materials. Klein saw science and technology as the saviour of architecture, because they promoted new forms and structures made from sculpting the air and other 'immaterial-materials'. He believed that *Air architecture* would actually improve the environment, positing that '*Air architecture* must be adapted to the natural conditions and situations, to the mountains, valleys, monsoons, etc., if possible without requiring the use of great artificial modifications' (Noever, ed. 2004). By creating *Air architecture*, Klein radically redefined the limits of architecture, asking why solid materials like stone, wood and brick should be the only materials in an architect's palette. By developing technologies for using (or, some may say, misusing) ephemeral materials for building, Klein created an alternative pathway for the architectural imagination. In the late 1960's, a group of artists including Robert Barry became associated with dealer Seth Siegelaub and started producing work that questioned the limits of art. Barry's series of works, known as 'invisible' art included *Inert gas series* (1969), in which a specific amount of gases (neon, xenon and helium) were released 'from measured volume to indefinite expansion' in the Mojave Desert (Wood, 2002 pp. 35-36). Lucy Lippard observed in *Six years: the dematerialization of the art object* that 'novelty is the fuel of the art market', and at the time of Robert Barry's *Inert gas series*, this 'fuel' was being burned at a rapid pace, constantly stretching the boundaries of the definition of art. By using the term 'dematerialization', Lippard attempts to remove art from its status as commodity by creating such ephemeral 'objects' of art like those including the natural expansion of gas, a substance that would be absurd to commodify. Artists like Barry were reacting against and attempting to create an alternative to the art market. However, over time, this work has not been removed from the art market. The ephemeral art movement was actually embraced by commercial galleries and dealers. As Lippard suggests, this market needed the fuel of these increasingly novel ideas (Lippard, 1968, p.31).

A connection to the market may have been necessary for the creation of the art and the survival of the artist, nonetheless it created a paradoxical situation in which the immaterial was moved into the object realm. The critical stance of the artist on the art market was compromised through the positioning of the work within the art market.

The Aer Exhibition

Today there are a growing number of contemporary art and social media projects from a multidisciplinary perspective that represent the beginning of an effort to give a voice to each one of us affected by poor air quality, to highlight the flaws in the current system, and to empower individuals to preserve and protect our fragile atmosphere. The *Aer* exhibition was curated by the author as part of her research and the featured artists are far from neutral about the issue of air and air quality (Polli, 2008). The artists in *Aer* all look critically at air issues and use various methods to raise awareness among the public. Some also take an active role by directly affecting the air quality and therefore human lives. Because air is invisible, artists are faced with the challenge of making the intangible real. Air pollution is a silent killer, and it is challenging to give a voice to the body's dependence on clean air. Most of the featured projects blur the line between art and activism, and all the projects aim to change public understanding of air as well as question accepted norms of ownership and responsibility.

Australian performance artist Sarah Jane Pell highlighted the body's transfer of air and our dependence on air as living, breathing beings. Her works explored the physical and emotional limits of the body. For example, *Interdepend* creates a closed-circuit life support system between Pell and artist Martyn Coutts, and *Undercurrent* presents a single performer contained within a sealed transparent dome with a finite amount of breathable air. These works are physically demanding for the performers and created an overwhelming emotional intensity for the public. Pell's works seem to give air a physical manifestation. This can be witnessed either through human interdependence or through a single womb-like containment that without breathable air would become a tomb. Pell's works seem to hold a vision of the future. This vision is apocalyptic: one in which the very air we breathe is a limited commodity. In the future, will the earth's fragile atmosphere continue to sustain us, or will we be forced to remain contained in controlled environments while our machines roam freely, reporting to us the world outside? By suggesting an alternative future of limited air, these works by Pell created a pathway that forced audiences to consider the important reciprocal relationship between humans and the earth's atmosphere.

The artist's team called Superflex have created a project for the purpose of influencing social change (see Colour plate xvii, Fig. C). Superflex worked in collaboration with Danish and African engineers on *Supergas*, which aims to provide a modest and efficient portable biogas system for families in Africa. Superflex identifies their artworks as tools, shaped by a social and economic commitment. The tool *Supergas* has helped individual families to become independent producers of energy with minimal time investment and without making dramatic changes to their culture. This transdisciplinary process of development involved the community on a deep level. Also, the design process didn't end with implementation, the tool itself was originally designed for flexible use, a kind of open-ended platform. *Supergas* captures organic materials that are an ordinary artefact of farming in order to promote individual energy empowerment and to protect the air from more polluting forms of energy production. The thought process that can take a polluting compound and with minimal costs turn it into an energy resource can be a contagious activity, in turn promoting similar independent and innovative cross-disciplinary and cross-cultural cooperation in the future.

In the 1960s, The US first implemented air quality monitoring and advisory systems to alert the public about dangerous levels of pollution. During days of poor air quality, public notification came bundled with the weather report and people were told to avoid going outside. While this 'one to many' kind of information exchange may work effectively for these kinds of warnings, other models in a networked environment could be exploited with respect to air quality. In an open platform, *Area's immediate reading* (AIR) by Pre-emptive Media (Beatriz da Costa, Jamie Schulte and Brooke Singer), the artists turned individual citizens into volunteer 'smog detectives' using a network of wireless pollution-monitoring devices. This open platform allowed real-time sharing of location and time-based information about pollution, health and the environment. Media was used as a strategy to open public dialogue.

Amy Balkin's *Public smog Offsets Tomorrow Today* (2007) project (see Colour plate xvi, Fig. A) addresses the commodification of clean air from the perspective of the market. Balkin is an artist whose works create metaphoric shifts, question social and political assumptions and take an activist stance. Her work often involves intensive legal, financial and political research. *Public smog* is a public park located in the atmosphere, of changing size and floating in an unfixed location. At first it seems like a fantasy! How can anything exist in such an ephemeral location? The premise of Amy Balkin's work references the economic system of emissions trading. Through her project, the 'global public' can purchase as many emissions allowances as possible on the emissions market. These carbon offsets are then retired, in other words they are taken off the market, making them unavailable to polluting corporations. By openly embracing the free market for the public good, Balkin presents a sharp critique of the system the project must operate within. Therefore she sees her 'public space' as the emissions trading market.

Balkin's work clearly questions the market and the solution she proposes is meant to be absurd. However, in the context of contemporary culture, the solution seems like a viable one. In fact it is very similar to the structure proposed by Feasta, where individuals buy and sell emissions credits on the market, and a certain amount of emissions credits are distributed for free to citizens. A group called TheCompensators* proposes the exact same solution as Balkin, claiming to have retired over 1500 EU emissions allowances (TheCompensators*, 2007). These solutions create potential problems grounded in the very idea of the market. Healthy markets may grow, but if people decide to buy emissions credits or clean air, the market may issue more emissions credits to balance the market and meet the demand. This process would force the public to pay ever-higher prices for clean air.

The difference between Balkin's *Public smog* and TheCompensators* projects lies in the fact that one identifies itself as an art project and the other as an environmental project, but the underlying metaphors are similar. By using the metaphor of a public park, Balkin's work allows viewers and participants to look at the system of emissions trading through a familiar lens. Most viewers understand the difference between public and private property in the context of land use. The privatization of air as if it was a public park is a metaphor Balkin used to influence a greater understanding of the problems that may emerge from an emissions trading system. Balkin invites public participation through the purchase of emissions allowances and offers an alternative reading of the *carbon trading* system, and therefore creates an alternative pathway for examining this market.

The message of *Public smog* becomes even clearer when seen in relation to one of Balkin's earlier works entitled: *This is the public domain*. In 2003, Balkin purchased a 2.5 acre parcel of land located in Tehachapi, California, intended as a permanent, international commons, free to everyone, held in perpetuity. Since there was no precedent in the creation of such a commons in the current legal system, Balkin's project involved a complicated legal process that explored solutions in both real property law and copyright law. Through this process, Balkin questioned the foundations of the existing laws and highlighted the disappearance of public space. Balkin has identified the project as an art project, and this classification is essential to her legal approach, one that explores the land as a creative work of art. Through this project, she joins a movement of people who move fluidly between the roles of artists, environmentalist and activist.

On December 11, 1997, the Kyoto Protocol was adopted by the US and 121 other nations, but not ratified by the US Congress. American industry forced the rejection, predicting 'disaster' if CO_2 reductions were enforced. In March of 2001, the US again pulled out of Kyoto, saying that complying would destroy the economy. Many US citizens disagree with their government's actions, and are concerned about rapid increases in global temperatures, ice melting and sea level rise, changes that the 2007 UN intergovernmental report on climate change states is 'unequivocal'. In another example, Ben Engebreth provides individuals in various US cities the chance to personally comply with the Kyoto protocol. Engebreth himself does not identify himself purely as an artist or call his latest project, *Personal kyoto* an art project, and his projects often operate outside of the art market on the Internet. *Personal kyoto* analyzes electric usage information and calculates an energy reduction goal of what the Kyoto Protocol might require for an individual. *Personal kyoto* allowed individuals to monitor electric use on a daily basis with the goal of reducing their personal consumption of greenhouse gases. Like Balkin's *Public smog*, *Personal kyoto* works within an existing system to empower public action and benefit. While *Public smog* takes on the publicly traded carbon offset system with collective action using a public space model, *Personal kyoto* looks to individual responsibility and accountability as a means to encourage global change.

Projects that focus on personal responsibility and embrace the philosophy of 'voluntary' emissions reduction may help raise awareness of the problem of CO_2 emissions among the general public and as such may have an impact on total emissions, but their focus on personal choice may detract from the urgent need to curb emissions now. Can the American individualist ideal (the ideals behind the problematic proposal made by the US to the EU which recently promoted volunteer emissions reduction) promote the changes needed? Voluntary emissions reductions may be a great idea on an individual level, but can they work on a global scale?

The paradoxical problems and metaphors that have been raised by these artworks are part of the system in which the works exist. They are either in the art world, with its gallery economy based on the buying and selling of works, or in the public art world, in which works can be supported by government or private interests, some works also operate in the semi-public forums of the market or the internet. These works bring up larger questions about the potential of art in a time of global environmental crisis, and more specifically the potential of art and science collaboration in creating alternative pathways to understanding and responding to climate change. By planting gardens inside of truck beds, artist Eve Andrée Laramée created a carbon-neutral fleet of three Mercedes Benz trucks *'Parks on Trucks': Project for the City of Aachen* (see Colour plate xvi, Fig. B). Along with bio-geographer Dane Griffin, she calculated the amount the trucks would drive so that their emissions would match the amount of air cleaned by the flatbed gardens. How far could these trucks travel so that they created no harm? In one case, she concluded it was no more than one-third kilometre per month! Andrée Laramée's work created an alternative pathway for addressing the problem of automobile emissions by presenting a potential solution. However, by showing that this solution was impractical, she emphasized the magnitude of the problem.

Climate change is a global problem that requires international cooperation. In the author's interviews with meteorologists and climatologists on projects interpreting weather and climate data, they have taken a very practical approach, that of the mitigation of inevitable climate change. In part, this practical approach is related to the damage already affecting the atmosphere. Even if CO_2 emissions were to stop tomorrow, they reference that climate change is predicted to continue for at least the next 100 years. Perhaps another part of the focus on mitigation might eventuate from an understanding that at the present time there is a lack of political will to do what is necessary on a global level to reduce greenhouse gas emissions. The projects in the *Aer* exhibition navigate the economic and personal politics of air and air quality. As these politics can be complex and controversial, Platform London, a group whose work crosses disciplinary lines to achieve social and ecological justice, attempts to blur the boundaries between art and activism. Their projects involve rigorous research, advocacy, public art and education, or various combinations of each. The global price of oil is set at London's International Petroleum Exchange, and their artwork entitled *Unravelling the carbon web* looks closely at two major players in the oil industry that have headquarters in London, BP and Shell. The project focuses on their activities in Iraq, the former Soviet Union and Nigeria. These have included the oil industry in Nigeria and the policy of Shell. A component of the project by Platform London, the *Remember ken saro-wiwa* project, was a tribute to the Nigerian writer and activist who led a nonviolent campaign against the environmental damage associated with the operations of Shell and other multinational oil companies in the Niger Delta. His execution by the Nigerian Military in 1995 provoked international outrage. Platform London then coordinated a coalition of organizations and individuals to contribute a series of living memorials to Saro-Wiwa, these included a book of poetry and a stainless steel bus made by Nigerian-born artist Sokari Douglas Camp. This growing project, aptly named *Unravelling the carbon web*, contains an archive of related news, historical documents and analysis, including fables that try to reach the conscience of the global oil industry.

Conclusion

The work of the artists in the author's curated exhibition, *Aer*, and the related art and activist projects discussed in this article, represent the beginnings of an effort to address the issue of air pollution from a multi-disciplinary perspective. In the 1960s, Yves Klein, Robert Barry, Hans Haacke and others developed artworks from ephemeral materials. By making artworks from air and water, these artists pushed boundaries and expanded the definition of art. At the time that Klein, Haacke and Barry were creating the ephemeral works discussed in this article, water and air were seen as public resources. However, by the early 1990s bottled water had become a popular item in stores and air pollution trading systems in Sulfur Dioxide and CFCs had already been implemented. Because artworks generally operate within various economies, whether they are gallery works or works of public art, the position of ephemeral artworks as private property may have unintentionally softened the public to the idea of selling bottled water and to the buying and selling of air. The context in which an artwork is presented: for example as a high-priced product in a gallery or in a public space, affects the extent of its message and the effectiveness of the work in responding to a global crisis like climate change.

Therefore, recent contemporary artists using ephemeral materials have responded to the idea of selling air by offering an alternative reading to the mainstream commercial messages that encourage marketing these resources. Contemporary artists presented in this article have used technology as a means of creative and critical intervention. Sarah Jane Pell (*Interdepend* and *Undercurrent*) has designed works that highlight the human body's impact and dependence upon air (see Colour plate xvii, Fig. D). Her works suggested the implications of an alternative future in which air is a limited resource. Eve Andrée Laramée (*Parks on trucks*) also used a vehicle to illustrate the potential of air, but that vehicle was severely handicapped by the constraint that it have no negative impact on the air quality. Through this work, Andrée Laramée illustrated the magnitude of emissions coming from each individual automobile compared to its physical footprint.

As has been shown through the controversies surrounding the creation of global markets that trade in air and through artists' critical responses to this controversy, there can be new mechanisms for communicating problems related to the environment in general and climate change in particular. From a top down perspective, carbon-trading systems may put the atmosphere under the control of a small number of large corporations rather than in the hands of the citizens that need to breathe air to survive. However, there may be another kind of trading system that artists can play a role in developing, one that facilitates a grass roots exchange of ideas in opposition to corporate control.

Towards that aim, *Supergas*, not only operated outside of the traditional art market, but also operated outside of the global energy market. *Supergas* functioned as a catalyst for social change by turning consumers into producers. Engebreth (*Personal kyoto*) drew attention to global efforts to reduce greenhouse gases and also re-directed the power of that reduction to individual citizens. Preemptive Media (*AIR*) also placed tools in the hands of citizens by empowering the public to record and monitor local air quality, and Amy Balkin (*Public smog*) critically questions the *carbon trading* system by suggesting a way for individuals to collectively subvert the system and return the air to the public domain.

Each human being is affected by poor air quality and climate chaos, and the response of governments to privatize the air may not solve the problem, but rather might create more difficulties. Several of the artists discussed in this article have created alternative pathways to highlight the flaws in the *carbon trading* system and to empower individuals to preserve and protect our fragile atmosphere. As has been shown in this article, artworks can serve as an alternative medium for promoting social movement and activism and as a social action that can lead to the development of new social interactions and structures.

References

Alberro, A & Buchman, S 2006, *Art after conceptual art*, MIT Press, Cambridge/MA.

Federal Communications Commission (FCC), accessed 21 October 2007, <http://www.fcc.gov>.

Flannery, T 2005, *The weather makers*, Grove Press, New York.

Gelinas, N 2007, 'A carbon tax would be cleaner', *Wall Street Journal*, 23 August, accessed 17 March 2010, <http://www.manhattan-institute.org>/html/_wsja_carbon_tax_would_be_cleaner.htm>. Glassie, J 2006, "Air index impressionism", *New York Times Magazine*, 10 December accessed 17 March 2010, <http://www.nytimes.com/2006/12/10/magazine/10section1A.t-2.html>.

Gore, A 2006, (1992), *Earth in the balance: Ecology and the human spirit*, Rodale, Emmaus/PA.

Hardin, G 1968, 'The tragedy of the commons', *Science*, vol. 162, no. 3859, pp. 1243-1248. p. 1245.

Intergovernmental panel on climate change (ipcc), 2007, *Climate Change 2007: The physical science basis summary for policymakers*, February, accessed 17 March 2010, <http://users.telenet.be/j.janssens/CommentsSPM4 web.pdf>.

Intergovernmental panel on climate change, working group II report: 'Impacts, adaptation and vulnerability' 2007, *Contribution of the working group II to the fourth assessment report of the intergovernmental panel on climate change: Summary for policymakers*, accessed 18 March 2010, <http://www.ipcc.ch/ipccreports/ar4 -wg2.htm>.

Joint economic committee 1997, *Study on tradable pollution emission*, US Congress, July 7, accessed 1 November 2007,<http://www.house.gov/jec/cost-gov/regs/cost/ emission.htm>.

Kanter, J 2007, 'Banks urging U.S. to adopt the trading of emissions', *New York Times*, 26 September, accessed 16 March 2010, <http://www.nytimes.com/ 2007/09/26/business/26bank.html>.

Klein, Y 2004, *Yves Klein: Air architecture*, Noever, P & Perrin F (eds), MAK Center for Art and Architecture, Los Angeles.

Kyoto Protocol 1997, United Nations framework convention on climate change, accessed 10 November 2007, <http://unfccc.int/kyoto_protocol/items/2830.php>.

Lippard, L 1973, *Six years: The dematerialization of the art object* from 1966 to 1972, Praeger, New York.

Lippard, L & Chandler J 1968, 'The dematerialization of art', *Art International*, vol. 12, no. 2, pp. 31-36.

Lohman, L 2006, 'Carbon trading: A critical conversation on climate change, privatisation and power', *Development Dialogue*, no. 48, September, pp. 1-360, pp. 19/54, accessed 16 March 2010, <http://www.dhf. uu.se/pdffiler/DD2006_48_carbon_trading/carbon_ trading_web.pdf>.

Perrement, M 2005, 'Corruption stalls government attempts to curb CFC trade', 14 December, *China Development Brief*, accessed 1 November 2007 <http:// www.chinadevelopmentbrief.com/node/371>.

Polli, A 2008, *Aer online exhibition*, accessed 16 March 2010, <http://greenmuseum.org>/c/*aer*/index.htm>.

Rimbach, J 2003, 'Oxygen bar in Atlantic City, N.J., feeds fresh air to tourists', *Free Republic*, 31 December.

Simms, A 2006, 'The great emissions rights giveaway', foundation for the economics of sustainability (feasta), *New Economic Forum*, March, accessed 16 March 2010, <http://www.feasta.org>/documents/ energy/emissions2006.pdf>.

Solomon, D 2007, 'Climate change's great divide', *Wall Street Journal*, 12 September, accessed 16 March 2010, <http://online.wsj.com/article/ SB118955082446224332.html>.

'Stratospheric ozone depletion 10 years after Montreal' 1997, *Natural Science*, 8 October, accessed 16 March 2010, <http://naturalcience.com/ns/cover/ cover4.html>.

*TheCompensators**, association to decrease emission allowances, accessed 16 October 2007, <http://www.thecompensators.org>.

Wood, P 2002, *Movements in modern art: conceptual art*, Delano Greenridge Editions, New York, pp. 35–36.

MEDIATED ENVIRONMENTS
COLOUR PLATES

▲ Figure A ▼ Figure B

Figure A: Edward Burtynsky, *Résidus de mine de nickel No 34,* Sudbury, Ontario, 1996, Épreuve à developpement chromogéne, 102 x 152 cm, Image © Edward Burtynsky, Courtesy Galerie Stefan Röpke, Köln/Flowers East Gallery, London.

Figure B: George Steinmann, *Montsegorsk,* Kola, Russia (from the series 'From-To-Beyond'), 1995, B/W Print, Blackberry juice (Rubus fruticosus L.), 12.5 x 18 cm, Image © George Steinmann.

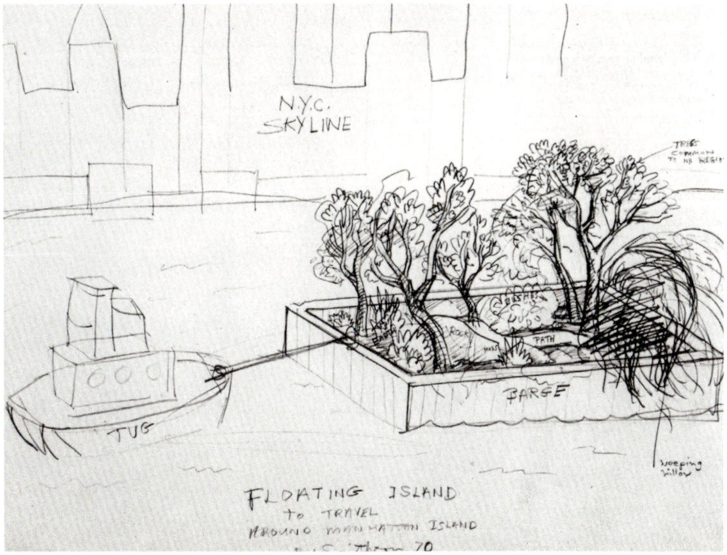

▲ Figure C

▼ Figure D

Figure C: Robert Smithson, *Floating Island to Travel Around Manhattan Island,* 1970, Graphite on paper, 47 x 60 cm, © 2009, ProLitteris, Zurich.
Figure D: Olafur Eliasson, *Your mobile expectations: BMW H2R project,* 2007, BMW H2R chassis, stainless steel, ice, and cooling unit, 140 x 560 x 240 cm, Installation view at Studio Olafur Eliasson, Berlin, Germany, 2007, Photo: Jens Ziehe, Courtesy the artist © 2007 Olafur Eliasson.

Figure A: *Nuage Vert,* HeHe, 2008, Photo: Niklas Sjöblom.

Figure B: *Nuage Vert,* HeHe, 2008, Photo: Niklas Sjöblom.

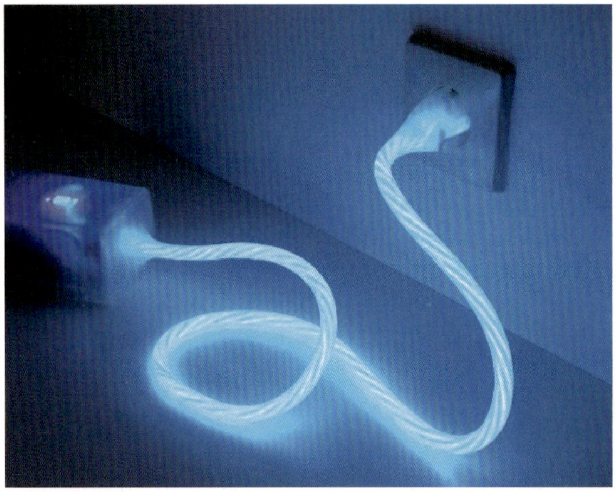

▲ Figure C

▲ Figure D

▼ Figure E

Figure C: *STATIC*, Power Aware Cord: Seeing Personal Energy Consumption, prototype. Project Team: Anton Gustafsson and Magnus Gyllenswärd, Photo: Magnus Gyllenswärd.

Figure D: *Flower Lamp* displaying low energy loads, lamp 'blooms'. By Front and Interactive Interactive Institute Project Team: Sofia Lagerkvist, Charlotte von der Lancken, Anna Lindgren, Katja Sävström, and Göran Nordahl, Photo: Anette Andersson.

Figure E: DIY Kyoto's *Wattson*.

▲ Figure F

▼ Figure G

Solid Blue
Standby / No event is currently underway

Solid Yellow
Warning / Day-ahead event warning has been issued.

Pulsing Yellow
Warning / An event will occur later in the day.

Solid Red
Activation / Event has been activated and is currently in progress.

Pulsing Red
Activation / Event in progress and another declared for the following day.

Solid Green
Testing / Demand response notification system is being tested.

Figure F: *Energy Orb,* or the PG&E Demand-Response Orb, Pacific Gas and Electric Co., 2006.
Figure G: Colour key, Ambient Energy Orb, Pacific Gas and Electric Company, sold through Ambient Devices (USA).

▲ Figure A

▼ Figure B

▲ Figure C

▼ Figure D

Part of the Survival Series,1970–1973 and introduced to create self sufficient farming techiques to feed an over populated world. Boston Museum of Fine Arts, as a part of the exhibition *Earth, Air, Fire and Water*

Figure A: Hog Pasture: R.W. Schumway's Annual Hog Pasture Mix, 1970

Figure B: Portable Earth Farming Series_Wheat.

Figure C: Portable Earth Farming Series_Wine.

Figure D Portable Earth Farming Series_Salad.

▲ Figure E

▲ Figure F

▼ Figure G

▼ Figure H

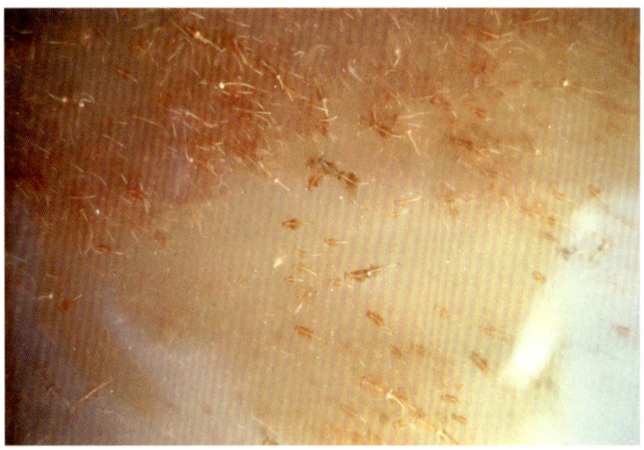

▼ Figure I

Ecosystems of the Western Salt works. 1971. *Art and Technology* Los Angeles Museum of Contempory Art, LA USA

Figure E: Four co-joined 10 foot by 20 foot ponds, seeded with algae Dunaliella make a changing colour field as the algae develop carotene in response to increasing salinity pond by pond.

Figure F: Brine shrimp eggs are added and after 30 days are harvested and re-harvested every 30 days thereafter.

Figure G: Brine Shrimp ready for harvest.

Figure H: The ponds become far more salty. The right pond turns white as the water completely evaporates.

Figure I: Salt is harvested.

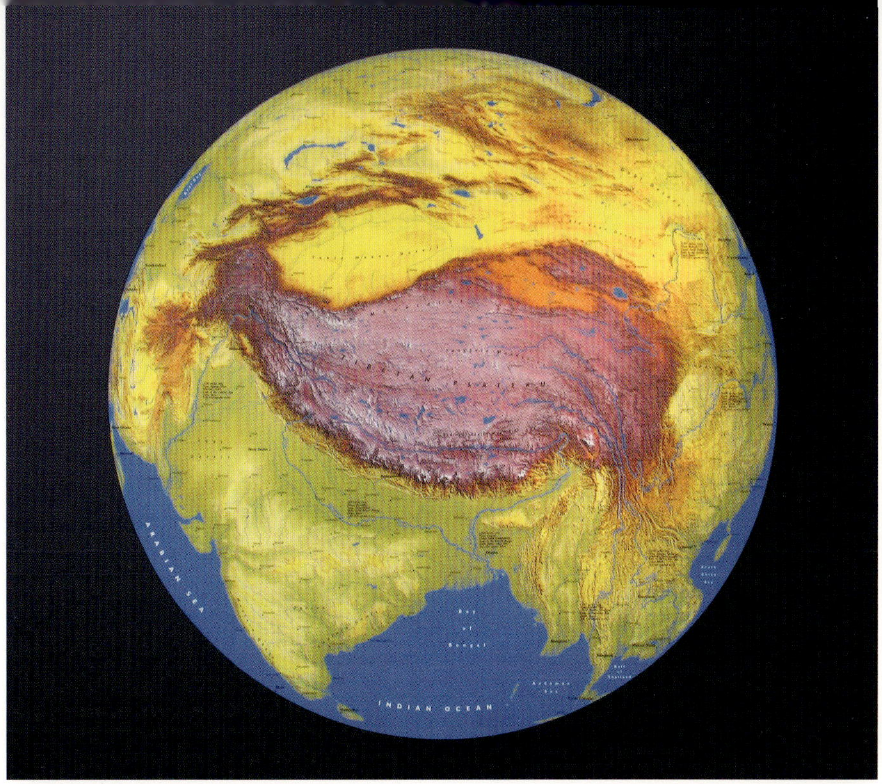

▲ Figure J

▼ Figure K

Figure J: *The Force Majeure: Peninsula Europe Part III:* Where a new complex forest ensemble is composed by using paleo-ecological research methodologies to rehabit the lands as far as possible, where snow and glacial melt formerly supplied the rivers with consistent flow. The ecological design will seek to create a sponge phenomenon, which would replace, in some measure, the original glacial melt, reducing the effects of flood and drought.

Figure K: *The Force Majeure: Tibet is the High Ground Part III:* Acknowledges that glacial melt, vastly accelerated by Global Warming, is putting the 7 great rivers that flow through the continent at risk for flood and drought. This work proposes, through an elaborate process of paleo-ecological research, to slowly replace the 2.4 million square kilometer plateau with a vast, water-holding, bio-diverse grassland/open-canopy forest ecosystem. The potential for carbon sequestration suggests that 6 gigatons of carbon can be sequestered per decade.

▲ Figure A

▼ Figure C

▲ Figure B

▼ Figure D

Selected (2x16x9 ratio) 3D Images from the Dome Format storyboard of Atmosphere One: Jill Scott and Andrew Quinn

Sequence One

The Water Cycle: the evaporation of molecules in the atmosphere

Figure A: A Tetrakaideacahedra (or Tetra based on the minimal space-dividing cell) rolls over the ocean, its movements and occupants being affected by evaporation.

Figure B: The Tetra becomes an Atmospheric Chamber: A researcher and a learner measure the water quality and carbon levels in the atmosphere.

Sequence Two

The Carbon Cycle: Photosynthesis and Climate History

Figure C: A small Tetra is constructed by a fabricator to enter the leaf of plant as Carbon Dioxide. The slow process of Photosynthesis into Oxygen can be witnessed by the audience.

Figure D: In a Tetra close to the leaf surface, a researcher and a fabricator talk about how the insect life and forest growth have been affected by climate change over time.

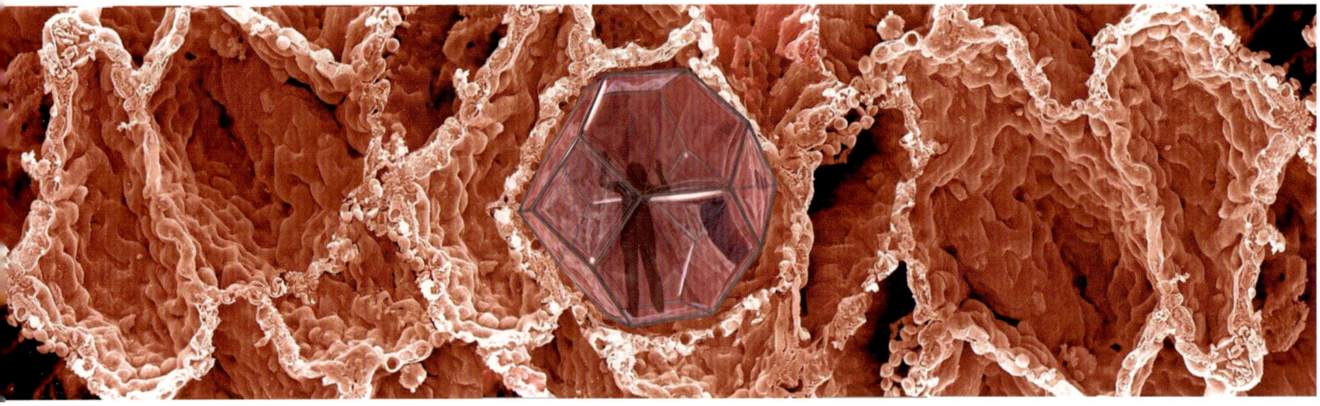

▲ Figure E

▼ Figure G

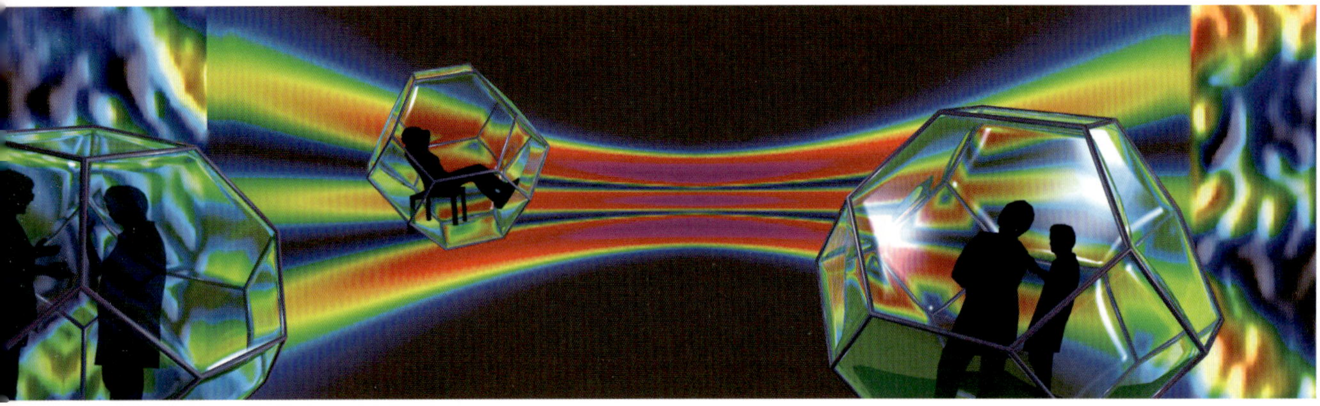

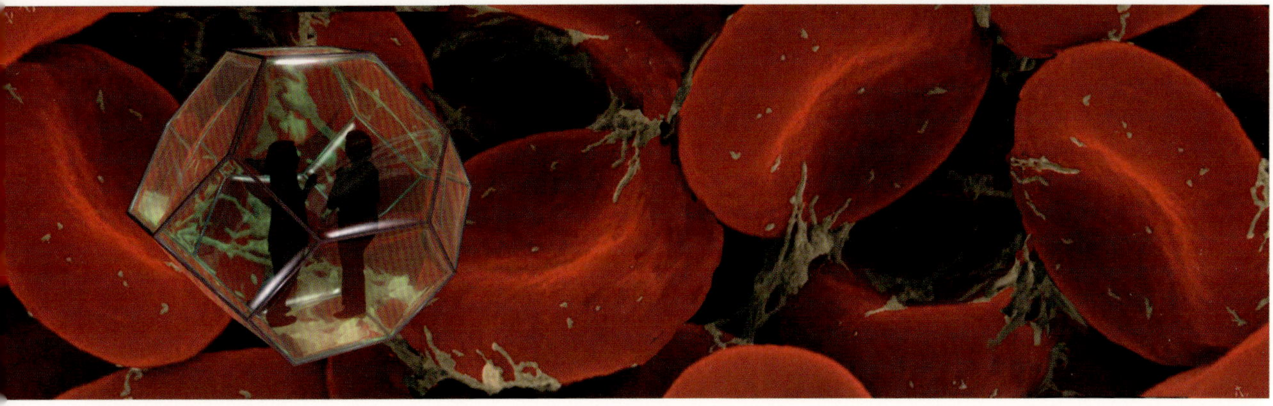

▲ Figure F

▼ Figure H

Selected (2x16x9 ratio) 3D Images from the Dome Format storyboard of Atmosphere One: Jill Scott

Sequence Three

The Oxygen Cycle: Energising the Body

Figure E: A shrunken Tetra with a learner inside travels through a set of Oxygen Molecules (o2) and asks the audience to breath in deeply.
Figure F: The Tetra is sucked down into the lungs while chasing the O2 molecule and it enters into blood stream though the alveoli. The learner asks the audience to all breathe out loudly.

Sequence Four

The Energy Cycle: The Sharing of Electrons

Figure G: Tetras behave like electrons travelling through an electric wire. Discussions occur about these processes.
Figure H: Hundreds of Tetras join together as a metaphor for our homes in sustainable cities, where alternative energy is shared between citizens.

▲ Figure A

▼ Figure B

Figure A: *Public Smog Offsets Tomorrow Today,* Douala, Cameroon, 2009, Amy Balkin.
Figure B: *Parks on Trucks: Project for the City of Aachen,* 1999, Eve Andrée Laramée in collaboration with the bio-geographer, Duane Griffin.

▲ Figure C

▼ Figure D

Figure C: *SUPERGAS/USER/UTA*, Cambodia,2001, SUPERFLEX.

Figure D: Sarah Jane Pell, *Under Current V,* The Bonnington Gallery, Nottingham UK 2004, Photo:graph Richard Graham.

Stills from the film *We Feed the World,* Austria 2005, Directed by Erwin Wagenhofer. Courtesy of Allegro Films.

Stills from the film *Food, Inc.*, USA 2008, Directed by Robert Kenner Courtesy of Magnolia Pictures

▲ Figure A

▲ Figure B

Figure A: *The Crossing,* Photo: Malcom Cross for Jill Orr (C) Latche Latche danceman, Peter Peterson.
Figure B: Jill Orr, *The Crossing,* Photo: Malcom Cross for Jill Orr (C) Jill Orr, nun.

▲ Figure C

▼ Figure D

▲ Figure E

▼ Figure F

Figure C: *Global Mind Project*, 'Spectacle of the Imaginary', Photo: Malcom Cross.
Figure D: *Global Mind Project*, 'Spectacle of the Imaginary', Photo: Malcom Cross.
Figure E: *Faith in a Faithless Land*, Photo: Naomi Herzog for Jill Orr (C).
Figure F: *Southern Cross – to bear and behold*, Photo: Naomi Herzog for Jill Orr (C).

▲ Figure A

▼ Figure B

Figure A: Apartheid Museum Johannesburg. Courtesy Wikipedia commons.
Figure B: Exhaust Sculptures. Photo: Urs Hochuli.

▲ Figure C

▼ Figure D

Figure C: Wooden structure outskirts of Johannesburg. Photo: Urs Hochuli.
Figure D: Johannesburg from above. Photo: Urs Hochuli.

▲ Figure A

▼ Figure B

Figure A: Minimising borders and maximising edges between nature and technology, FoAM, 2008.
Figure B: The term cultivation is at the root of the word culture.

▲ Figure C

▼ Figure D

Figure C: Solar powered cricket. Luminous Green, Belgium, 2007.

Figure D: 'A problem cannot be solved by people who are concerned with only one or another of its parts', Fukuoka, 1978.

▲ Figure A

▲ Figure B

▲ Figure C

▲ Figure D

▲ Figure E

▲ Figure F

Examples of Emergency Design

Figure A: *Rendering Freedom*, © Anthony Ling / Seasteading Institute
Figure B: *Oasis of the Sea*, © Emerson Stepp
Figure C: © Greenpeace
Figure D: © Dietmar Mathis / Feuerwehr Rankweil
Figure E: Auroville Copyleft Wikimedia commons
Figure F: *Homeless Shelter*, © Yana Milev, Kyoto 1999

▲ Figure G

▲ Figure H

▲ Figure I

▲ Figure J

▲ Figure K

▲ Figure L

Examples of Emergency Design

Figure G: *Case Study Homes* © Peter Bialobrzeski

Figure H: *Antartic Village – No Borders* © Lucy + Jorge Orta

Figure I: *Les enfants du Don Quichotte*, on the Capitole place, Toulouse, France, May 2009. Foto © Ludovic Courtès, 2009

Figure J: *Identify me*, © Yana Milev, Berlin 2009

Figure K: *Waiting for the Guards* © DarkFibre

Figure L: *Sandbag shelter* © Nader Khalili / Cal-Earth <http://calearth.org>

Figure A: The Neon Bone Yard 2009. Art wasted, waste as art, Jim Venturi.

Figure B: Las Vegas in the late 1960s, Denise Scott Brown and VSBA.

Figure C: Example of 'Shack Chic', township residents in South Africa creating lively interior spaces with what is available.

Denise Scott Brown

Figure D: Shoes made from recycled tires.

RE-CONNECT

Angelika Hilbeck

We are currently experiencing the simultaneous decline of essentially all fundamental systems human societies rest upon. As the climate undergoes dramatic changes and biodiversity still disappears at unprecedented rates, our economic, health and food production systems also falter.

While the reasons for the failing of these systems are rooted in uncountable disconnections, its manifestations are connected. In this chapter, I look into some of these disconnections and at how the operational environments in human societies have been mediated to the point of manipulation so that an asymmetrical system has emerged for one sole purpose: monetary profits and greed. Novel approaches and concepts for remediation must be conceived and implemented quickly. The arts have a prominent – if not key – role to play in this implementation as it seems to be one of the last disciplines left with the largest degrees of freedom for creativity, novelty, action, exposure and provocation. One field that seems to have taken on such a role is film. I also discuss here why documentary films have significantly increased over the past decade and their role in the context of environmental and human health decline.

Fig. 1: The domino effect of the collapsing systems sustaining human civilization and existence

The new role of documentary films

The unfolding consequences of human intervention and prematurely introduced technologies are finding roots in the conscious of global human societies. The public need and desire to gain better understanding in the intricacies and complexities of the underlying mechanisms of the current failing systems is best reflected in the increased popularity of documentary films. Until about two decades ago, the role of documentaries was primarily educational tailoring mainstream knowledge for the general public about natural phenomena or scientific-technical innovations. Documentaries such as those by Sir David Attenborough[1] about the evolution of the earth and various global ecosystems were, and remain, very popular and won prestigious awards. While this educational role of documentaries still remain, the genre is increasingly complemented by documentary films that take on an investigative, revealing and exposing focus, more often than not questioning mainstream science and established knowledge. Such investigative documentaries continue to gain great popularity, and some of the most well-known films of this genre are listed in Table 1. The most highly acclaimed example is the documentary film *An inconvenient truth* by Davis Guggenheim, featuring former US vice president Al Gore as the main character who reveals the reasons and controversies around climate change. This film ran in mainstream theatres around the world and reached millions of viewers and it received the Academy Award in 2007. This factor significantly contributed to Al Gore receiving the Nobel Peace Prize together with the scientists from the IPCC[2]. This did finally establish the fundamental relationship between environmental degradation and world peace.

Date of Release	Film Name	Film Maker
27. October 1983	Koyaanisqatsi – Life out of Balance	Godfrey Reggio
2004	Future of Food	Deborah Koons
21. May 2004	Supersize me	Morgan Spurlock
14. July 2004	Life running out of control (TV)	Bertram Verhaag
21. January 2005	Darwin's Nightmare	Hubert Sauper
30. September 2005	*We feed the world*	Erwin Wagenhofer
31. August 2006	Inconvenient truth	Al Gore
17. November 2006	Fast Food Nation	Richard Linklater
8. June 2007	Black Gold	Marc and Nick Francis
9. November 2007	A crude awakening: The oil crash	Basil Gelpke Ray McCormack Reto Caduff
10. October 2007	The 11th hour	Leonardo di Caprio Nadia Conners
11. March 2008	The world according to Monsato (TV)	Marie-Monique Robin
12. September 2008	Flow	Irena Salina
2008	Food Fight	Christopher Taylor
25. April 2009	King Corn	Aaron Woolf
4. June 2009	*Food Inc.*	Robert Kenner
31. July 2009	Tapped	Stephanie Soechtig Jason Lindsey
9 September 2009	Crude	Joe Berlinger
21 September 2009	The Age of Stupid	Franny Armstrong

Table 1. A list of popular documentaries released since 1983.

While this list of documentary films is neither complete nor comprehensive, it does indicate an increase in frequency and it shows the breadth of topics dealing with unsustainable resource extraction and abuse of both nature and humans alike. While in the 1980s only one documentary made it into mainstream theatres and received international recognition, none of that calibre was found in the 1990s. However, 19 investigative documentaries were released in the past 10 years with 5 international releases in 2009 alone. So, this trend seems to be still unabated.

These are investigative documentary films that have enormously helped to reveal the disconnections and 're-connect the dots', thus, enabling a broad audience to become informed citizens and realize that many, if not most, of these developments are not in their interest. Although the range of listed documentary films includes many topics, my focus will be on agriculture, food production and bioscience. Two very popular, fairly recent documentaries will be used as illustrative examples: *We feed the world* and *Food Inc.* (see Colour plate xviii-xix) These two films stand in a continuum of other investigative and expository documentary films, because at least 8 more documentary films dealing with food and water issues are listed in Table 1. *We feed the world* and *Food Inc.* were selected because each was surprisingly and exceptionally successful in reaching the public – one in Europe and the other in the US. Although both have similar messages to convey and overlap in the featured issues, they also have a number of differences.

Revealing the disconnections: its drivers and profiteers!

Both documentaries show how the surrender of agriculture and food production has dictated profit-maximization and lead to the current predatory system of unsustainable methodologies jeopardizing our collective existence. This 'profit-first' model is grounded on the notion that societal development is exclusively based on the economic system taking care of all human needs. Economic incentives drive or overrule all other systems shaping human societies, from ecosystems to social systems. The idea is that if you put a price tag on everything, including ecosystem and social services, it will gain economic value and, even basic supplies like food and water can be treated and traded like household appliances and cars.

> '... water is a foodstuff like any other, and like any other foodstuff it should have a market value. Personally I believe it's better to give a foodstuff a value so that we're all aware that it has its price, and then, that one should take specific measures for the part of the population that has no access to this water, and there are many different possibilities there.' (Peter Brabeck, CEO Nestlé, *We feed the world*, 1:28 minutes – 1:30 minutes).

As corporations become richer and more successful, do they create jobs and make society sufficiently rich, so that public good would come about by itself? According to the current 'supply and demand' model, essential things, including food stuffs, would be produced (cost-) efficiently and go where they are needed and, ultimately, trickle down to those who have less, eventually also lifting their standard of living! Similarly, also environmental concerns and unsustainable production methods would eventually be solved out of an 'economic logic' as it would be in the interest of corporations not to erode their own base. One is hard pressed to find a segment of human activity in western societies where the 'profit-first' model has not been applied and has not caused a stage of crisis to some degree. But this model turns out to serve only a minority and fails for the majority of the global human society. It promotes exploitative environmental behaviour to the point of collective self-destruction. We are now learning that 'need' and 'demand' are quite separate issues and that high demand of affluent citizens does not trickle down to satisfy the 'needs' of the poor. In the market economy world 'demand' translates into 'want' and, most importantly, what can be paid for it. But 'wanting' something and 'needing' something are completely different things. Today's global economy boils down to a system of 'supply and want', or perhaps some 'supply and demand' as long as one has the financial means but little 'supply and need'. It fails completely for those who do not have money and need things. 'Profit maximization is the murderous strategy!' (Jean Ziegler, UN Special Rapporteur on the Right to Food, *We feed the world*).

In order to keep this decoupled market system striving, the economy 'mediates' the environment in a way that it satisfies and generates a sufficient number of consumers whose consumption behaviour in turn re-enforces an increasingly centralized, monopoly system run by a handful of global corporations who control the entire production chain from raw material to cars, field to fork - and beyond. This in turn provides them with a degree of non-democratically sanctioned political power that cannot be overestimated. This power massively and disproportionately influences the shaping of our future, blocks progress, and hinders progressive solutions towards a sustainably functioning world. They have so effectively established a 'revolving door' strategy where corporate employees switch back and forth between corporations and their overseeing regulatory authorities that they are essentially writing their own rules. *Food Inc.* shows multiple cases of top level management employees or lawyers working for one of the biggest biotech companies, Monsanto, taking up top level positions at the Food and Drug administration (FDA) and the Environmental Protection Agency (EPA)[3] and *vice versa*.

Therefore, a giant self-reinforcing system has emerged over the past five to six decades that causes people to become increasingly disconnected from the production of their goods, their environment, their food and, finally, their own bodies. Both documentary films reveal how these disconnections were brought about.

Agriculture

After World War II, we re-designed our agricultural and food production systems, shifting from the primary goal of producing food and feed to the goal of monetary profits. This was achieved by increasing productivity in terms of yields-for-profit, literally, at any costs. With the help of chemical pesticides and cheap oil, cheap commodities and processed foods were brought to many in the industrialized world. By systematically externalizing the negative side effects of this industrialized agricultural production system to society at large, unparalleled profits to chemical and oil companies and their linked distributing and retailing corporations could be raised. The resulting unprecedented global corporate power and their financial resources allowed them to use all means available to mediate the societal and political environment by deeply ingraining the subliminal message into societies, that there is only one way to produce sufficient affordable food for all – the industrial way[4]. Thus, global companies effectively mediated the societal and political environment, and the striking fact that we have in fact fed less and less people since the mid 1990s, when this industrial, profit-first model was instigated, went largely unnoticed. Instead, we have produced more and more raw material for industrial purposes of, and for, the rich (e.g. FAO 2009, IAASTD 2008, Patel 2008).

Both documentary films show the soulless and cruel mechanized production systems of industrial agricultural factories that reduce living subjects, plants and animals alike, into inanimate objects. *Food Inc.* reveals how by disassembling the complexities of running a farm enterprise into the sum of mindless, repetitive, assembly line style activities, the farm has been turned into a factory. This strategy has allowed farmers to reduce the operational costs because huge agricultural factories can now be run by unskilled, uneducated, unprotected, and easily replaceable, cheap labour. Workers who often neither understand, nor care, for the entire process. Farmers, consequently, lose ownership and become disconnected from their purposes. Additionally and perhaps more importantly, the control and oversight over the entire production systems of these huge agricultural factories resides with a handful of skilled, educated people, engineers for the most part, who 'oversee' these operations from a remote office via computer control and give orders to technicians and workers. Of course, also these operators and engineers become largely disconnected from the purpose of food production and aim to maximize profits. In this system, it does not matter anymore to an engineer whether he or she helps design devices and assembly lines for the production of hairdryers or for the mass-killing of animals that are handled like commodities.

Food

Logically, processed food stuffs from these commodities follows the same industrial, profit-first model. First, all commodities (predominantly soy beans and maize) are profitably and scientifically disassembled into their smallest marketable compounds only to be re-assembled again into novel adventurous combinations in profitable food processing factories to what Nestle (2007) calls 'Techno-Food' or Pollan (2008) 'edible food-like substances'. In *Food Inc.*, Pollan cites these food stuffs as 'clever rearrangements of corn', and 17 years ago, Fussell described this same disassembling-rearranging strategy in her highly comprehensive book on maize as follows:

> 'From the perspective of industrial farmers, corn is of value only as it can be transformed chemically into whatever commodity is most in demand. The methodology of nineteenth-century chemistry underlies the refining of corn as it does the refining of oil: analyze the system, fragment the parts, quantify the parts and synthesize at will. In such a system organic plants are but raw material for the processor, who fabricates products for which the manufacturer creates the demand.' (Fussell 1992 p 356)[5]

As in industrial agriculture, unprecedented global corporate power and essentially unlimited financial resources have allowed the involved global food processing industries to mediate the societal and political environment by deeply ingraining the message that this food was 'modern', 'better' and 'healthier' than the original or its whole food bases. As Nestle (2007) demonstrated in a well researched book on food politics in the US, the primary mission of food companies is still to sell products. Therefore, 'nutrition becomes a factor in corporate thinking only when it can help sell food' products. Alternatively, Pollan (2008) tries heroically to defend food from the food industry on the one side and nutritional science on the other. Both massively optimize their profits by making the simple process of eating and food at large as complicated a matter as possible. This strategy has profoundly confused many people in western and western-influenced societies to a point where they do not understand anymore what is good for them to eat, when, and why (Pollan 2008, Nestle 2007). It has also caused the lack of regulation and oversight of what types of 'edible food-like substances' an industry can produce and lax limitations regarding the possible health claims[6]. Thus, the consumers became disconnected from food making and the purpose of food ingredients – a slow and subtle process hardly anybody noticed. This way, simple dishes based originally on perhaps 5 ingredients contain a multifold of that, with names even an educated consumer cannot recognize. Take the example of bread. Who would think that a bagel, which many people believe is made of flour and water, a little yeast, some salt and sugar and perhaps some added goodies like nuts or berries, can indeed contain as many as 35 ingredients[7]. This confusion leads to disempowerment and a disconnection from food *per se*, creating new dependencies on consultants and engineers. What used to be age-old folk knowledge has been transformed into a scientific exercise that only a professional, academically trained nutritionist can master – most of whom are closely enmeshed with regulators and industries. It is no surprise that these 'edible food like substances' do not actually suit our biological requirements and needs.

Impacts on human health

The profit-first model turns food-manufacturing businesses into industrial processing factories that produce bizarre 'edible food like substances', which in turn generates the 'clientele' for the allied pharmaceutical corporations that make their profits from treating the symptoms of the victims of these 'foods'. As industrial food consumption increased, so did the negative impact on human health. According to the Center for Disease Control (CDC)[8], obesity and its related health problems, like diabetes, have reached epidemic proportions in western societies and continue to climb. However, these highly disturbing developments on human health are largely spun as an external, self-inflicted but certainly disconnected issue (Nestle 2007, *Food Inc.*). By luring low-income families into eating unhealthy fast foods, which are made artificially cheaper than whole foods (through highly subsidized maize and soy beans), income, or education level becomes the best predictor of obesity and its associated human health conditions such as diabetes and high blood pressure.

> 'We didn't even think about healthy eating because we used to think everything was healthy. Now, that I know that the food is really unhealthy for us, I feel guilty giving it to my kids. [...] When you have only a

> dollar to spend and you have two kids to feed either you go to the market and try to find something that's cheap or go just straight to the drive-thru and get two small hamburgers for them.' (Maria Andrea Gonzalez, low-income immigrant family; *Food Inc.*)

The importance of mediating the environment towards education and changes in eating habits and nutrition is being increasingly understood by mainstream medical science such as the Center for Disease Control and Prevention (CDC) in the US, as the opening statement on their obesity website leaves no doubt:

> 'American society has become "obesogenic", characterized by environments that promote increased food intake, non-healthful foods, and physical inactivity. Policy and environmental change initiatives that make healthy choices in nutrition and physical activity available, affordable, and easy will likely prove most effective in combating obesity.' (<http://www.cdc.gov/obesity/index.html>)

Today, a broken system has emerged: one that works better for corporations than for individuals by maximizing people's sick lifespan and inventing new diseases for the healthy. These require expensive treatments causing a boom in anti-aging and beauty treatments, pharmaceuticals and clinics.

Science and research

Consistent with the profit-first model, scientists have re-structured public science and research agendas towards serving corporate interests rather than public interests. Today, unknowingly or unaware, most scientists subscribe to a corporate driven science agenda, with the best intention to contribute positively to society. They wish that 'some' good will come from their work (Bioscience Resource Project (BRP) Commentary 2007). Public sector science has been re-designed through innumerable public-private-partnerships to cater primarily to these corporations. If public interest is served it is mostly coincidental and always indirect via the products the same industries sell to them again. So, societies often pay twice: for sponsoring and enabling the development of a product via tax money and the product sold to them for the full price that includes the development costs, while the profits, of course, remain with a selected circle.

While these developments are by no means restricted to the field of biotechnology, most of the currently pressing environmental, economic and human health issues crystallize in biotechnology. Here, the application and deployment of research is also driven by a handful of powerful global corporations, all of which are global chemical corporations. In his 2-part analysis of the 'failure of science' with regard to the genetic engineering of food, Lotter (2008a, b) warns of a 'major conflict in science'. Likewise, the BRP commentary (2007) sees an 'agenda gap in science'. Both the BRP Commentary (2007) and Lotter (2008b) locate the primary reason for this development to be the 'major changes in the relationship between research universities and private industries since the early 1980s, characterized by increased bilateral dependence, networking of scientists from the two sectors, and commercialization of university research'. Research programs were restructured during that time from a non-proprietary 'public goods' model to one that focuses primarily on the corporate, proprietary good (Etzkowitz 2005, Welsh and Glenna

2007, Krimsky 2003). Slaughter and Rhoades (2004) coined the term 'academic capitalism' to describe the surrender of science to market ideology. Lotter (2008)[9] saw the ramifications of the restructuring of science towards the corporate-good model in the following ways:

- Tolerance by the scientific community of bias against and mistreatment of non-compliant scientists whose work results in negative findings for transgenics, including editorial decisions by peer-reviewed journals, as well as tolerance of biotechnology industry manipulation of the information environment (confirmed by a recent article in the journal Nature and Nature Biotechnology by Emily Waltz 2009).
- Monopolization of the make-up of expert scientific bodies on transgenics by pro-industry scientists with vested interests in transgenics.
- Deficient scientific protocols, bias, and possible fraud in industry-sponsored and industry-conducted safety testing of transgenic foods.
- Increasing politically and commercially driven manipulation of science within federal regulatory bodies such as the FDA.

Lotter delivered well-documented examples to support each of these charges. He shows, for example, that the USDA dispersed $1.8 billion for crop biotechnology research to universities between 1992 and 2002, of which one percent ($18 million) went to 'risk-related research'. Most of the funds went to researchers who closely cooperated with the developers of GM crops as they have complete control over the research material through patent rights. In her book *Food Politics*, Nestle (2007) identifies this shift from public, to corporate-influenced science in the field of nutrition. She locates there some of the driving causes behind the decline in food product quality. Similarly, bio-safety issues for human health and the environment are only included in the business equation of large biotech companies as 'safety' helps to sell a product and, neatly, embeds it into the product development process.

Social impacts

Both films reveal that the cruel and abusive logic of production and consequent handling of animals and plants, is connected to the mistreatment and abuse of human beings within the same industrial processing model. These abuses range from exhibiting the inhumane and appalling living conditions of African migrant workers in agricultural systems in southern Spain, to the dangerous working conditions of Mexican migrant workers in slaughterhouses in the USA.

> 'A culture that just views a pig as a pile of protoplasmic, inanimate structure to be manipulated by whatever creative design a human can foist on that critter will probably view individuals within its community and other cultures in the community of nations with the same type of disdain and disrespect and controlling type mentality.' (Joel Salatin, Polyface Farms, Shenandoah Valley, Kentucky in *Food Inc.*)

By utilizing footage taken with hidden cameras on employees, Robert Kenner exposes the treatment of workers in the largest slaughterhouse of the world, Smithfield, in North Carolina. Here, most employees are illegal immigrants who have no rights or status, and are subjected to dangerous working conditions. The film features police raids of these known illegal immigrants, thus, making formal lay-offs conveniently obsolete. One call to the local police will take care of any blame. While illegal immigrants are deported, the hiring company is hardly ever questioned. As Fussell (1992) noted in her book on maize:

> 'In such a system, organic plants are but raw material for the processor, who fabricates products for which the manufacturer creates the demand. Equally, consumers are raw material for processing and consumption by the manufacturer. The consumer becomes the consumed.'

Secrecy and lack of transparency in agriculture, food production and science

This concentration of power and money inside the hands of a few global corporations allows the privatization of public knowledge, so it becomes intellectual property. Openness and transparency in both the industrial production process as well as the scientific process have drastically declined over the recent two decades. While this is perhaps a reaction of the involved industries to the increasing criticism and discontent about the way they produce food and their conduct in general, such investigative documentaries are instrumental to help to raise awareness about food. According to Robert Kenner, his film was not at all intended originally as what it became.

> 'My original concept derived from a curiosity about representing the multiple voices and points of view of the people who bring food to our tables. I was taken by surprise by how much my original concept changed during the making of the film.' – 'I felt as if I'd stumbled into an Orwellian world of behind-the-scenes wire-pullers controlling a fundamental aspect of our lives – the food we eat – which operates in near-total secrecy thanks to the fear it instills in people who know about it.' – 'I gradually realized that, while I had set out to make a film about food, I was now making a film about unchecked corporate power. [...] I didn't realize when I started that I was really making a film about freedom of speech, and I didn't know that I would spend the next few years of my life working with first Amendment lawyers.' (*Food Inc.* 2009, the book edited by Karl Weber, p. 321)

Closely connected, science and research is controlled by secrecy agreements with public sector scientists, as are the scientists who work in the field of industrial agriculture and food production. If scientists do not sign such secrecy agreements, they do not get access to their needed research materials or the financial means to conduct, for instance, bio-safety research. Strangely enough, today, this kind of research is funded by the industries that develop them. This fundamentally puts freedom of science and the independent assessment of safety of industrial products at stake. Unsurprisingly, after decades of installing this corporate-good, profit-first model in techno-science, only a few scientists remain who have retained the necessary distance and capacity for critical reflection and scientific inquiry. Sadly, this attitude is neither wanted nor rewarded anymore! In reality, independent scientists who publish data that do not support corporate interests and voice scientific views dissenting from those of the industries and their allied science circles, are being subjected to massive campaigns aiming to discredit and silence them or oust them from their positions (Waltz 2009 a, b). Today, a climate of secrecy, suppression and fear characterizes so many fields of techno-science and, foremost, the so-called 'life sciences' including biotechnologies and molecular biology (Editors Scientific American 2009, Pollack 2009, Waltz 2009a,b). This is particularly disturbing as this ostracization includes assessments of safety and the risks of their commercial products: research which is absolutely critical for public and environmental health today and in the future.

Additionally, the art of spinning scientific findings, generating uncertainty and casting doubt has been perfected by corporate public relations firms and global consulting companies (Michaels 2008, p. 372) with the aim to muddle and undermine regulations and regulatory decision making. So-called 'product defence' groups have emerged that are professionalized in this field and trained during the battles over tobacco smoking and lung cancer[10]. Already, the lack of proper consideration of ecological science in the application of technologies such as gene technology was lamented by ecologists a number of years ago[11] (Snow et al. 2004), but their voices were unheard. This lack has seriously undermined the science for the public good and progress of humanity, while endowing privileged circles in techno-science with enormous, non-democratically legitimated power.

Differences

The director of *We feed the world*, Erwin Wagenhofer, takes on an educational and exposing role. This is also illustrated by the fact that his website offers a professional education package specifically for high-school students. The director of *Food Inc.* takes on a more activist role and aims to build a movement, also through his website[12] where the film maker calls for action and provides a platform for voicing opinions, organizing events and disseminating relevant information.

Some footage overlaps in both films. For example, the assembly line processing of live baby chickens. However, the aims and style differ between both films. *We feed the world* has no off-commentator and relies entirely on the statements by the people who are running the operations. By doing so, along with informing the viewer, they also reveal their striking degrees of personal unhappiness and frustration about the situation. This film connects the dots explicitly for the viewer by dividing the film into chapters with headings as for example[13]: 'Why our chicken are eating up the rainforest and a quarter of the Brazilian population is starving[14].' The film does not agitate or polarize the viewers but relies on the power of letting them watch the industrial operations and the explanations provided by those who run them. The viewer is expected to build his or her own opinion. This strategy worked surprisingly well, and *We feed the world* has become one of the most popular documentary films in Austria. It far exceeded the expectations of its makers (Grasser, DVD)[15].

Food Inc. combines the voices of the filmed people with off-commentators who were introduced in person to the viewer at the beginning of the film, like Michael Pollan and Eric Schlosser. Both are well-known, popular figures in literature and journalism as well as activists for a paradigm shift in food and agricultural production in the USA. However, the most powerful statements also come from the people who expose their feelings of powerlessness and tell the camera about the degree of control corporations exert over them. The only 'farmer' who seems to be content with his situation had actually accepted his re-defined role not as an independent farmer but rather as an employee of Tyson, one of the 5 big industrial chicken producers in the US. Vince Edwards complies entirely with their rules, he relies on their technology and money and is simply executing their production strategy.

> 'We have a contract with Tyson. They've been growing chicken for many, many years. And it's all a science. They got it figured out. If you can grow a chicken in 49 days, why would you want one you got to grow in three months?' (Vince Edwards, *Food Inc.*)

Vince Edwards had also complied with the 'recommendation' of Tyson to not allow the film crew into the chicken houses to film how they were kept. While he personally could not see anything wrong and would have been more than happy to have his chickens filmed, he followed this 'recommendation' by Tyson.

Food Inc. uses many sophisticated animations that explain the underlying connections that would be difficult to see in reality. For example, Kenner shows the disassembling of maize into a myriad of chemical compounds that are added to new types of processed foods.

Summarizing conclusions

Discontent is growing. Many people feel that something is wrong with the way we grow and produce our food. Because the exploitative profit-first economic model is now applied to all fundamental systems of human societies, the system has now reached its peaks: peak wealth for a small minority, peak oil, peak water, peak industrial food - leaving only one direction to go – downward. With global warming and the financial collapse leading the way, agriculture, food and health are following. Investigative documentaries are serving an important role by revealing and exposing the underlying mechanisms and connecting the dots for the viewer of this vastly complex system of global dimensions. This not only explains the increasing popularity of such investigative documentary films, they actually serve the immediate need of people. Moreover, the modern medium of film making allows directors to produce such films with more affordable sophistication.

In *We feed the world*, the director Erwin Wagenhofer interviewed the CEO of Nestlé, Peter Brabeck, who revealed his personal state of denial and lack of insight in the failure of the system that his global oligarchy, as Jean Ziegler calls them, has helped to establish. Stubbornly, Brabeck points to the successes of his strategy and argues that its failures are due to 'bad' implementation of this otherwise working strategy. His honesty is perhaps one of the best sarcastic achievements of this film as the viewers can easily observe how lost and disconnected such corporate leaders are from the fall-out of the system that has made them immensely rich. Most memorable are the closing sentences in *We feed the world* spoken by Brabeck and left uncommented. It became stunningly clear for the viewer how the corporate elite is imprisoned in a world of market- and profit-logic severely restricting their intellectual options for progressive solutions and options beyond and above the current system.

Some questions still remain open and unaddressed. How can we progress in the face of such powerful blockers and stakeholders who seem to be determined to pursue the path of self-destruction? Why don't any of the documentations extend their lines of dot-connections to include two further very important groups of stakeholders in this field: pharmaceutical companies and public sector science? I have attempted to point to the intimate relationship of the pharmaceutical corporations to their fellow agricultural and food processing counterparts who generate its 'best customers'. Ironically, most chemical /biotech companies, who for example produce poisonous pesticides and genetically modified crop plants, are also producing pharmaceuticals in related branches of their global agglomerates.

Options for the way forward

There seem to be two pressing issues involved at this time. One deals with the search for production models that could serve as basis for development at a large scale that would alleviate the failures of the current model. The other deals with the big question: What are the options for action for the majority of people? People who realize that the system must change, but are incapable of bringing about this change because the ruling elites are unified in a state of denial. Elites, which are tied down by the corporate control of transnational companies, whose power has surpassed that of many, or most, sovereign nations.

Alternative production models

Food Inc. features two contrasting models or solutions: On the one hand there is the large US-wide organic corporation Stonyfields Inc.[16] and, on the other hand, the small decentralized farming operation of Polyface Farms[17] run by the Salatin family. The Polyface farming model clearly calls for a more fundamental shift in production and distribution towards a local, decentralized system. For example, Polyface Farm refuses to ship products outside of their vicinity and encourages people to look for other local farmers. The owners of Polyface Farms, the Salatin family, have no desire to increase their operation and deal with large retailers such as Walmart. In contrast, the once small organic family dairy farm Stonyfield went the opposite way. They bought into the economic logic of scale and chose to work with Walmart and were bought out by the large transnational corporation Danone. Although they follow organic standards, when it comes to processing yoghurt and transport, they have followed the current economic model of growth based on a large scale centralized distribution system. Their sales increased significantly when Walmart decided to sell their products. Today, Stonyfield Inc. is one of the few big corporations in organic milk production – without using pesticides, antibiotics and abusing people, all of which deserves enormous credit. But we still need a public discourse on which of these models can best serve our needs and also retain a small ecological footprint. Only then can we affect change and gear the science agendas towards people's needs again as well as develop optimized production systems.

Progress in the face of blockades

Critical documentaries have succeeded in revealing and deconstructing the underlying reasons leading to the global decline of ecological and economic systems. It seems they also can generate momentum and move people to the point of catapulting themselves out of the vicious spiral and their involuntary complicity to exist with such a problematic system. These critical documentaries lead the way and can have a tremendous role in connecting the disconnected issues of ecology, economy and socio-politics. I argue that scientists need to join efforts for the conception and implementation of new concepts with creative film makers and other artists.

We need to develop transdisciplinary teams to engage the public in a world that hovers 'between complete anxiety and a total incapacity to predict or imagine consequences as seen in human-provoked environmental changes and aggressive power struggles' (Saitô 2006). What we share is the collective desire to not be destructive, and not to be lured into complicity and complacency with the powers and logics of predatory behaviour and calculus. Artists are needed to help in the quest for space for transcending disciplinary boundaries. As Saitô (2006) suggests: 'Today the artist's constructive intervention is to scrutinize commonly profit-driven processes of collaboration to address the socio-political dilemma in a world obsessed with short-sighted results.' This is the perfect pretext for 'collaborative art' – a shift from bringing art to the people, to instead working with the people to create art (Sowder 1995). We have a joint quest for sustainable progress and a future beyond greed.

Notes

1 <http://www.imdb.com/name/nm0041003>.

2 Intergovernmental panel on climate change of the United Nations.

3 *Food Inc.* Michael Taylor, 1984-1991 at King & Spaulding, he served as lawyer advising Monsanto on genetically modified food labelling. In 1991, he moved to the FDA as deputy commissioner for policy where he oversaw FDA's decision not to label genetically modified foods. Once that was achieved he moved back to Monsanto in 1998 until 2000 as vice president for public policy.

4 'Corporate interest in agriculture and the way agriculture research has been conducted in land grant institutions, with a lot of influence by the chemical companies and pesticide companies as well as fertilizer companies – all have been playing an important role in convincing the public that you need to have these inputs to produce food, (Ivette Perfecto, Professor for Ecology, University of Michigan – <http://www.flag-sa.org/blog/2008/08/organic-farming-can-feed-world.html>).

5 In the late 20th century corn transformed from a food or feed crop to a raw material competing in uses with crude oil or petroleum. In 1987, the National Corn Growers Association declared that 'anything made from a barrel of petroleum can be made from a bushel of corn.' Today out of 10'000 items of a regular grocery supermarket in the US, 2500 contain corn in one form or another and the website lists over 70 products that use corn of those ranging from beer, cosmetics to paint or varnish to pharmaceuticals, tires and yoghurt. Fussell stated in the 1990s that less than 1% of all corn is actually eaten as food. 85 percent is converted into animals and the rest is used for industrial purposes (Fussell 1992).

6 'Emerging science seems to suggest that substance x [a vitamin in a functional food product] may add to breast health' – statement heard by author in a commercial on a country radio station in Wyoming in July 2009.

7 Ingredients of a randomly chosen brand of bagels in a US supermarket lists > 35 mostly highly processed ingredients obviously making this a profitable 'edible foodlike substance'. Ingredients include: wheat flour, malt barley flour, niacin, ferrous sulfate, thiamin mononitrate, riboflavin, folic acid, water, blueberry bits (sugar, corn flour, dextrose, corn starch, soybean oil, fructose, dried blueberries, natural and artificial flavours, wheat starch, citric acid, salt red 40, blue 2, blue 1, green 3), sugar, wheat gluten, salt, yeast, mono-diglycerides, guar gum, calcium propionate (a preservative), corn syrup solids, molasses, enzyme, soy oil,

ascorbic acid.

8 Center for Disease Control CDC – <http://www.cdc.gov/obesity>.

9 <http://www.ijsaf.org>/archive/16/1/lotter2.pdf>.

10 'They [product defense groups] combine science with public relations to help clients avoid regulation and litigation. [...]. The intent is to cast doubt on real science. The industry has deep roots in the fight over tobacco.' David Michaels, January 2009, <http://www.fastcompany.com/magazine/132/manufacturing-doubt.html>.

11 'Ecologists, agricultural scientists, molecular biologists, and others need broader training to address the above recommendations. We strongly encourage greater multidisciplinary training and collaborative, multidisciplinary research on the environmental risks and benefits of GEOs' (Snow et al. 2004).

12 Comment by M. Marvier 2004: 'Given that the current trend in biological education is to move toward ever more specialized curricula, calls for multidisciplinary training seem to be falling on deaf ears. But having a narrow background can lead to some highly undesirable consequences. For example, I recently met a scientist from India who was working to genetically engineer an endangered fish so that it might better tolerate waters that had become intensely polluted with heavy metals. With just a little training in ecology, this molecular biologist would likely have recognized the foolishness of his research ambition-after all, having one species of fish tolerate heavy metals would only mean those metals could be accumulated and passed up the food chain, possibly even to humans. The need for breadth in biological training simply cannot be overstated. Sadly, [...], the gap between the recommendations made in the ESA position paper and reality is huge' <http://www.twnside.org.>sg/title2/service113.htm>.

13 <http://www.takepart.com/foodinc>.

14 'Why Tomatoes travel 3000 km through Europe and Africans are drawn to the rich northern countries and our vegetables end up on Africa's markets'.

15 E.g. 'Best documentary' 2006, The Guild of German Art House Cinemas (about 300 member cinemas, largest such association in Germany).

16 <http://www.stonyfield.com/>.

17 <http://www.polyfacefarms.com/>.

References

Bioscience Resource Project, 2007 'The agenda gap in science', February, accessed 18 March 2010, <http://www.bioscienceresource.org/commentaries/article.php?id=13>.

Editors, *Scientific American* 2009, 'Do seed companies Control GM crop research?', August, accessed 18 March 2010, <http://www.scientificamerican.com/article.cfm?id=do-seed-companies-control-gm-crop-research>.

Etzkowitz, H 2005, 'The rise of the entrepreneurial university', *International Journal of Contemporary Sociology*, vol. 42, pp. 28-43.

Food and Agriculture Organisation (FAO) 2009, 'The state of food insecurity in the world: Economic crises – impacts and lessons learned', Rome, accessed 18 March 2010, <http://www.eeo.ed.ac.uk/postgraduate/MSc/envdev/intdev/files/FAO_food_security_2009.pdf>.

Fussell, B 1992, *The story of corn*, University of New Mexico Press, Albuquerque,

IAASTD Global Report 2009, 'Agriculture at a Crossroads', B McIntyre, H Herren, J Wakhungu & RT Watson, (eds).

Kenner, R 2009, 'Exploring the corporate power behind the way we eat: the making of *Food Inc*', in K Weber (ed.), *Food, Inc.: How industrial food is making us sicker, fatter and poorer, and what you can do about it: a participant guide*, Participant Media, New York

Krimsky, S 2003, *Science in the private interest: Has the lure of profits corrupted biomedical research?* Rowman & Littlefield. Lanham/MD.

Lacy, S (ed.) 1995, *Mapping the terrain: New genre public art*, Bay Press, Seattle/WA, p. 126.

Lotter, D 2009a, 'The genetic engineering of food and the failure of science – Part 1: The development of a flawed enterprise', *International Journal of Sociology of Agriculture & Food*, vol. 16, pp. 31-49.

Lotter, D 2009b, 'The genetic engineering of food and the failure of science – Part 2: Academic capitalism and the loss of scientific integrity', *International Journal of Sociology of Agriculture & Food* vol. 16, pp. 50 – 68.

Michaels, D 2008, *Doubt is their product*, Oxford University Press, also in *Scientific American*, vol. 292, June 2005, accessed 18 March2010, <http://www.scientificamerican.com/article.cfm?id=doubt-is-their-product>.

Nestle, M 2007, *Food Politics: How the food industry influences nutrition and health*, University of California Press, London/UK.

Patel, R 2008, *Stuffed & starved: The hidden battle for the world food system*, 398 edn, Melville House Publishing, New York.

Pollack, A 2009, 'Crop scientists say biotechnology seed companies are thwarting research', *New York Times*, publ. 19 February, accessed 18 March 2010, <http://www.nytimes.com/2009/02/20/business/20crop.html>.

Pollan, M 2008, *In defense of food*, Penguin, New York.

Saitô, MW 2006, *Engaging the public: Dialogical art and frameworks to collaborative environments*, Momentarium, accessed 18 March 2010, <http://www.momentarium.org/research/collaboration.pdf>.

Slaughter, S & Rhoades, G 2004, *Academic capitalism and new economy: Markets, state, and higher education*, Johns Hopkins University Press, Baltimore/MD.

Snow, AA, Andow, DA, Gepts, P, Hallerman, EM, Power, A, Tiedje, JM & Wolfenbarger, LL 2005, 'Genetically engineered organisms and the environment: Current status and recommendations', *Ecological Applications*, vol. 15, pp. 377-404.

Waltz, E 2009a, 'GM crops: Battlefield', *Nature*, vol. 461, pp. 27-32.

Waltz, E 2009b, 'Under wraps', *Nature Biotechnology*, vol. 27, pp. 880-882.

Welsh, R & Glenna, L 2007, 'Considering the role of the university in conducting research on agri-biotechnologies', *Social Studies of Science*, vol. 36, pp. 929-942.

HEAT: ART, PEOPLE & CLIMATE CHANGE

Jill Orr

The premise of the performance work and this essay is, that through awareness of historic, cultural and local relations to any given place, lie the seeds of human stewardship that I believe is an important ingredient for social change regarding climate change solutions.

This essay reflects on my work as a performance artist who engages with the cross-cultural relations in specific sites, as a means to address the behavioural shifts implicit within solutions to climate change. I have created socio-poetic environmental performance, installation, photographic and video responses to many different performance projects that engage in sites within Victoria, Australia.

It is within this scope that my work can most effectively contribute to the interface between art, science and the community.

The understanding of both the issues of climate change and potential solutions through awareness and action can be seen as an interface between the accessibility of science and the idea of empowerment through action. The feminist phrase, 'the personal is political' has resonance here because the groundswell of active involvement in whatever field holds personal attraction, is more likely to endure and develop local solutions shared by global networks. Part of this process is addressing blockages that prohibit interaction between people. Some blockages manifest in historical long-standing attitudes regarding people and place, where severe disadvantage through racism, poverty, genocide and lack of education are felt as trauma.

The identity of Indigenous people cannot be separated from their ancestral land. Their challenge has, since colonisation, been one of societal recognition of their spiritual relations to land. The country of Australia, since settlement, has been irrevocably transformed from bush land into farmland and owned by non-Indigenous farmers and governments. The Indigenous struggle for cultural acknowledgement and land rights have in the last several years seen some successes. Each claim must demonstrate unbroken ancestral links to the land in question. These rights enable communities to practice ceremonial and cultural traditions on that land as they attempt sustainability in an economic and cultural sense. These communities face urgent issues of health, education and employment. The struggles for recognition and the acknowledgement of atrocities in the hands of white society have been acknowledged by the Rudd Government in the symbolic act of an apology in 2008 (Rudd 2008).

The process and the scars of inter-generational alienation from their country, impacted further by the stolen generations where governments took children forcibly from their families are still felt. The last incidence of forced removal was officially in 1969, however unofficially the practice continued much after this <http://reconciliaction.org.au>. The trauma associated with this practice is within living memory and still impacts all Indigenous people. The rate of suicide, incarceration and substance abuse is well documented and attributed in part to the stolen generations inter-generational trauma (Human Rights and Equal Opportunity Commission Report, 1997). Against this background The Australia 2020 Summit: The Future of Rural and Regional Australia (Australia 2020 Summit 2008), also recognises that Indigenous Australians manage one fifth of the land in Australia. By contrast there is an unsubstantiated urban myth that some Australians feel an environmental saviour in the hands of Indigenous land-care. It is vitally important that Indigenous knowledge is listened to and included within sustainable solutions. However it is another question to think that Indigenous communities can carry this responsibility for the entire country. The complex double paradox is part of a cultural construction played out by a guilty mainstream whose romance often fuels aspects of a quick fix to climate change by invoking the romantic colonialist image of the 'noble savage' in tune with the land.

C.C. Lamberg-Karlovsky, Director of the Peabody Museum of Archaeology and Ethnology, Harvard University writes:

> 'If past images, whether written or photographed, were permeated by attitudes of colonialist superiority, racism, or the idealised notion of the innate nobility of the "savage", what then of our present perspective? [...]
> These may be no more than our wishful projections onto other peoples, past and present, in an effort to ameliorate the problems of our own day.' (Lamberg-Karlovsky 1986)

We need to remain alert to the fact that Indigenous communities have had recent government intervention in the guise of child protection against sexual abuse. The troubling lack of education and health services, suicides and unemployment put a reality to any romance that Indigenous land management can save us all. Each locale is different with its specific environmental attributes. We all face this challenge and we all can contribute on a local level within our immediate environment.

Sustainability is at the core of these cultural misconceptions. However, awareness and acknowledgment of difficult historical truths must occur before and/or simultaneously with, work on environmental sustainability if we are to succeed in achieving solutions. These processes are long underway yet the hurt and history run deep, and this is where transdiscourse is a vital approach. Not one person, group, tribe, place, company, political party or country can effectively embrace all there is to know or form one single input. The process is multi-faceted, multi-disciplinary and inclusive.

Both Indigenous and small town sustainability is implicated by, in and through the relations to the land which has formed and informed identities. These different cultural representations often occur in the same location and are the subject of several works that explore cultural aspects of sustainability.

The works I will discuss are *The Crossing*, *The Southern Cross – to bear and behold*, *Faith in a faithless land* and The *Global Mind Project, 2010*. At the heart of each work is the challenge faced and pathways that are opened through the process of performance.

All aspects of life are on the table, as the Copenhagen Meeting on Climate Change in December 2009 demonstrated. The African and other developing nations have clearly demonstrated that their countries will be affected first by increases in global temperature and they require equal consideration and assistance. Yvo de Boer, Executive Secretary of the United Nations Framework Convention on Climate Change has said: 'Politically, there is a high degree of mistrust between developed and developing countries. Yet climate change cannot be tackled with a lack of trust' (de Boer 2009).

The issue of trust is tested in the creation of *The Crossing*, which is a micro-version of the enormity that faces international relations in dealing with climate change solutions on a global level.

The Crossing

I am an outsider, a visiting artist and although I have emotional and spiritual ties to Mildura, a regional city whose ancient Murray River frames the town, my idea did require immense consultation. I was inspired by Lock Island – a partially artificial island in the Murray River – to create the performance event *The Crossing* (see Colour plate xx, Fig. A & B).

The Murray River is distressed. Much of its water has been over allocated to irrigators who have grown most of the nation's food. Paradise was created from the desert by controlling the rivers flow since the late eighteen hundreds. Currently up and down stream of the lock system the water levels are low, impacting entire ecologies. The politics of water is delicate as many growers leave the land which quickly returns to the red-earthed desert. It is within this context that *The Crossing* takes place.

The river is important to the many Indigenous tribes which were abundant before 1830. White settlement brought with it small-pox that decimated thousands of Aborigines who were also displaced through land clearance and over-hunting. The First Nations peoples and their lands changed irrevocably. This is the historic site of the river crossing for many Indigenous tribes passing North, South, East and West of there. The name Koorie refers to all Indigenous Australians that traditionally occupied Victoria and New South Wales. Within Koorie identification there are many different tribes. The Latche Latche and the Barkindji tribes, who live on both sides of the Murray River, were involved in the performance.

The work is inspired by local stories about cross-cultural relations to place, and incorporates early colonial institutional characters that had direct connections with the Indigenous population, such as the missionaries, who established several missions in the region. They provided food, shelter and education in return for salvation. At times this was a fraught relationship. The performance characters representing this are the nun and the missionary. The bush nurses arrived in Australia in the late eighteen hundreds and worked amongst both white settlers and Indigenous communities. Their midwifery saw the births of numerous Indigenous babies on the earth floors of the mobile tent hospitals. Their role was felt necessary by the state because many of the Aboriginal birthing practices required access to their land. The Latche Latche and Barkindji female elders with whom I spoke are testament to this.

The Crossing leads audiences across time to include the contemporary 'Lost Malaysian' who is neither coloniser nor colonised. His dissociation is his lack of connection to this place, a symptom of globalisation and immigration. Performed by Tony Yap who is a Malaysian trance dance master, the dance form is earthed and yet draws on an energetic transfer during the performative process. There is also a contemporary 'white tree spirit' who is an amalgam of my own childhood Celtic fairies and Australian bush spirits translated by the dancer Emma Strapps. Emma is trained in Butoh dance, which similarly draws on a strong-earthed connection.

The present reality is the Koorie children who dance their ancient River dance in the place of their ancestors. The dance is performed in short repetitions that build on a vibratory call from the earth through the feet to absorb, release and connect through the present to their ancestral spirits. Each dance form is different yet connected through a cross-cultural intention of unifying the body, mind and spirit to the place. I was most interested to place these dance forms together as a symbolic act of co-existence where each contributes to the overall work without compromise. This is symbolic of the broader social challenge towards inclusive collaboration that requires trustworthy and respectful recognition of difference as the first base towards socio-ecological change.

The collaborative structure may hold a key

Collaborations with Australian Indigenous people require great transparency of intention, clarity of ownership, respect of Indigenous cultural heritage and clear methods for creating, in this instance, the collaborative performance event. Given that the work also included other performers from non-Indigenous backgrounds I worked with the idea of creating small performance cameos where the performers made works to specific briefs. This is well understood in the contemporary performance language but it was a first for the Mildura Koories. While speaking with the Latche Latche dance man he revealed that he was illiterate, so all of my prior correspondence was not understood. Having said that, he was a master of improvisation and our communication was largely felt. Trust was vital and this enabled an extraordinary opportunity for symbolic healing to occur. I will elaborate on this shortly.

The Mildura Koorie's task was to design and perform their sections with no interference by me. In this way a clear space was made and they chose how to represent themselves thus giving respect for their artistic integrity. This was a crucial factor. It demonstrated trust and my own commitment to a sincere collaboration. We also discussed the context in relation to the other performers. This principal I believe is a vehicle for developing transdiscourse on a deep level that can contribute to human stewardship. Creative processes whether in the arts, industry, science and community proceed when trust is felt. This method worked and enabled intuitive improvisation to develop.

The Performance

Audiences encounter the bush nurse who tells stories of births and deaths, both Indigenous and non-Indigenous. The audience encounters the missionary who has sunk into a delusional rage with his forsaken God. His mission to convert the heathens is constantly witnessed by the Latche Latche elder who is an ever-present shadow. This dance man called his role the 'black shadow'. He knew this concept not from theory but from life experience.

There is the colonial woman and her children who act as guides for the audience.

The converging dance scene where the young Koorie dancers perform their totem dances accompanied by the didgeridoo played by a Latche Latche musician, was central to the performance. Entering this scene is the white tree spirit followed by the Lost Malaysian, dancing his transformation. The missionary rudely bursts onto the scene, where he blasphemes, abuses and pounds his bible, and is abruptly stopped by the nun who throws a bucket of water over him, sending the missionary to the ground. The dance man was a silent master of ceremony who swiftly and with stealth, symbolically decapitates all intruders.

This 'punctum moment' (Barthes, 2000 (1981), p. 27), to apply Roland Barthes term for photography, is this:

> What would happen if colonisation did not occur?

I was tested here through the moment of improvisation. Would I (we) enable this action? Yes. Energetically speaking this moment of truth, the moment to speak, had happened. Powerful in that minutes prior, was the result of 200 years of colonisation. It stopped. The act of retribution, in a moment of performance symbolism, was felt by a largely Koorie audience. Sighs and laughter of deep appreciation rippled throughout. The healing between black and white, Indigenous and non-Indigenous, occurs when the truth of history is acknowledged. Climate change solutions and cultural transformation are part of the same challenge where difference is an inclusive and active ingredient.

The pathway through participatory agency is difficult to assess. In the moment there was a feeling of enthusiastic appreciation, however as our daily lives resume and the stark differences in privilege are experienced, I am left hoping that the participating children and audience may have experienced the collaboration positively. Perhaps it was only myself and the non-Indigenous performers who gained invaluable insights into our differences. I will never know given that evaluations are written reports and any real response is couched in efficient terms. The schools and adults involved did respond enthusiastically in person and in grant acquittal reports, however the depth of experience will take time. Success will be an Indigenous culture that is culturally and economically sustainable and which works equally within the broader Australian society.

Socio - poetic Images

The Southern Cross – to bear and behold and *Faith in a faithless land* are both filmed in the same location of Mitre Lake. The works are influenced by the same local history but two distinct characters, the missionary of *Faith in a faithless land* and myself in a white dress coat in *The Southern Cross - to bear and behold* portray the two works. The results and implications are quite different because the intention behind the missionary is imbued with history as it resounds in a contemporary context. Myself, as an ambiguously costumed contemporary figure, draws on the present socio-environmental challenges. Both works imply the environmental and cultural overlays at Mitre Lake. Denig refers to Bruce Chatwin's *Songlines* and quotes: 'Stretching across the continents and ages: that wherever men have trodden they have left a trail of song: and that these trails must reach back and forth in time and space' (Chatwin in Denig 1996 p.120).

Denig describes Western, Eastern and Indigenous meta-narratives as songlines where memory traces and oral traditions converge, intersect and part at different points in time across the ages.

The well documented historical connection between the star formations of the *Southern Cross* as the navigational tool that guided the tall ships into the Southern Hemisphere and ultimately on to the Australian shores has a crucial connection to both works. The paradox that lies between the traces that overlay Indigenous ancestral life on the land are written over by colonial settlement that is again written over by the current environmental distress symbolised at Mitre Lake.

To consider the effect of our labour in the positive and negative aspects and behold the infinite beauty of nature reminds me that we are very small standing beneath the night sky. The observations of the night sky are navigated from the earliest sextants to massive telescopes and from satellites to brainwave scans. These are mediated technologies that enable past discoveries and present desire to propel future knowledge. The impetus can be seen as a duet of imagination and desire propelling forward action.

> 'Quantum physics obliges us to take seriously what has been a more purely philosophical consideration: that we do not see things in themselves, but only aspects of things. What we see is an electron path in a bubble chamber, not an electron, and what we see in the skies are not stars any more than a recording of Caruso's voice is not Caruso. By revealing that the observer plays a role in the observed, quantum physics did for physics what Darwin had done for the life sciences: it tore down walls, reuniting the world with the universe' (Ferris 1998).

Mediated environments, landscapes and ecologies are not actual places. They are representations framed by apparatuses and interpreted and refined through the assistance of technology. With this in mind, the cultural context also informs what is framed and mediated. My direction of the camera's viewfinder frames and captures the socio-poetic images of *Faith in a Faithless Land* and The *Southern Cross – to bear and behold* (see Colour plate xxi, Fig. E & F). The resulting images are informed by the physicality of Mitre Lake, as I struggle across the oozy surface embodying the historic and cultural overlays.

I have employed another methodology in creating these works. Essentially the photographs are documenting my performances for the camera. The intimate collaboration here is the employment of a photographer. I cannot trust the sulphurous mud and intensity of the flame to a shutter release cable but I do have full confidence in the photographer, Naomi Herzog, to capture what I present. I have witnessed the word 'environment' change from an elite left wing concept, informed by courageous science in the 1960s and 70s, to a household word in 2010. This has occurred because thirty years of discussion, action and politisation has affected a paradigm shift. More change is still necessary. The environment is mediated. The environment has become the subject of transdiscourse.

However the local environment is the place where you trip over and skin your knees, where you sneak the first kiss with grassy evidence on your jumper, where the old man with rabbits in a sac on his back is really a baby snatcher out to get you (A very 1950s image). This environment is imbued with memory and corporeality. It lives. That for me is a crucial link between people and place that is the conduit between science, culture and transdiscourse. This is a local experience that must pulse with immediate relevance within each locale to penetrate the gloss of mediated states and the actual science.

The Southern Cross - to bear and behold and Faith in a faithless land.

> 'There is never one moment when past dissolves completely, leaving a new landscape in its wake.' (McKenna 2002 p. 202)

Mitre Lake sits at the base of Mitre Rock that is part of Mount Arapelis in Western Central Victoria. It is the tribal home to the few remaining Djurid Balug people of the Wotjobaluk Tribe. I acknowledge their ownership. This landscape is both an ancient theatre within which the human drama unfolds, and is in reality a harsh bottomless deposit of oozy black clay covered by a salty crustaceous surface. It is sulphuric and luminous and has been mined for its salt in the past. Mitre Lake does resemble hundreds of dried up salt lakes that have been caused by drought and erosion. However Mitre Lake is natural, and has the ability to dramatically and temporally record the traces of life that are captured on its surface. This surface is like a mirror, reflecting both the ancient and recent past and mirroring the potential future. It is full of presence and implicit absence.

The Australian land, as with other lands, must have been alien for the missionary whose constancy was the test of their own faith bearing the Cross of Christian colonisation. Mitre Lake appears to be another desert whose iconic biblical burning bushes do not even grow so the measure of epiphany resides in footsteps that are washed away in the occasional storm. The missionary trudges through the mud bearing the Cross of Salvation and carrying the word to whom ever will listen or is vulnerable to bribes of sugar, flour and redemption. The Indigenous people were particularly vulnerable.

Values and belief systems run as simultaneous threads that share the same locale. Together and different, inclusive and exclusive, witnessed by the light of the stars which observe, as we do, the dramatic environmental consequences of our forward march towards progress and economic growth. The stars, to which I have given a consciousness for purposes of human empathy, run to another tune which is that of an intergalactic and cosmic rhythm through time. Nature's rhythm is not bound by faith or profit or the millisecond that is our existence. Charles Darwin's insights seem to be unmatched in terms of survival of the fittest through adaptation.

The *Southern Cross – to bear and behold* is an image of hope as central to humanity's desire for a positive ecological future. Both faith and hope are integral to manifesting ideas and energising change, which in this instance is cultural, scientific, economic and historic. 'The land is hot, so hot that your protection bursts into flames' (Orr 1989). I wrote this when creating the first burning umbrella image, *Walking on planet earth*. I have revisited the image of a burning umbrella for the central image of *The Southern Cross - to bear and behold*. The new image has a different resonance and yet the transformative quality of fire is the energy of positive action both of the heart, body, mind, and desire, acting within and not only on, the environment. There is both apocalypse and renewal. To bear and behold the renewal is the task ahead.

We are framed by the screen, which is and has been our reality for most contemporary visual language. As a visually literate collective we know the difference between hype and sincerity and between emotional engagement and passive watching. The role of art here is at the intersection that evokes the poetic through which multi-layers of meaning can be interpreted. Art highlights facts that are interpreted and understood and highlights consumerism from which there is little escape. Media as technological criticism and media as a form of art and communication take place as an aspect of the entire mediated landscape. I think it is feasible to say that we do know the difference between mediated intention because we have become masters of screen interpretation as a daily experience.

I would like to think that the change of behaviours necessary to achieve climate change solutions are benefiting from mass ideological, educational and scientific information programs through technology. David Attenborough has embedded inaccessible ecologies as an intimate screen experience that forms an active part of our indirect experience of the natural world. Without his and other documentaries, vast audiences would not know about the diversity of life on Earth. He has formed a link between locales that have become integral to the way we see the world. Media Art can take this to a different place where interactivity, and transdisclipinary discourse is the modus operandi.

History tells us of less sophisticated technologies in the service of both democratic and autocratic population manipulation. How can media art contribute in a less manipulative manner? The answer may be in the fact that artists do not hold, nor wish to hold power over others. The concern of most artists is to contribute to an open debate through visualizing, representing and mirroring their world as a reflection of who we are and what we may become. This identity does not involve power over others, although it can and does articulate the mechanisms of power. In his *Introduction to Walter Benjamin* on modern media, Jennings, states; 'In technology a physis is being organized through which mankind's contact with the cosmos takes a new and different form.' Jennings continues; 'One path is the path of violence that leads, for the collective, to the "nights of annihilation" of World War I. And the violence wreaked by technology is not merely martial and collective; it inheres in every individual encounter as well. Benjamin never lets the reader forget the overwhelming, indeed annihilating effect of the new apparatuses upon the human body and its senses. [...] Benjamin's belief that certain properties of technological media as such hold within them the potential for social change' (Jennings 2008, p. 12).

The Global Mind Project 2010.

I was invited by the artist, Karen Casey to respond to her *Global Mind Project* (see Colour plate xxi, Fig. C & D) with a performance that took place in Melbourne at Federation Square in January 2010. The *Global Mind Project* is a Media Arts and Brain Sciences initiative by Karen Casey in partnership with software designer, Harry Sokol.

Using unique video effects software to generate real-time audiovisual effects from brainwaves, *Global Mind Project* aims to creatively interpret mind-states, to be presented as live screen art and online performances. The project is the culmination of several years of research and development, initiated in 2004 with testing at the Brain Sciences Institute, Swinburne University of Technology in Melbourne. *Global Mind Project* will be an online access for performance web casts and ultimately a means to facilitate viewer interaction in the form of direct mind interactions with the artist and others <http://www.globalmindproject.com>. The idea of a global mind had an instant attraction particularly because it is a global mind that I believe is the unifying and activating force of our time for environmental change. I see this metaphysically as well as through practical online forums. My interest is the space in between the body and high-end technology as a means to ground human physicality as the 'trans-medium' between the actual environment and mediations representing it. We have received valuable feed back from this event where audiences, being a mixture of invited guests and the general public, ranged from amazement to disappointment. There is a great expectation that technology will not only be amazing but that it will fix all. Perhaps this may be so.

There is a dilemma with the rapid development of technology and the consuming public. For example even the film *Avatar* after its initial completion, was constructed again with new, updated technology. The *Global Mind Project*, low budget in scope, exists due to Karen Casey, whose singular artist's vision is complemented by Harry Sokol's software development with neuro-headsets from Emotive Systems and the three performance artists. We came together united by the potential of an idea. I think that the sustainability of life on Earth is a complex mix of high-end innovations and more humble attempts to realize pathways forward. It is all necessary in the mix. This art, mediated online, is one of many initiatives that contribute to transdiscourse.

The *Global Mind Project*, *Spectacle of the Mind*, was a live performance that utilizes high end brain wave technology to demonstrate the performer's mind changing the projected images as part of the live action. This was also streamed online. The potential to screen the live performances, simultaneously on public screens in other countries, for example, New York, London, Tokyo etc., is only a matter of funding and co-ordination. The memorable 2000 New Years Eve that was telecast across the globe visualizing each countries entry into the new millennium is an example of this working. The important difference of The *Global Mind Project* is the performance of and making visible, states of mind through the subtle communication of an individual, through brain wave technology, to the global and local collective. This is very different to the collective celebrations of the New Year.

My performance for The *Global Mind Project*, *The spectacle of the mind*, drew on the corporeality of the human body as a site between high-end technology and late eighteenth century magic shows. I am fascinated by the unseen made visible, which in part is achieved through the effects of the headset where there is a quality of magic and disbelief when viewing this. Is this really affected by brain waves? I wanted to contrast this with historic magic shows where the trickery was almost believed, and charlatans were many. The global mind is also about a spiritual dimension discussed earlier in this chapter, where people and place are spiritually connected. This being a dimension that is within the cultural connection to sustainability. I read *the spectacle of the mind* as the cipher between the body, mind and spirit that is sited within magic and technology.

Using the illusion of a Houdini escape from a large trunk-like coffin, I am released by my assistants, Craig Peade and Ben Cittidini. We are each dressed in late old-style mourning costume, except my head gear visibly incorporates the headset, placing the old-style magic theatre in the hi-tech present. I am handed a handkerchief into which I spit. This is the first important gesture of embodiment and projected visceral truth. (A live video close up as a cut away, dissolves through the brain wave images on screen). Craig is disrobed down to his long johns whilst the other gently wipes his eyes, nose, mouth etc. With each wipe the newly wet handkerchief is hung in the vertical trunk. This process continues as Craig's body is wiped all over and the numerous handkerchiefs become fluttering white cloths within the trunk. Blood was smeared over his chest and stomach. The crying, laughing, sneezing, digesting, expelling and bleeding body was on display as vulnerable, fragile and immediate. The spectacle was pure theatre with smoke machines puffing and false blood at the climax; belief and disbelief, spectacle and reality are on display. My task with the headset is not only to create actions that are programmed to alter the projections with movements from the jaw, face, hands, arms and full body. I am also evoking historic mediums where the trance state is an altered state of consciousness often associated with séances and physical phenomena. The trance state is similar to meditation such as a slowing of the heart beat, slow deep breathing and altered brain patterns. It is also similar to the performance state <http://www.voicesofspirit.co.uk/pages/about-trance.htm>.

I was evoking Madame Blavatski who was a renowned medium in the eighteen hundreds. She was trained by masters from Tibet and established Theosophy which she called 'The knowledge of the divine'. She explains that 'Brotherhood is not a mere ideal. It is in fact in nature on the spiritual plane. [...] We assert that the divine spark in man being one and identical in its essence with the Universal Spirit, our "Spiritual Self" is practically omniscient, but that it cannot manifest its knowledge owing to the impediments of matter. Now the more these impediments are removed, in other words, the more the physical body is paralyzed, as to its own independent activity and consciousness, as in deep sleep or deep trance, or, again, in illness, the more fully can the inner Self manifest on this plane. This is our explanation of those truly wonderful phenomena of a higher order, in which undeniable intelligence and knowledge are exhibited' <www.blavatsky.net>. In this way the brainwave interaction on the screen becomes less impeded by matter because it is conducted via the electrical impulse from the brain. Madame Blavatski had her detractors who accuse her of racism, particularly anti-Semitism. She was accused of being a charlatan, a fraud and an imposter in 1885 and was cleared of these claims in 1996. She is an unreliable character in the face of science but her influence through metaphysics and theosophy is broad amongst believers. I find her work on states of mind an apt counterpoint to use within a performance of high technology, body and *the spectacle of the mind*. Madame Blavatski is not necessarily made known to the audience. She is one of the influences to my own actions as a 'brain wave medium'. Perhaps in another incarnation of this work her presence may be acknowledged.

In the closing action Ben takes the handkerchief that I spat in from the trunk and shows both sides as dry to the audience. He neatly folds it and returns it to his pocket thus proving that forces of evaporation were at work. Amidst plumes of theatrical smoke we leave the stage. The live action was cut from the live camera at different times onto the images on screen. In that way the audience could see the brainwaves altering the projected video images, my assistants performing viscosity and myself as the brain wave medium. The video images were set in four sequences; firstly, fiery landscapes that became flash points into another world. Then there were images from spittle that became immense landscapes and cosmic travel, followed by the journey through intestines with pulsing cellular action and lastly the heart as bloody pumping and pulsing cells. Each brainwave interruption changed the images by enlarging holes and orifices, changing speed, creating multiple and overlapping perspectives. The images were evocative and not realistic in any way.

Summary

In conclusion, the nature of each work discussed is collaborative, cross-disciplinary and contributes to the broader transdiscourse on mediated environments. The images created as the lasting results of the performance experience have their own 'aura' where engagement is different and yet essentially the same as the live experience. Viewers take away the images as memory and issues as points of debate. The continued presence online as an interactive environment adds to the existing international forums through individual, group and interdisciplinary cross linkages.

The Crossing, *The Southern Cross - to bear and behold*, *Faith in a faithless land* and The *Global Mind Project* are examples of media art contributing to sustainable development through socio-poetic issues. Facts can only say so much before they become alienating, dry statistics. Humanity thrives on the imaginary, where stories, narratives and shared cultural expression can be the spark that energizes multiple forms of creative manifestation.

References

Australia 2020 Summit, 2008 *The Future Of Rural And Regional Australia* April accessed 11 March 2010, <http://www.australia2020.gov.au/topics/rural.cfm>.

Barthes, R 2000 (1981) *Camera Lucida*, transl. by R Howard Vintage Classics, Random House, London.

de Boer, Y 2009, Executive Secretary United Nations Framework Convention on Climate Change, *What can and must be achieved at Copenhagen*, address to the New York Bar Association 23rd September, accessed 17 March 2010, <http://unfccc.int/files/press/news_

room/statements/application/pdf/090923_speech_new_york.pdf>.

Denig, G 1996, 'Songlines and Seaways', in *Performances*, Melbourne University Press, Victoria, Australia.

Ferris T 1988, *Coming of Age in the Milky Way*, Morrow, New York. *Global Mind Project* 2010, ABC arts online, 22 January, accessed 17 March 2010, <http://www.abc.net.au/arts/stories/s2799320.htm>.

Human Rights and Equal Opportunity Commission Report 1997, *Bringing them Home - Report of the National Inquiry into the Separation of Aboriginal and Torres Strait Islander Children from Their Families April 1997*, accessed 3. March 2010, <http://www.hreoc.gov.au/social_justice/bth_report/report/ch1_part1.html>.

Jennings, M 2008, Benjamin, W, *The work of art in the age of technological reproducibility, and other writings on media*, Jennings, MW, Doherty, B & Levin TY (eds), Belknap Press of Harvard University Press, Cambridge/MA.

Lamberg-Karlosky CC 1986, Foreword exhibition catalogue *From Site to Sight: Anthropology, Photography and Power of Imagery*, Peabody Museum of Archaeology and Ethnology and the Department of Anthropology, Harvard University: Banta M, Peabody Museum Press, Cambridge MA.

McKenna, M 2002, *Looking for Blackfellas Point: An Australian History of Place*, UNSW Press, Sydney NSW.

Orr, J 1989, *Jill Orr*, Australian video art archive (avaa), <http://www.videoartchive.org.au/jorr/>.

ReconciliACTION Network 2007, *Stolen generations fact sheet*, 28 July, accessed 18 March 2010, <http://reconciliaction.org.au/nsw/education-kit/stolen-generations/>.

Rudd, G. 2008, *Apology To Australia's Indigenous Peoples*, 13 March 2008, accessed 3 March 2010, <http://www.aph.gov.au/house/Rudd_Speech.pdf>.

Voices of spirit: S Tyler-Walters, *About Trance*, <www.voicesofspirit.co.uk/pages/about-trance.htm>.

SOUTH AFRICAN URBAN SPACE: A 'MEDIATED' ENVIRONMENT

Therese Steffen

Ivan Vladislavić's Portrait with keys: the city of Johannesburg unlocked.

'We are stories. It's a notion so simple even a child could understand it. Would that it ended there. But we are stories within stories. Stories within stories within stories. We recede endlessly, framed and reframed, until we are unreadable to ourselves.'

'I am looking forward to seeing Jo'burg from the air. As the aircraft lifts you out of it, above it' it becomes, for a moment, comfortingly explicable' (Ivan Vladislavić, Portrait with keys: the city of Johannesburg unlocked, 98-99).

Urban literary and visual culture is a condensed artistic way of both addressing and stylistically expressing socio-historical facts and societal change. Literary and visual art in South Africa is no exception to this rule. A range of cultural texts critically and aesthetically reflect urbanizational processes in South Africa since the beginning of the (English) literary tradition in the 1880s. By the beginning of the 21st century, a burgeoning artistic attention has been paid to the city in South Africa. Contemporary South African authors and artists, among them writers Ivan Vladislavić or Phaswane Mpe, and artists William Kentridge or Willem Boshoff, respond to the tremendous move toward the city as both setting and subject that has occurred since the demise of apartheid boundaries after 1994.

This contribution seeks to analyze the prolific creative processes and their mediality in Ivan Vladislavić's literary texts with a focus on the city of gold, the 'disorderly', 'elusive' metropolis of Johannesburg (Nuttall, Mbembe, 2008). A polycentric and international city with a hybrid history that continually permeates the present, Johannesburg,

Jo'burg or Jozi, has become a place of intermingling and improvisation, a city that is fast developing its own brand of cosmopolitan culture in (South) Africa. Before delving into Ivan Vladislavić's Portrait with keys: the city of Johannesburg unlocked (2006), a socio-historic context will set the ground for a more informed understanding of Vladislavić's text as 'mediated' environment.

South African urbanity as text and context to creativity and mediality

Urbanization is a worldwide phenomenon that affects the future of any population in its economic, political, societal, and cultural development. This rapid progress of a global urbanization began already in the 20th century with a 10% growth of the urban population by 1900, to approximately 30% by 1950, to almost 50% by 2000. Today more than 70% of Europe's, North-, and Southamerica's population lives in an urban environment; in Asia and Africa numbers have risen to 40%, respectively 35%. By 2030 more than two thirds of the so called Third World population will be living in urban areas. Africa is no exception to the rule, quite the reverse: The African Continent features the fastest increase in urbanization. By the beginning of the 21st century rural life styles have increasingly lost out to urban attraction and sophistication. Thus the city, even the metropolis or, the megalopolis, in the case of Cairo, Dakar, Lagos, or Johannesburg, has changed the way of life throughout Africa. According to politicians and researchers alike, these urbanization processes with their positive and negative side effects will be the most challenging tasks to be mastered in the future. Their handling will determine how the Continent at large develops. (Cf. 'Living the City'; Center of Competence in African Studies, University of Basel, 2008)

Next to economic, sociological, historical, or anthropological studies, fiction and art – i.e., imaginary processes at large – analyze lives and living conditions as they are, or should be. The human/humane condition, alike. Fiction particularly reflects upon individual and public conflicts of the past and present, creates and mediates an environment full of dreams deferred or, rarely, fulfilled and develops utopian solutions to deadlock situations. In fact, cultural texts critically and aesthetically respond to urbanization processes in South Africa since the predominantly agricultural and mining country in the 19th century has become industrialized and urbanized, attracting rural inhabitants – both black and white – to cities, ports, and manufacturing centers. By regarding all nonwhites as but temporary city dwellers, the national Apartheid government tried from 1950 to 1985 to stem the tide of rural depopulation. Though the South African Apartheid regime imploded almost twenty years ago in 1990, the city of Johannesburg still shows the tracks and scars of racial, social, and spatial segregation. The metropolis Jo'burg at large, thrives on its multicultural heritage, yet, socially and ethnically defined spaces and boundaries remain more or less intact. While wealth seeks security in fortress-like gated communities, poverty populates the margins of the urban sprawl. In short: Black and White have not yet bridged the gap. 'Jo'burg Now! Baustelle Südafrika', an exhibition at the Wiener Architekturzentrum, (5 August – 27 September 2004; no catalogue), did highlight both, the great potential of the city as well as the numerous difficulties inherited with its past. While Jo'burg uncontrollably grows on its periphery, depopulated 'dead' business districts define the inner city. Urban pseudo-sophistication posing in tall Disney-world-mimicry, confront and control the surrounding townships. Those still live on their craft of imagination, recycling, and improvisation. Since 2001, however, new urban planning has sought to transgress such traditional boundaries. If the densely populated borough of Alexandra lies adjacent to the luxurious new business district of Sandton in the sharpest of possible contrasts, current housing projects try to alleviate this class tension with new buildings constructed close by on the less affluent side. Social housing areas are also built to enliven the inner cityscape and to reduce an ever increasing crime rate. Thus, traditional townships like Soweto are increasingly linked with the city's urban infrastructure today. Next to these absolute necessities in post-apartheid urban planning, also visions of a better future find their artistic expression in the re- or new design of parks and public squares. The Walter Sisulu Square, e.g., speaks the language of the 'Freedom Charter' (Studio MAS), whereas the Soweto-neighbourhood Kliptown features a monument symbolizing equality, freedom, and openness as an identity-furthering architectural device. A similar policy governs the newly constructed premises on Constitution Hill which is located between the downtown area and the densely populated ghetto Hillbrow. On Constitution Hill, OMM Design developed the Nation's Constitutional Court to embody the new spirit of South African democracy. Even the grand trial hall is kept transparent. Hence, Johannesburg continues to live on and with its stark contrasts. It is a seething cauldron of the old and new, the rich and poor, the black and white plus everything creative and thriving in-between as well. Artists, among others, designer Athi-Patra Ruga, explore and perform in these de-territorialized no-man's lands, and imbue dilapidated inner city districts with new artistic meaning in an act of cultural re-territorialization.

Two particular buildings should exemplify a current 'Jo'burg'- tension: Gold Reef City and the Museum of Apartheid (GAPP Architects 2002), (see Colour plate xxii, Fig. A).

While Gold Reef City allows the visitor to experience the different historical stations of South Africa - gold digging here has degenerated into a touristic amusement next to a Casino - the Museum of Apartheid, completed in 2002, represents the flip-side of the golden Rand. With its prison-like high white walls the museum symbolizes stark confinement and detention on both sides. Paradoxically, a white cube preserves the darkest part of South Africa's history in a small spatial slot. Though confined now, apartheid is thus caused to live on in public memory. Johannesburg's current struggles to move beyond apartheid's dual strategies are best summarized by Achille Mbembe:

> 'With the end of legally sanctioned segregation, Johannesburg is nowadays a metropolis increasingly forced to construct itself out of heterogeneous fragments and fortuitous juxtapositions of images, memories, citations, and allusions drawn from its splintered histories. Some of its fragments seem to recall the post-colonial city form in Africa. The latter is characterized not so much by decay as by the coexistence of divergent elements of different origins brought together in a space whose limits are constantly made and remade. Life, here, is lived under volatile conditions. [...] It is possible to observe such developments in present-day central Johannesburg

> or in Hillbrow. For the most part, the white population has abandoned these areas, leaving behind an infrastructure now occupied, inhabited, or used by blacks in ways sometimes radically different from its original purposes.' (2004, p.399)

Johannesburg loses its original contours, is reduced to an empty set, or, paradoxically, gains depth. By forcing the city to open up, this process of deframing and enframing has set different repertoires of spatial imaginations and practices into collision (2004, 400), (see Colour plates xxii-xxiii)

Thus, Johannesburg resembles other African cities in the aftermath of decolonization: the most modern and formal compete with rural informality representing a compositional process marked by polyphonic dissonances. (Mbembe 2004, 400) Indeed, contemporary Johannesburg is undergoing a massive spatial restructuring not unlike the one that occurred under apartheid. In the central business district, worn-out structures are competing with government-sponsored building projects. Elsewhere, growth is fuelled by private capital for middle- and upper-income residents, insurance companies, banks, and corporations. (Mbembe 2004, 393) One of these examples, a luxury township in the green suburbs of Northern Johannesburg, Melrose Arch, is a private development by the Sentinels Mining Industry Retirement Fund. It is an eighteen-hectare office, retail, residential, and recreational complex near the mega-malls of Sandton and Rosebank. Melrose Arch is a new upscale city within the city, a clean well lighted place. (ibid., 394) According to relevant advertisements, its security belt is outstanding:

> 'Melrose Arch is surrounded by a fiber-optic ring that offers high-speed access to the Internet. Buildings, basements, and public spaces have been specially designed for high-cellular reception. This technological sophistication extends to security. When its three-part security system rollout is completed, Melrose Arch will be protected by a total of one thousand cameras of which there will be twenty-nine Digital Sprite multiplexers, 240 cameras plus fifteen high speed domes, 224 input matrixes, five workstations, and a supervisor station' <www.dedicatedmicros.com>.

In an act of paradigmatic spatial transition, luxury communities such as Melrose Arch or Montecasino are displaced from the old city center to the outskirts. No longer central but marginal, Melrose Arch or Montecasino have thus turned into empty placeholders for the representation of white supremacy, eroded by time rather than remembered by it. That is why they are largely the manifestation of the failure of the racial city to assimilate the passage of time. Theirs is an architecture no longer of (Edwardian or modernist) mimicry but of 'hysteria', as Marder so aptly said, understood as a form of suffering from 'reminiscences, repressed memories that fail to be integrated into the psyche'. (Marder in Mbembe, 402) In the process, they develop a form of 'regressive forgetting', itself an attempt to ward off the movement of time.

South African urbanity unlocked by Ivan Vladislavić: the premises

The fiction of one of South Africa's most stimulating writers to emerge from the transnational period, Ivan Vladislavić, shows a keen awareness of these dilemmas inherent in the process of giving spatial or concrete representation to the transience of memory. In 1998, he co-edited with Hilton Judin, *Blank: Architecture, Apartheid and After*, a kaleidoscopic view on architecture in South Africa's changing cityscape as an economic, sociocultural and aesthetic signifier. His concern with space and spatial dimensions at large permeates his entire oeuvre so far, but remains under-evaluated.

Vladislavić's career as a fiction writer began in 1989 with the publication of a collection of short stories entitled Missing Persons. His reputation grew with his first novel The Folly (1993). In the post-apartheid era he has published Propaganda by Monuments and Other Stories (1996). His second novel The Restless Supermarket (2001/2) was followed by his third one, The Exploded View (2004) and The Model Men (2004). Willem Boshoff appeared in 2005, and Portrait with Keys: The City of Johannesburg Unlocked in 2006. If we consider the time-frame in which Ivan Vladislavić's writing career has been taking shape, 1989 until present, we notice that it exactly spans what has earlier been referred to as the period of 'official' transition (from 1990 to 1994) and its not less transitional aftermath that extends the transition and societal transformation. Hence, Ivan Vladislavić's work is deeply imbued with the process of urban space as 'mediated' environment.

Ivan Vladislavić, of Croatian origin, was born in Pretoria in 1957 and has lived in Johannesburg since 1977. He is the paradigmatic urban eyewitness of citiscapes' transition, roaming the uneasy areas of alarms, electric fences and security guards, exploring the contested boundaries between those who lock themselves away and those who remain outside. Yet, in consistently living, walking and writing in-between stereotypical dichotomies he follows in his father's footsteps. Already he was an ardent city mapper as the author recalls his urban upbringing in Pretoria:

> 'When I was I child, my father, a city man through and through, a lover of walking and driving, finely attuned to change in the world around him and therefore able to give directions with creativity and precision taught me that it never harmed anyone to have a map in hand. [...] Since then, experience has taught me, [...] that getting lost is not always a bad thing. One might even consider misdirecting a stranger for his own good.' (Portrait with Keys, 16-17)

I will argue that Ivan Vladislavić is a most careful observer, with a naturalist or 'social realist's' eye in his acute rendering of telling details of the transitional process. Yet, at the same time he also remains committed to the 'social cause', only the parameters that define the 'social cause' have changed since 1994. Although his observing and reasoning is at its core a moral one, his reasoning is based on fragmentary, contingent notions of morality. It is derived from a morality that acknowledges the limits of the notions it is based upon - such as race, culture, class, gender distinctions-and hence also acknowledges its own limits. For these reasons the author's perspectives on the cityscape shift constantly. While both Vladislavić and his protagonists seem to be mapping Jo'burg, running errands, observing, meeting, greeting, avoiding people, this continuity of an itinerary is cut willingly by the camera I/eye. In changing its view points and cultural perspectives often, at times abruptly, in selecting representative scenes and settings of change, transition, waste and decay, the camera I/eye does not only discover and uncover the hidden, the unseen but also comment and criticize developments from a critical distance. Thus highlighted and juxtaposed by Vladislavić, the cityscapes portrayed in shorter or longer snapshots, i.e., numbered paragraphs of varying length, gain a high level of spirited visual and verbal credibility.

Johannesburg's urbanity unlocked: Ivan Vladislavić's Portrait with keys

So far the most inclusive city-sequence by Ivan Vladislavić was published under the title Portrait with keys: the city of Johannesburg unlocked in June 2006, an archive of writings on a segment of Johannesburg that has been walked, observed and reflected upon over the years and partly published in smaller cycles earlier. Portrait with keys: the city of Johannesburg unlocked 2006 consists of 138 numbered short texts/snapshots, each addressing life and architecture in transition in Johannesburg. The time frame stretches from recollections of the late 1970s to the immediate present. The protagonist is, in most instances, Ivan Vladislavić himself, although there are dozens of other characters with whom he shares encounters and interactions.

Portrait with keys: the city of Johannesburg unlocked – Vladislavić's perspectives on the cityscape always shift – comprises two parts: Point A (snapshots 1-78) and Point B (snapshots 79-138) offer a double perspective. Whereas Point A ends with the protagonist(s) leaving Johannesburg on a flight, Point B begins with the take-off of a plane to Johannesburg. The spatial and temporal gap between suggests both closeness to and distance from home, yet the snapshots continue in the same vein in Point B. They are finely-crafted interlinked shorter or longer texts that reveal Vladislavić's fascination with architecture in transition, i.e., the places people choose to live and the things they seek to create: 'Every day I trawl along my habitual routes ready to be startled by something else I have missed until now' (Pwk, 164). His skill at handling subtle social commentary from small details and larger cityscapes as well is evident throughout his oeuvre. He is also a highly innovative montage technician in modernist and postmodernist ways as he cuts and pastes key passages or snapshots from one short story cycle to another, from a novel back to a short story and vice versa. Thus, the reader is taken along on various itineraries, yet via repetition and reiteration is being offered continuity within contingency.

Beyond the driving and walking continuum of the protagonist's itinerary/ies through Johannesburg, the sharply cut and juxtaposed scenes allow the reader to form their own remorselessly accurate, engaged and detached individual stops in a city in transition. The message is clear: Jo'burg cannot be perceived other than as a kaleidoscopic panopticum. Consequently, Portrait with keys: the city of Johannesburg unlocked closes with an index of various 'Itineraries' the reader can choose from. (195-199). They are classified as L=Long; M=Moderate; S=Short and offer the following 'Itineraries': 'An accidental island' (L); 'Artists' book (M); 'Beggars and sellers' (M); 'Body language' (M); 'Branko' (M); 'City centre' (L); 'Closer together' (M); 'Engaging the Gorilla' (L); 'Falling' (see 'Walking'); 'Gardens' (S); 'Ghosting through' (S); 'Home territory' (L); 'Insecurity' (see 'Security'); 'Liars and thieves' (M); 'Memorials' (M); 'Object lessons' (L); 'Old lives' (S); 'Painted walls' (S) see also Walls; 'Safe and sound' (L); 'Security' (L); 'Self storage' (L); 'Street addresses, Johannesburg' (L); 'Trade secrets'

(L); 'Underground' (S); 'Walking' (L); 'Walls' (S); 'Water' (S); 'Writers' book' (M); 'Young lives' (M).

Ivan Vladislavić's inspiration for his thematic indexing is Humphrey Jenning's great compendium of readings, Pandemonium 1660-1886: The Coming of the Machine as Seen by Contemporary Observers. Pandemonium, however, in John Milton's Paradise Lost, a word which Milton coined from the Latin pan (all) and demonium (demons), is the capital of Hell, literally the place of all demons. With the passage of time, the word came to mean any place of wild disorder, noise, and confusion. This idea is subtly emphasized with Milton's choice of Mulciber as the architect. Mulciber was another name for Hephaestus, the Greek God of the Forge, who was tossed from Olympus by a drunken Zeus. Mulciber is consequently a figure of some ridicule and not the most likely architect to build a lasting city. One other aspect of the construction of Pandemonium – and particularly in view of Johannesburg – is worth consideration. Mammon and the other devils find mineral resources including gemstones in their search for building materials. This discovery of resources suggests that the Hell Milton has imagined is a multifaceted and timeless place that might as well refer to Johannesburg/Egoli: the place of gold and diamonds. (Cf. John Milton, Paradise Lost, Book 1, lines 756 ff.) Yet, Ivan Vladislavić's unique montage technique of intertextual echoes, of cutting and pasting identical snapshots or entire cycles in new thematic strings is distinctly his own. (Cf. Author's Note, Portrait with Keys, 201-203) Not only does he achieve cohesion via recognition and reiteration but in doing so, he also parallels and reproduces the cityscape's architectural mimicry – every colonial town imitates former architectural styles, from Edwardian to high modernist. Thus, Vladislavić creates and recreates his own vivid mimesis of Johannesburg in transition via his recycling cut-and-paste-style of his texts. 'By "mimesis", we should – according to Stephen Halliwell- understand a capacity to identify oneself or establish similarities with something else while at the same time inventing something original.'

Let us turn to a 'medium journey', an itinerary of my own selection. The numbered snapshots for closer inspection that first formed the carefully edited cycle 'Jo'burg' for GRANTA (2006), are also integrated in Portrait with keys: the city of Johannesburg unlocked (2006). Snapshot numbers below refer either to this latter edition (Pwk), or to 'Jo'burg' the cycle published in GRANTA (2006): ('Jo'burg'). In analyzing selected snapshots, we shall trace the protagonist's concerns, the places in transition visited, revisited, and ultimately changed, the safety measures involved, the contention between private and public space felt and endured, in short, his environment 'mediated' in a series of literary snapshots so visual and precise that they function almost as a picture gallery. The opening snapshot of Ivan Vladislavić's Portrait with Keys (Pwk) leaves no doubt. In this sprawling South African metropolis you are either in or out: in or out of your premises, your working or leisure environment, your sports club, even your public library. This cutting and unremitting boundary-drawing divides the air as sharply as the opening or closing of a bank safe. No imaginary 'third-space' betwixt inner and outer space allows for musings, thoughts or tardiness. Valuable items, including your body, must be protected by all means as the opening lines state with utmost clarity:

> 'When a house has been alarmed, it becomes explosive. It must be armed and disarmed several times

> a day. When it is armed, by the touching of keys upon a pad, it emits a whine that sends the occupants rushing out, banging the door behind them. There are no leisurely departures: there is no time for second thoughts, for taking a scarf from the hook behind the door, for checking that the answering machine is on, for a final look in the mirror on the way through the hallway. There are no savoured homecomings either: you do not unwind into such a house, kicking off your shoes, breathing the familiar air. Every departure is precipitate, every arrival is a scraping-in. In an alarmed house, you awake in the small hours to find the room unnaturally light. The keys on the touch pad are aglow with a luminous, clinical green, like a night light for a child who's afraid of the dark.' (Pwk, snapshot 1, 15)

The unanimous procedure of locking/unlocking is still the entrance ticket to a city in the vicinity of the Witwatersrand, with its university, its history of gold and diamonds, its businesses. Doubtlessly the legacy of a socio-politically discerning system, before, during, and even after 1994, still governs the have and have-nots.

Ivan Vladislavić does not only dissect the lives of his contemporary 'Jo'burghers' within their protective walls, he observes the city's visual changes in their opening and closing systems at large. He keeps mapping both the horizontal and vertical spaces and places in their making and breaking. The history of the Carlton Center in the former business district Hillbrow is a striking example of a landmark in decay (Pwk, 29-32). Thus the private and the public spaces are not only explored but change becomes obvious in the everyday-performance or closure of Johannesburg's buildings, still the country's financial and economic center. Life however, in alarmed premises seems to be unnatural. The gated innocence of a white affluent community appears dimly and clinically lighted, as if this innocence needed the protection of a bell-jar afraid of the darker realms of experience outside. It is as if white people are forced to hibernate in strangely well-lit places. An increasing anxiety manifests itself in increasing safety measures:

> 'Johannesburg is a frontier city, a place of contested boundaries. Territory must be secured and defended or it will be lost. Today the contest is fierce and so the defences multiply. Walls replace fences, high walls replace low ones, the highest walls acquire electrified wires and spikes. In the wealthier suburbs the pattern is to knock things flat and start all over.' ('Jo'burg', snapshot 2, 129; Pwk, snapshot 131, 173)

> 'Around here people make the most of what they've got; the walls tend to grow by increments. A stone wall is heightened with prefab panels, a prefab wall is heightened further with steel palisades, the palisades are topped with razor wire. Wooden pickets on top of brick, ornate wrought-iron panels on top of plaster, blade wire on top of split poles. These 'piggyback walls' are nearly always ugly. But sometimes the whole ensemble achieves a degree of elaboration that becomes beautiful again, like a page in the Homemaker's Fair catalogue. [...] The tomason of access is our specialty. There are vanished gateways everywhere. On any street, you may find a panel in a wall where the bricks are a different colour or the courses poorly aligned, indicating that a gap has been filled in. A garden path leads to a fence rather than a gate. [...] The most common tomason of access by far is the metal hinge' ('Jo'burg', snapshot 2, 129; Pwk, snapshot 131, 173-74).

One of the chief signifiers of urban change is the 'tomason', a small token:

> 'The term "tomason" was coined by Genpei Akasegawa to describe a purposeless object found on a city street. He has tracked and tagged hundreds of them in Japan and other parts of the world. A tomason is a thing that has become detached from its original purpose. Sometimes this detachment may be so complete that the object is turned into an enigmatic puzzle; alternatively, the original purpose of the object may be quite apparent and its current uselessness touching and amusing. Tomasons thrive in the man-made world, in spaces that are constantly being remade and redesigned for other purposes, where the function of a thing that was useful and necessary may be swept away in a tide of change or washed off like a label. They are creatures of the boundary, they gravitate to walls and fences, to entrances and exits.' (Pwk, snapshot 123, 163-64)

Jo'burg was, and still is, a gold digging settlement. Since 1886, a gold digging mentality has survived various periods of transience. In Vladislavić's words:

> 'Gold was discovered on the Witwatersrand in the winter of 1886. [...] Commissioner Street, the backbone of the city, follows the old wagon track between two of the first mining camps, from Jeppestown in the east to Ferreirasdorp in the west. So the city's spine was fused to the Main Reef, the subterranean gold deposit that called it into life. Today, going down Commissioner into the high-rise heart of Africa's richest city, I am reminded that here we are all still prospectors, with a digger's claim on the earth beneath our feet.' ('Jo'burg', snapshot 3, 130)

Gold digging remains the governing mentality, or rather, necessity for a large part of the population, that leads to the stealing and ultimate destruction of a charming heirloom casket full of lapel badges, 'badges of identity' and 'simple markers of a life story' handed down to the protagonist by his grandfather, to father, to son, and then gone. This white line of identification is definitely broken. Intriguing is the secret lock of this casket the poachers later could not open.

> '... a wooden casket half the size of a pencil case, decorated with forest scenes made of inlaid segments of stained wood, now faded to a perpetual autumn. There was a secret mechanism for opening the drawer, a wooden switch concealed beneath a small tile that could be slid aside-it fitted so perfectly you could not even insert a fingernail into a crack, you had to moisten the tip of your finger and pull gently. Pressing the switch caused the drawer to spring open.' ('Jo'burg', snapshot 4, 131)

Though the casket recalls the secret mechanisms of an alarmed house, it got stolen by the two poachers to whom the protagonist gave food in his apartment, a strong and painful moment of recognition and transition. A teenager and his younger brother, both in rags grabbed what they could in his apartment while he was fetching food for them. Later, he found but splinters of the box nearby. 'Frustrated by their inability to open the box, they had smashed it.' (ibid., 131)

From this personal realm of loss and frustration the sequence moves on to Jo'burg's public places in transition, the city's parks and scenic waterways: the pond at Rhodes park or Bruma Lake. Without doubt, these 'whites only' days spent in 'Berea

Park' or 'Oppenheimer Park', full of artificial landscaping adjusted to white tastes, are also gone forever. Vladislavić stresses various aspect of colonial mimicry.

> 'In Johannesburg, the backdrop is always a man-made one. We have planted a forest the birds endorse. For hills, we have mine dumps covered with grass. We do not wait for time and the elements to weather us, we change the scenery ourselves, to suit our moods. Nature is for other people, in other places.' ('Jo'burg', snapshot 5 132)

> 'We are happy taking the air on the Randburg Waterfront, with its pasteboard wharves and masts, or watching the plastic ducks bob in the stream at Montecasino, or eating surf 'n' turf on Cleopatra's Barge in the middle of Caesar's.' (ibid., 132)

With his great sense of irony the author further links 'wildlife' in the parks with the new 'wildlife' of the metal hunters or scrap dealers as they poach the monuments of white supremacy piece by piece:

> 'Johannesburg has an abundance of wildlife, and the poachers have taken full advantage of the open season. They've bagged a bronze steenbok from Wits University; a horse from outside the library in Sandton (first docking the beast, to see if anyone would mind, and then hacking off its head like Mafiosi); a pair of eagles nesting near the Stock Exchange; and another steenbok in the Botanical Gardens at Emmerentia. [...] Of course, urban poachers are not just hungry for horseflesh: any old iron will do. They are especially fond of the covers on manholes and water mains.' ('Jo'burg', snapshot 6, 133)

These urban poachers not only literally deconstruct white monuments in public spaces, they also act according to the 'gold digging mentality' of the Jo'burg of 1886. Roughly one hundred years later, they dig and poach no longer gold in the mines underneath but the white pioneers' historic monuments. Nightly brigades deconstruct the theme parc of suprematist nostalgia and in order to sell the metal on the black market, even Herman Wald's Leaping Impala, the 'eighteen animals in full flight' got chopped off, piece by piece out of Ernest Oppenheimer Park, although these animals were 'set to survive the century unscathed' ('Jo'burg' 133; PWK, snapshot 93, 127-129). What is left are empty pedestals. The protagonist's laconic comment on this this is: 'get the jump on the poachers by selling the booty yourself.' ('Jo'burg'134)

Next to the nightly poachers are the daily beggars, among them 'The man who paces up and down outside the Gem Supermarket like a creature in captivity' ('Jo'burg' 134). He is astonishingly picky when:

> '... the woman emptied the change from her purse into his palm. He examined her offering curiously. Before she could walk off, he began to pick through it and give the smaller denominations back to her. After a moment's puzzlement, she held her hand to accept the rejects. She seemed fascinated by the exchange.' ('Jo'burg', snapshot 6, 134)

Was he ungrateful, even insulting, or just teaching a lesson to the affluent buyers who could be more generous? It is important to note that Vladislavić's narrator neither judges nor ever mentions the skin colour of his characters involved. Yet, after this particular moment of rejection of presumably white generosity, the sequence turns to its central piece, that offers a modicum of peace and good hope for those enfolded.

> 'A stoep in Good Hope Street. The deep-blue garden wall holds a precise measure of the twilight still. [...] We have been talking and laughing for hours, putting our predicaments in their place, finding ways to keep our balance in a tide of change. We could fetch fresh beer glasses from the door of the fridge, but these warm ones, stickily fingerprinted and smelling of yeast, suit this satiated conversation better. We speak the same language.' ('Jo'burg', snapshot 7, 135)

This is obviously a white world in which one may retreat from the cityscape in transition and its challenging moments. At large, the protagonists claim:

> 'This is our climate. We have grown up in this air, this light, and we grasp it on the skin, where it grasps us. We know this earth, this grass, this polished red stone with the soles of our feet. We will never be ourselves anywhere else. Happier, perhaps, healthier, less burdened, more secure. But we will never be closer to who we are than this.' ('Jo'burg', ibid.)

One day, the protagonist visits the Johannesburg Public Library to read up on Max the Gorilla, the zoo's most famous resident – he caught and bit poachers and policemen alike – and is, instead, absorbed in the trivial mystery of a strike going on. But before we can enter the Library, we must accompany the visitor through an underworld of 'safety parking' in great transition.

> 'Stepping up from the Harry Hofmeyr Parking Garage. This vast basement, where in the years past you'd have been lucky to find a bay, is all but empty. [...] Every new building in Johannesburg has secure, controlled, vehicle-friendly entrances and exits. The well-heeled – who naturally are also the well-wheeled – should be able to reach point B without setting foot in the street. The malls are hemmed in by parking garages. Complexes of apparently independent buildings, designed to simulate the neighbourhoods of a conventional city, are undermined by huge, unitary garages that destroy the illusion. Superbasements. Older buildings have to adapt to the new requirements.' ('Jo'burg', snapshot 8, 136)

At the Public Library the obvious reversal is refreshingly ingenious: while the black schoolchildren who are now the main users of the facility stroll arm-in-arm up the broad staircase from the library gardens or gather in the grand lobby to giggle and whisper, the few white suburbanites who still venture here park underground and slip in up the back stairs.

A longer snapshot devoted to the Carlton Center is a swan song on Jo'burg's big monument of modernist architecture. Built in the early 1970s the skyscraper's decay is Jo'burg's most telling monument of transition:

> 'Every month for the past fifteen years, on the second Thursday of the month, I have met my brother Branko for coffee at the Carlton Centre. I could chart the life and death of this great complex by the sequence of coffee shops which came to serve as our regular meeting-place over the years: from the Koffiehuis, where the waitresses were got up as Dutch dairymaids in clogs and lace caps, to the Brazilian Coffee Shop, where the cups and saucers arrived and departed on a conveyor belt. ('Jo'burg', snapshot 10, 137) Then, in the mid-Nineties, the car park began

> to shrink. The demand for parking fell, level by level, like a barometer of change in the city centre. The people with cars were clearly going elsewhere. [...] In May 1998, when I turned into Main Street there was a chain slung across my usual entrance. [...] (HOTEL CLOSED. [...] When I resurfaced into the chilly air a little later, a fierce white light caught my eye. Welders in overalls were sealing off the canopied entrance of the Carlton Hotel behind a palisade fence.' ('Jo'burg', snapshot 10, 138; (Pwk, snapshots 11-12, 29-32)

The following snapshot is also dedicated to the topic of people meeting downtown. Louise, a friend, now teaching at the Twilight Children's Shelter and the protagonist knew each other as editors at Ravan Press in O'Reilly Roady. They would meet at the Florian in Hillbrow. This Venetian coffee house offered English boarding-house fare. It is the dying Louise who introduces the protagonist to something unexpected about the world that always filled her with an infectious wonder. Once she tugged him over to the balcony at the Florian to point out the iron covers on the water mains set into the pavements:

> 'Did I know these spaces below these covers, where the meters were housed? Well, the poor people of Jo'burg, the street people-we did not call them 'the homeless' in those days-the tramps, car parkers and urchins, used them as cupboards! They stored their winter wardrobes there, and the rags of bedding they used at night, they preserved their scraps of food, their perishables, in cool shade, they banked the empty bottles they collected for the deposits. It tickled her – she laughed out loud, just as if the idea had poked her in the ribs – that such utilitarian spaces should have been appropriated and domesticated, transformed into repositories of privacy for those compelled to live their lives in public.
>
> [...]There was a maze of mysterious spaces underfoot, known only to those who could see it. And this special knowledge turned them into the privileged ones, made them party to something in which we, who lived in houses with wardrobes and chests of drawers, and ate three square meals a day, could not participate.' ('Jo'burg', snapshot 13, 141)
>
> 'It's pathetic,' I said, 'that people are so poor they have to store their belongings in holes in the ground.' 'No it's not. It's pathetic when people don't care about themselves, when they give up. These people are resourceful, they're making a life out of nothing.' ('Jo'burg', snapshot 13, 142; Pwk, snapshot 31, 50-51)

This is one of the touching passages when due homage is being paid to the resourcefulness of an invisible group of people, when change and transition are measured in different ways. The next snapshot, repeated in various cycles, belongs to the itineraries 'safety' and 'security'. It is aptly positioned before the great private birthday party at the home of the protagonist and his wife Minky. Upon this occasion, security is more important than food and the guestlist. Here is the beginning of an impressive list of locks and safety measures.

> 'The range of steering locks available in South Africa is impressive the wild Dog, the MoToQuip anti-theft lock, the Twistlok, the SL2 Auto-Lok, the EagleClaw by Yale, the Challenger [...] All these locks work on the same principle: they are attached to the steering wheel and immobilize the vehicle by preventing the wheel from being turned. The locks also have the same basic design. [...] The association with wild ani-

mals known for their speed, strength or ferocity is also found in other areas of the security industry: tigers, eagles and owls appear on the shields of armed response companies, and rhinoceroses and elephants in the logos of companies that supply electrified fencing and razor wire.' ('Jo'burg', snapshot 14, 144)

The final snapshot in my itinerary entitled 'Mediated Environment' could be called 'Transdiscourse in Johannesburg' as it performs an exchange between human beings, utterly beyond and despite safety measures and linguistic means. It is a secret understanding of giving and taking, a day's beginning with sharing necessities. Between metal security bars a human/humane alarm system keeps ringing and banging in the early morning hours. With a clock-like regularity a black face keeps popping up behind the bars until the white person draws the bedroom curtains, gathers the small change destined to reach the other side. In the beginning of this daily ritual of exchange the begging face showed up like a brief identity marker, a synecdoche, as if the donor would/should honour an individual rather than a representative of the many needy. The ritual has, at last, two human beings reaching out to the tip of their extremities.

> 'He rattles the metal catch on our back gate every third or fourth day. When I lift the curtain at the bedroom window to see who's there, he shows his face between the iron bars of the gate like an identity card. He used to say his name, but now he has fallen back on this visual shorthand. Even in the gloom, I recognize his white peaked cap. I go out and let the money fall into his cupped palm. He squints at me through the bars and drops a little curtsey. Neither of us say a word. We have been reduced to a simple mechanism of supply and demand. Occasionally, I spy on him as he leaves counting the coins, stepping out quite confidently. I think he is pretending to be a backward rustic to keep my sympathy.' ('Jo'burg', snapshot 17, 149; Pwk, snapshot 98, 136)

In conclusion, I argue that Ivan Vladislavić with his snapshots of and itineraries through Johannesburg achieves a 'renewal of perception' (Gaylard 2005). The reader's perception both of objects in the visible tangible world and of the words that represent those objects – words and worlds that can be collected, listed, taken apart, reassembled, contracted, expanded, augmented and otherwise manoeuvred, will be changed forever. Yet, Vladislavić's rendition and listing of specific objects is not an act of disengagement from the wider political reality, quite the reverse. His works also acknowledge the political dilemma that the unequal distribution of those objects implies.

In rendering urban transition into visual texts mediated through language, Ivan Vladislavić has become one of the foremost chroniclers of Johannesburg. Further, he establishes a transdiscourse not only between the visual and the literary, but also between colour and class bars. He sees, understands and condenses the perceived as through a camera I/Eye. Thus, Portrait with keys: the city of Johannesburg unlocked indeed opens up the 'elusive' and 'entangled' metropolis in multifarious ways and keeps remapping neighbourhoods and Johannesburg at large. Thus, Portrait with keys demonstrates the prolific creative processes and their mediality in an exemplary way.

References

Barnard, R 2006, Apartheid and beyond: South African writers and the politics of place, Oxford University Press, New York / London.

Bond, GC, & Gibson, NC (eds) 2002, Contested terrains and constructed categories: Contemporary Africa in focus, Westview Press, Boulder/CO.

Gaylard, G 2005, After colonialism: African postmodernism and magical realism, Wits University Press, Johannesburg.

Graham, S 2007, 'Memory, memorialization, and the transformation of Johannesburg: Ivan Vladislavić's The Restless Supermarket and Propaganda by Monuments', Modern Fiction Studies, vol. 53, no. 1, Spring, pp. 70-97.

Halliwell, S 2002, The Aesthetics of mimesis: Ancient texts and modern problems, Princeton University Press, Princeton/NJ.

Mbembe, A 2004, 'Aesthetics of superfluity', Public Culture, vol, 16, no. 3, pp. 373-405.

Mbembe, A & Nuttall, S 2004, 'Writing the world from an African metropolis', Public Culture vol. 16, no. 3, pp. 347-372.

Milton, J 2007 (1674), Paradise Lost, BK Lewalski. (ed.), Blackwell, Malden/MA.

Morphet, T 1997, Review of Ivan Vladislavić 'Propaganda by Monuments and Other Stories', World Literature Today vol. 71, no. 2, pp. 444.

Nuttall, S 2004, 'City forms and writing the "Now" in South Africa', Journal of Southern African Studies, vol 30, December, pp. 740-747.

Nuttall, S 2009, Entanglement: Literary and cultural reflections on post-apartheid, Wits University Press, Johannesburg.

Nuttall, S & Mbembe, A, (eds) 2008, Johannesburg: The elusive metropolis, Wits University Press, Johannesburg.

Said, EW 2000, 'Invention, memory and place', Critical Inquiry, vol. 26, no. 2, winter, pp. 175-92.

Viljoen, H & Van der Merve, CN (eds), 2004, Storyscapes: South African perspectives on literature, space & identity, Peter Lang, New York.

Vladislavić, I 1998, 'Street Addresses, Johannesburg', I Vladislavić, & H Judin (eds), Blank: Architecture, apartheid and after, NAI Publishers, Rotterdam.

Vladislavić, I 2000, 'Interview with Ivan Vladislavić', by Christopher Warnes, Modern Fiction Studies MFS, vol. 46, no. 1, spring, pp- 273-281. p. 280.

Vladislavić, I 2005, 'Jo'burg', Granta 92: The view from Africa, I Jack, (ed.), Granta, London, pp. 129-149.

Vladislavić, I 2006, Portrait with keys: the city of Johannesburg unlocked, Portobello, London.

LUMINOUS GREEN

Nik Gaffney and Maja Kuzmanovic

Luminous Green is a series of gatherings about possible futures; about a human world, that is enlightened, imaginative, electrified and most importantly – living in a fertile symbiosis with the planet. Luminous Green encourages transdisciplinary discussions and collaborations between people from all walks of life, including artists, designers, academics, activists, social entrepreneurs, economists and policy-makers. The objective is to spawn inspiring conversations, contacts and propositions using holistic methods for looking beyond (and beneath) conservation and sustainability. Everyone who becomes involved in these gatherings is interested in making their work and life an example of resilience, innovation and inspiration.

Present Continuous

Current local, translocal and global communication patterns seem to be reflecting the turbulent conditions of our ecological, economic and social habitats. The media, in their myriad shapes and forms, provide variously coloured lenses through which to watch this turbulence. Mass media, with their focus on easily digestible sound bites of information, often oversimplify the interrelatedness between issues in an attempt at clarity. Information found on the internet can be rich and varied, often requiring a healthy dose of scepticism concerning the tangled paths of interpretation and translation from (original) sources. Social media can provide a diversity of opinions, experiments and other curiosities. Plenty of consumption, plenty of communication and plenty of action, adding additional strange attractors to existing chaotic situations. A leitmotif throughout the various communication channels is a (quite legitimate) sense of urgency. Frequently the responses to this urgency take the form of the fallacy 'We must do something. This is something. Therefore, we must do it'. It is not clear how much (if any) thought goes into considering the wide range of answers to the more involved questions such as – what can be done; what can be done now; what can be done now that is relevant; what can be done now that will set the foundation for future improvements; and most importantly, what can be done that won't end up making things worse?

Much of the current thinking about the sustainability of our lifestyles is predominantly future focused – in 2020, by 2050, in 5, 15 or 50 years – things will change for the better (according to neo-liberal optimism), or for the worse (according to some scientific projections, or deep green pessimism). In the mean time, the future has arrived and begun to unravel into the past, quietly and unnoticed. In the rush to predict or change the future, we all too easily neglect the present, the only time in which we can actually influence and exercise our possible futures. By becoming more consciously present in the 'here-and-now', we can begin to discern a continuous string of present moments stretching into the mythical 'long term'. We cannot sacrifice the present for an unattainable future, yet we cannot retreat into an 'innocent' past which spawned our present problems. So, the question becomes; what can we do to live more fully in the present, work toward a more luminous future, while drawing inspiration from the past?

Capitalism and technological optimism

Our present is technologically driven and thus we will need to address cultural, political and environmental issues through a technological lens. However, technology itself is not enough. It is a blunt object, an undirected automaton without human will, desire or interest. Any technological lens needs to be focused by 'enlightened' intention, and that intention illuminated by an understanding that humanity is an integral part of the natural world we inhabit. We have nowhere to go if we leave our 'blue ball-of-a-home' (Horvitz 2002). Futuristic, technological progress alone cannot save us from natural disasters, or lead towards a sustainable future.

Another lens, frequently used to examine contemporary issues is that of the market economy. The optimism that market-based approaches will solve our environmental and social problems has been dampened somewhat by the financial crisis of 2008, but it still strongly colours the view. The financial crisis demonstrated in devastatingly unpredictable fashion that global systemic failures can occur even in the heart of the sector that is built as a market 'on its own terms'. This should provide a double-edged warning about global markets, for both those who are quick to defend and those who are even quicker to denounce. On one hand, we cannot let something essential to our survival, something so uniquely precious as our only life support system be driven by market forces, which are barely understood and frequently exploited. A worrying aspect of applying economic models to the environment, or society at large, is that these models often ignore parts of an exchange that are difficult to measure or directly quantify as 'externalities', things existing outside of a transaction. In a closed system, such as our self-regulating, self-sufficient biosphere, there can be no externalities. On the other hand, the financial crisis also demonstrated how interconnected, interdependent and global our technological systems for valuing and allocating resources have become. It would be folly to dismantle such a system hastily, especially if the alternative is to replace it with something even more feudal (protectionist cartels, local warlords or robber barons for example). Global capitalism, if it is to survive (which is a big 'if' for some) must evolve in the face of complexity, assume redundancy and resilience rather than efficiency, scarcity and fragility (Taleb 2007).

Ecology of Solutions

If there were simple technological or market 'solutions' to these various crises, we would, no doubt, have instigated them already. However, the political and social systems that are struggling to confront long-term, systemic, life threatening problems appear as unconcerned as the metaphorical frog, not noticing itself boiling to death. Any 'solutions' still left available to us collectively, are going to be complex (but not necessarily complicated) and messy. We may not have the luxury to make incremental changes any longer, but that should not paralyse us. There are many, many small reciprocally connected changes that can work in synergy (in the Fuller sense) to form larger, longer-term systemic and cultural shifts. What distinguishes such changes from individual incremental 'fixes' is an illuminated understanding of connectedness and interdependence between them. Developing an ecology of imperfect, complimentary solutions, rather than striving to perfect a single one which might work in some indefinite future. Thereby we not only spread the risk, but also open up possibilities to unexpected and previously unimagined outcomes.

Permaculture (Holmgren 2002) provides a compelling example of how to successfully apply an 'ecology of solutions' to growing food and increasing biodiversity. In its simplest form, permaculture provides a method of gardening that focuses not only on the desired crop, but nourishes the eco-system on which it depends. The resulting gardens (also known as 'food forests') develop into robust self-sustaining systems, able to provide an abundance of food for humans, animals and plants, while requiring a minimum of inputs over the long term. While there is ongoing discussion over how widely these principles can be applied (Holmgren 2002), the Permaculture design principles[1] that guide this type of farming are a recurring inspiration to people from all walks of life, interested in approaching today's challenges from a 'whole systems' perspective. Using permaculture principles, we can approach design (or any other human endeavour) as a whole system, where each element contributes to the whole. The role of humans in this system is to continually observe the whole (from within, since we are a part of the system ourselves) and consider our actions, which influence individual elements, while contributing to a global dynamic balance. In the words of the natural farmer and former microbiologist, Masanobu Fukuoka, 'the ultimate goal of farming is not the growing of crops but the cultivation and perfection of human beings' (Fukuoka 1978).

Culture and Cultivation

The term cultivation[2] is at the root of the word 'culture' in many Indo-European languages. Culturing still refers to the growing crops or cultivating biological materials (bacteria, yeasts or tissues) in artificial conditions, but most commonly when we talk about culture, we talk about the cultivation of human beings – our thoughts, behaviours, actions, communities and ultimately our (collective) consciousness. The arts, sciences and spiritual traditions, can all be considered technologies of cultivation, fuelled by collaboration between different people. In permaculture (as well as other holistic approaches to the world) cultivation of the environment and transformation of culture are active and continuous, interrelated processes within the same system. Undoubtedly, the cultivation of environments and cultures will contain a diversity of (sometimes contradictory) approaches – a concoction of technological, economic, environmental and cultural ingredients in various measures. Bringing together a plethora of diverse approaches will require compromises to be made, vested interests divested, opinions changed, lifestyles restyled and new, 'unholy' alliances will need to be formed (and, if we play our cards right, a phoenix may rise from the ashes).

> 'A problem cannot be solved by people who are concerned with only one or another of its parts. To the extent that the consciousness of everyone is not fundamentally transformed, pollution will not cease' (Fukuoka 1978). (see Colour plate xxv, Fig. D)

Another important lesson from permaculture is that cultivation begins with the immediate surroundings of the human dwelling – starting in the kitchen, with the herbs on the windowsill, spreading into mixed patches where vegetables, fruit and 'weeds' are grown in guilds (Holmgren 2002). From the edges of these patches, larger trees grow to form full-blown forests, in whose protective shade a variety of shrubs, creepers and herbaceous plants can find a home. Even though cultivation of the whole forest is the goal, the first 'zone' (the home) in which humans spend most of their time and effort is the zone the closest to our everyday life. Similarly, for most people global turbulence only becomes apparent when it adversely affects our daily lives – whether it is ongoing droughts, flooded basements, xenophobia, credit crunch, heat waves, unemployment, or food insecurity.

Guild Culturing

While the complexity and the vastness of global issues may remain as abstract figures and threats, with occasional news reports of disasters in far-off lands, we remain collectively paralysed (or simply apathetic). In order to make necessary changes, cultivating a more illuminated culture, the various crises need to be dealt with simultaneously on a global (ecological) and a human (personal) scale. Changing cultures requires finding appropriate levels at which individual contributions can be most effective. To further the comparison with permaculture, we need to find social and cultural equivalents of guild gardening – where, while sustaining our individual selves, each of us performs functions that also contribute to the development of the guild as a whole.

We need complimentary, and often redundant actions on all levels. For example, people focused on global policy are involved in negotiating treaties, such as the Kyoto and Copenhagen Protocols; simultaneously, computer enthusiasts are putting together initiatives such as AMEE, DIY Kyoto or pachube; philanthropists are organising global initiatives to co-ordinate green energy investments and social entrepreneurship; designers are reinventing products as sustainable services; industrial manufacturers are sharing information about their supply chain, using methods inspired by Open Source. While all of these are laudable pursuits, not one could succeed in isolation. Across cultures and disciplines, we learn and borrow from each other, refine, adapt and transform solutions as required. We can then apply them in domains that are close to us, that we experience on a daily basis and that we can work with on a scale that is most appropriate to our own situation. In other words, they

Fig. 1: Moderated World Cafe session. Luminous Green, Singapore 2008

Fig. 2: On Non-Human Agency. Luminous Green, Singapore 2008

become living and lived solutions. They are reused, reduced and recycled through direct human experiences, becoming more robust and resilient through each iteration.

Luminous Green

Could it be that the seeds for a more 'illuminated' culture can already be found in existing human undertakings, but that the 'medium' (culture, society, technology, etc.) in which these seeds can grow needs to be better developed? Starting with this premise, FoAM initiated a series of gatherings under the name 'Luminous Green'. We decided to seek out motivated, curious and open-minded people and bring them together with equally motivated people from other fields and cultures. People who care about the world as a whole, who are keen to play an active part in its evolution, are open to constructive criticism, curious about new perspectives and willing to share their knowledge and resources. Luminous Green brings these people together in an environment where they are first and foremost required to be themselves – inspiring and inspired individuals, with a multitude of stories and experiences. The gatherings are non-hierarchical, participatory situations that are designed to bring about unexpected connections, between people who may otherwise never come in contact with each other.

By leaving the culturally assigned 'roles' behind, it is important that the Luminous Green participants meet without preconceptions, institutional, or political affiliations – that they meet each other as fellow human beings, carrying a mixed bag of opinions, taboos, habits and other curiosa. We believe that personal dialogues, engaged one-on-one conversations (leading to many-on-many conversation) can inform a wider, clearer understanding of the complexities within which we live. Through various sessions and experiments, we want to encourage the participants to share their stories, inspirations and goals, find common (and uncommon) ground, challenge stereotypes and presumptions. Writers, activists, politicians, economists, inventors, investors, scientists, designers, artists, beekeepers, farmers,

Fig.3: Props used to visualise the state of the world in 2050. Luminous Green, Singapore, 2008.

Fig.4: Proposing session topics. Luminous Green, Belgium, 2007.

mycologists, bureaucrats and other enthusiasts are welcome to question, confront and support each other, in a polyphony of voices. For example, an enlightening discussion arose when four people (an artist, biologist, policy maker and an activist) touched on the topic of GM crops. In the beginning of the conversation, they assumed they would agree with each other, but as they touched upon specific cases and their complexities, the discussion brought up several opposing views which didn't fit neatly into their exiting understandings. Because they had already established a warm relationship with each other during the previous evening, everyone was more willing to listen and postpone judgement. Thus the conversation enabled them each to learn something new. By seeing the topic in a different light (from other people's perspective), having a much richer understanding, not just of GM crops, but of topics they had previously thought unimportant for their own practices, such as trade relations, controlled experiments, weather patterns or bio-art.

Imagining, greening and illuminating possible worlds

The Luminous Green philosophy is grounded in the belief that the world as a whole and all its parts can become more luminous – illuminated, electrified and imaginative, while nourishing a lush, fertile, green environment. We refute the nihilistic and fatalistic view of deep ecology, or that of religious rupture preaching passivity because it's all out of our hands anyway. We disagree with the 'hairshirt' green polar opposition of consumerism that legitimises suffering, denial and sacrifice, yet neither accept the short sighted capitalist approach of continuing 'business as usual'. Such business as usual will create a future for those who can afford it, while continuing the relentless consumption of natural resources for disposable, wasteful lifestyles. However, Luminous Green can find interesting seeds in all of these approaches, so rather than siding with one or another dogma, it seeks to form 'unholy alliances' between the elements that are most vibrant and potentially life-giving. We believe that the communities best

Fig. 5: Shojin Ryori lunch session hosted by Enso Kitchen. Luminous Green workshop, Singapore, 2008.

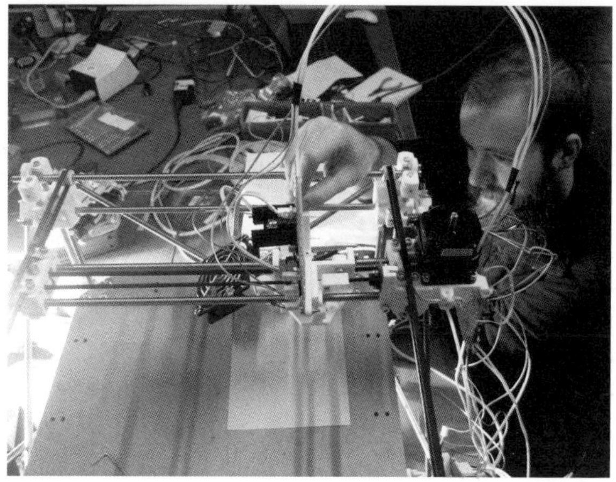

Fig. 6: Constructing the RepRap – A Self Replicating Rapid Prototyper, FoAM, 2007.

equipped to deal with current instabilities will be founded through unexpected couplings of people with divergent interests (that may have temporarily converged), able to work as equal partners, regardless of their specific cultural, professional or social backgrounds. Luminous Green is one of the places in which we hope such connections can be formed. At previous gatherings, an environmental activist and a liberal economist found new perspectives on disparate issues, while chatting about their common passion for mountain climbing; an artist and an engineer exchanged approaches to child rearing; a scientist and a farmer compared notes on tissue culturing. Each of these people took their new insights away with them, to foster and share further.

In order to encourage these connections to be formed in a gathering of limited duration, we are continuously experimenting with different forms of participatory learning and sharing. We began by drawing on 'Open Space Technology'[3], enriching the dry 'market place' planning with active storytelling techniques from alternate reality gaming, engaged dialogues from appreciative inquiry, visualisation methods from graph theory and most importantly remembering to be welcoming hosts. The most important condition of the Luminous Green events is that everyone feels that they are the right people at the right place and that whatever happens, each of them are responsible for making it happen. We want to move the groups and the events from passive consumption of preexisting knowledge, to active participation in its creation and reflection. If this condition is fulfilled, all those involved create an environment where the 'agenda' is open enough to bring burning issues to the fore, in productive discussions, exercises, or experiments. Social and aesthetic aspects of the gathering are crucial parts of the programme, to help tensions and arguments to be dissipated. We have striven to make Luminous Green a non-confrontational environment that enables encouraging difference and conflicting opinions to coexist, while dissent and play are encouraged to avoid the traps of 'group-think'. Sharing meals is as important as sharing ideas. Dancing, doing hand-stands or offering massages can be interspersed with hands-

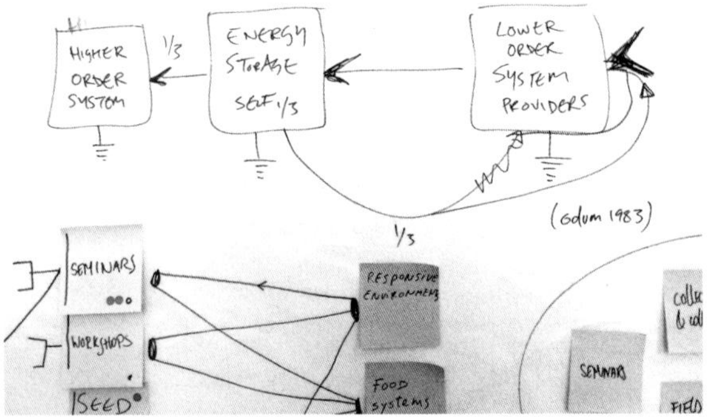

Fig. 7: Designing processes from a whole systems perspective, using permaculture principles. FoAM, 2008.

Fig. 8: Sociometric exercise. Luminous Green, Belgium, 2007.

on tutorials about DIY photovoltaics or theoretical sessions on topic ranging from Biomimicry (Benyus 1997) and *Carbon trading* to Frugality. (see Colour plate xxv, Fig. C)

A Luminous Green gathering is neither a radical environmentalist camp, nor a glitzy, self-congratulatory, green-gold business event. It is an edge habitat – like a coastline where marine and land-based eco-systems meet - a fertile and diverse, yet often contradictory space of inconsistencies; an entangled, productive chaos, designed as such to provoke discussions and questions that otherwise rarely get raised. The selected participants rarely mix in their daily lives and we don't expect everyone to agree with each other, but a respectful questioning of each other's practices and beliefs is a healthy thing to do – it can dissolve arrogance, isolationism and xenophobia.

During the Luminous Green gatherings, we aspire to grasp what kinds of behaviours and cultures can be brought forth from a fertile chaos, without a predefined schedule or outcome. We count on the inventiveness of the participants to translate the discussions and experiments into workable conclusions for their own contexts. In order to put these conclusions into practice, the participants are always a mixture of people from the creative sector, academia, policy and business. While the latter are engaged in many debates about environmental and social instabilities, it is rare that artists and designers are invited to contribute to the 'serious' solutions (although this is slowly changing). At FoAM, we found it unacceptable that the very people who are able to influence culture are often overlooked as a part of the solution. The creative sector shapes public spaces and events, designs materials, processes, systems and situations, within academia, industry and civil society. People working in creative fields are used to tackling complex issues that are often difficult to measure and quantify – cultural values, creative processes, or human experience. Such issues can not be easily reduced to statistics, or easily mapped to equations in a carbon calculator, however, they must be considered in order to incite necessary changes in human behaviour. During Luminous Green we recognised that there are at least three important things that the creative sector can contribute to possible solutions: an integrated approach to unwieldy problems, experience with participatory processes that can bring forth unexpected outcomes and the ability to make beautiful things (see Colour plate xxiv, Fig. A).

Integrated approach to complex issues

We would argue that it is not possible to tackle any one of the currently critical issues in isolation - they all form part of the same larger problem - that we have created an existentially unstable, fragile system. This problem can be tackled more effectively if we approach it from multiple perspectives, simultaneously and systematically, using integrated, holistic approaches. To paraphrase Einstein, we cannot solve a problem using the same kind of thinking that caused it. What we need are not individual remedies for only the most urgent issues, but fundamental behavioural and cultural changes, across the board - through all social structures and economic strata. On a daily basis, there are many issues that require our immediate attention, such as providing conditions for a dignified life for everyone in a global society; the distribution of food, fuel and other natural resources; ensuring a physical, social and psychological well-being of our communities; restoring and maintaining an ecological balance, and so on. These challenges cannot be solved using analytical methods alone. They require creative leaps, heuristic trial and error (along with other methods used in design research), as well as solid public experiments to ensure the feasibility and durability of the proposals. All these techniques form part of the creative process and are practised by artists, designers, architects and others on a daily basis.

Applying methods and techniques from creative processes to any currently critical issue can help us 'think out of the box' and perhaps find solutions where they are least expected. Design advocates such as Tim Brown, Bruce Mau, John Thackara, Olafur Eliasson, or Bruce Sterling are working with industry and policy-makers in this ongoing search. Their works have already proven the value of involving designers in rethinking the supply chain processes (including whole life-cycle analysis), rapid prototyping, iterative development, etc. Creative practitioners are not usually paralysed by complex problems – they are seen as inspirations, opportunities for positive change. By working with complexity, we may surprise ourselves and solve multiple problems, produce work with multiple benefits – for example, by designing one specific 'sustainable' touristic experience, we necessarily touch on transport and travel, food production and distribution, preservation of natural beauty and cultural heritage, health, etc. The cumulative effect of working with complex problems (often in transdisciplinary teams) should help make the works more inclusive, systemic and holistic, incorporating both quantitative and qualitative methods, with no 'externalities' and no 'aways'.

Transdisciplinary artists, scientists and collectives, such as SymbioticA, Angelo Vermeulen (cf. BioMODD), Bernard Lahousse (cf. 'foodpairing'), Radioqualia (cf. 'Radio Astronomy') or Project ATOL (cf. 'Makrolab'), tackle complexity by dissolving or permeating boundaries between traditional disciplines. At FoAM, we encourage the development of this community of generalists, looking to synthesise knowledge from a variety of domains. In our opinion, this can be a slow, long and often frustrating process. It took centuries to fragment knowledge into a myriad of useful specialisations, so we expect it will take a while to reconnect the weave. However, we suggest that this process is invaluable for creating more holistic, sustainable human cultures able to live with complexity while understanding the need for specialisation.

In Bruce Sterling's manifestly grandiose espousal of the guiding principles for the Viridian Design Movement, there is a single, salient 'Viridian Research Principle' that encourages Viridians to 'Walk Through the Walls of Knowledge Guilds – The boundaries that separate art, science, medicine, literature, computation, engineering, and design and craft generally are not divine. These boundaries are socially generated. Research techniques are not identical, nor are results all equally valid under all circumstances; quantum physics isn't opera. There exists a sensibility that can transcend intellectual turf war with no loss of rigour. If you choose to do it, you can step outside the boundaries history makes for you. You can walk through walls.' (Sterling 2001)

Participatory culture

One of the notable differences between the environmental movements in the 1970s and today is that we are beginning to understand that prescribing universal solutions and telling people what to do, doesn't work. There may be as many approaches to problem solving as there are problems. What we are looking for today are ways in which everyone can become an active participant and work on finding specific solutions. Anyone should be willing to proactively think and engage – everyone's help is needed – from those in academia, industry or the professions, to enthusiastic amateurs with a do-it-yourself approach. There is an overload of information out there and while access to it becomes easier, there is still a need to be able to cut through the jungle of nonsense to build knowledge relevant to our own lives and environments. Rather than 'The Solution', we should be looking for ecologies of solutions, interdependent and robust, nourished by local conditions, with strong trans-local ties able to evolve through collaboration and trust.

The creative sector has extensive experience with participatory forms of culture. In particular, media and electronic arts have moved toward engaging audiences as co-authors using a wide range of methods and formats: from performative interventions in public spaces (e.g. Future Farmers, Blast Theory) and happenings focusing on relational aesthetics (e.g. Boo Chapple, Arabeschi di Latte), to games (e.g. Sixtostart, Tale of Tales), interactive environments (e.g. Time's Up, FoAM) and community workshops and festivals (e.g. Constant, CityMined). Design has become instrumental in engaging 'end-users' as participants in the design process itself, from being passive consumers to becoming active producers. Social design engages communities to rethink their daily habits (e.g. Participle), product design becomes a relational service industry (e.g. Elephant Design, Reprap), the black boxes of digital tools are broken open and placed as tool-kits into the hands of their users (e.g. Tinker.it, Bricolabs), materials and structures are becoming adaptive and responsive to external stimuli (e.g. Loop.ph, Textile Futures). Each of these examples respond to a present need, while also working to change people's attitudes towards culture – from passive to active, from consuming to experiencing. Aren't these precisely the attitudes needed to address some of the most pressing problems of our times?

Beautiful things, delightful stories

One of the cultural challenges for the near future is a de-cluttering of the world from unnecessary 'stuff' – things we don't want (such as e-waste or MMTCDEs[4]), but also many of the things we believe we want (like cars, electronic gadgets, throw away cups, or cheap, breakable furniture). How much of this stuff is truly fulfilling a need, enhancing our experiences, improving living conditions? How do we select what to make, what to unmake and what not to make in the first place? How can we influence these decisions when they are made on a global scale, influenced by large marketing machines and single-issue lobby groups? In the final Viridian note, Bruce Sterling proposes a set of criteria for 'uncluttering' our surroundings by a process of categorisation, and elimination. (1) 'Beautiful things' able to fill your life and the life of others with meaningful aesthetic experience; (2) 'Emotionally important things' whose story you want to remember in order to share with others; (3) 'Tools, devices, and appliances that efficiently perform a useful function.' (4) 'Everything else'. Keep, improve or acquire things in categories 1, 2 and 3 & get rid of everything (yes, everything!) in category 4. (Sterling 2008)

Tools and technology are often on the agenda and, since we are tool-using animals, will necessarily form a part of our approach to problem solving. Aesthetics and storytelling pop up less frequently in environmental and policy debates, but they are key components of cultural experiences (and therefore cultural change). Again, it is the creative sector that has extensive experience with these domains. We make things that people want to consume, surround themselves with and immerse themselves in. Beautiful things in all their sounds, colours, textures, tastes, smells and movements can focus us fully on experiencing the present moment, while simultaneously feeling connected to 'something larger', to the continuum of beautiful and mysterious things that stretches through time immemorial. Without aesthetic experiences, any specific solutions to today's problems will remain in the sphere of the functional and will expire over time. If a solution is beautiful as well as functional, if it touches people not only intellectually, but also on emotional and even spiritual levels, it has a chance of more profoundly influencing people's thoughts, behaviours and cultures. In Buckminster Fuller's words:

> 'When I am working on a problem, I never think about beauty. I only think about how to solve the problem. But when I have finished, if the solution is not beautiful, I know it is wrong.'

Just as technology alone won't suffice, beauty on its own isn't enough. Beautiful things can clutter the world in many new and exciting ways, but only some of these things will end up becoming culturally significant, and socially meaningful – when they become used, shared and integrated into the social fabric as stories, gifts or experiences. Eventually this 'stuff' becomes wholly consumed, worn out through extensive (re)use, transformed and repurposed, ripped apart to become 'compost' for new stories and experiences. 'consumable' is the truest sense of the word – consumed, until matter dissolves, absorbed into a story that endures.

'The process of unfolding goes step by step, one pattern at a time. Each step brings just one pattern to life; and the intensity of the result depends on the intensity of each one of these individual steps.' (Alexander 1979)

Looking inward

There is much that creative practices can offer to the world, but there is also much work to be done to make current practices more environmentally and ethically sustainable. On the simplest level this means refining the material conditions in which we work - choosing non-toxic materials, using renewable energy sources and carefully examining our supply chain. This is no different from the responsibility of every other person on the planet. More specifically, we can look at how the practice itself needs to be transformed to inhabit and embody some of the ideologies that we propose. This involves questioning our methods, formats and artefacts along with examining the integrity of our own everyday lives. The creative sector can become a laboratory for possible futures, in which we can experiment with different models of working, living and sharing. Moving beyond critiquing and commenting on the sorry state of the world, to generating different realities, starting with our own workspaces, studios or living rooms. Natalie Jeremijenko (cf. 'Environmental Health Clinic'), Marko Peljhan (cf. 'Makrolab'), Kate Rich (cf. 'Feral Trade') and Heath Bunting (cf. 'The Status Project'), for example, provide a range of creative activities which encourage us to embark upon the long journeys towards new realities. Luminous Green aims to be a temporary point of exchange where such possible futures can be learned, examined, supported or critiqued. We want to encourage people to combine existing efforts, share knowledge and bundle resources. To involve people operating on the outskirts of the creative sectors, as well as those who may have forgotten that we exist. We aim to integrate rather than separate, clarify rather than reduce, working towards a shared abundance, rather than enforced scarcity.

Inconclusion

Luminous Green gatherings are conceived as complete experiences, where we aim to stimulate the participants intellectually and emotionally, in both material and spiritual spheres. Our goal is to immerse ourselves in an imaginative present to be able to envisage possible futures. We don't try to force any particular future, nor conclude with a five point action plan. The real outcomes of Luminous Green are the lasting impressions on the participants' lives – whether through a new collaboration, inspiring directions, an exciting relationship, or something else that none of us expected. None of this can be designed into the programme, but what does help is a carefully prepared context, an inspiring setting, a friendly group of people and a good dose of attention. Everyone at Luminous Green is encouraged to be completely present and committed to the experience. When this happens, we become aware of what's really at stake and what role we can play. According to Masanobu Fukuoka, 'we have come to the point at which there is no other way than to bring about a movement to bring nothing about' (Fukuoka 1978). Then, from the centre of nothingness, we can begin to see more clearly what it is that we can do to become more luminous.

Acknowledgements

Luminous Green <http://luminousgreen.org> and groWorld <http://fo.am/groworld/> were initiated by FoAM <http://fo.am>, organised in collaboration with the Guild for Reality Integrators and Generators <http://grig.info>, supported by the Flemish Authorities, VAF, Design Singapore, ISEA2008 and the Culture 2000 Framework of the European Commission. Our thanks goes to the numerous individuals and organisations around the globe who have made these initiatives possible.

Notes

1 Permaculture design principles: (Holmgren 2002)
   - [1] Observe and interact.
   - [2] Catch and store energy.
   - [3] Obtain a yield.
   - [7] Design from patterns to details.
   - [8] Integrate rather than segregate.
   - [9] Use small and slow solutions.
   - [10] Use and value diversity.
   - [11] Use edges and value the marginal.
   - [12] Creatively use and respond to change.

2 From Latin cultura (growing, cultivation) and colere (to tend, cultivate).

3 See: <http://www.openspaceworld.org>, also known as Unconference, or FooCamp.

4 Million Metric Tons of Carbon Dioxide Equivalents.

References

Alexander, C 1979, *The timeless way of building*, Oxford University Press, New York.

Benyus, JM 1997, *Biomimicry: Innovation inspired* by nature, William Morrow & Co, New York.

Fukuoka, M 1978, *The one-straw revolution: An introduction to natural farming*, Rodale, Emmaus/PA.

Holmgren, D 2002, *Permaculture: Principles and pathways beyond sustainability*, Holmgren Design Services, Hepburn, Australia.

Horvitz, R 2002, 'Whole earth culture', article originally written for the conference *Divočina jako fenomén integrální kultury* (Wilderness as a phenomenon of integral culture), Klenová, Czech Republic, 4–5 May, accessed 17 March 2010, <http://wholeearth.com/history-whole-earth-culture.php>.

Owen, H 2008, *Open Space Technology*: A user's guide. 3rd edn, Berrett-Koehler, San Francisco.

Sterling, B 2001, 'The viridian principles', *Whole Earth*, Summer, accessed 17 March 2010, <http://www.wholeearth.com/issue-electronic-edition.php?iss=2105>.

Sterling, B 2008, 'The last viridian note', *Viridiandesign* (website), accessed 17 March 2010, <http://www.viridiandesign.org/notes/451-500/the_last_viridian_note.html>.

Taleb, NN 2007, *The Black Swan: The impact of the highly improbable*, Random House, New York.

Wilson, PL & Weinberg, B (eds) 1999, *Avant gardening: Ecological struggle in the city & the world*, Autonomedia, Brooklyn/NY.

EMERGENCY DESIGN – NEW SEMIOTIC ORDERS OF URBAN SURVIVAL

Yana Milev

The concept of emergency design draws together various design, media and socio-cultural phenomena first observed in association with marginalized living spaces; as such, it has become a matter of growing public debate.

Introduction

In 2006 I launched the research project *Emergency Design – Design Strategies in Zones of Anomie*. This soon developed into a long-term research platform focusing on four distinct areas: states of emergency, catastrophes, concepts of emergence, and designs for survival. The roots of this Emergency Studies Project go back to the end of the Cold War and the beginnings of political post-modernism, a time when many of the issues now confronting us began to crystallize: new types of (asymmetrical) war, economic crises, natural catastrophes in the wake of global climate change, new orders of precariousness – nomadism, human super-fluity, poverty – and new strategies in the media and protest movements. Behind these phenomena lay further developments: the war on terror, data control, collapsing financial markets, the spread of corporocratic business, the extension of new economic zones in the form of war zones etc. What this amounted to in terms of public awareness and discourse was a new type of urban catastrophe.

The Emergency Studies Project has found expression in a number of events and publications: the 'First International Symposium on Emergency Design' took place at Zurich University of the Arts (ZHdK) in 2006; the proceedings were published by Springer (Wien/New York), who also published the first of a four volume series entitled Emergency Empire/Emergency Design in 2009. A museological series, 'talks inbetween emergencies', has meanwhile been set up in cooperation with the Center for Art and Media, Karlsruhe. The present essay aims to provide a concrete survey of emergency design, defining illustrating and discussing five new semiotic spaces of urban survival and living. (see Colour plate xxvi-xxvii, Fig. A - L)

Perspectives

Civil law – emergency as a state of exception

The dictionary definition of 'emergency' – a neologism derived from the Latin *emergere* (to arise or bring to light) – is 'a serious, unexpected and often dangerous situation requiring immediate action' (New Oxford 1998). Applied to civil society, the political concept of a state of emergency is modern, arising only after the end of the Second World War:

it denotes not the situation itself but the revocation of the laws hitherto governing a society and their replacement with special 'emergency' legislation to counter the situation. The authority to declare a state of emergency in situations of war, civil catastrophe or the like, and to impose such jurisdiction is based on the concept of national sovereignty; it implies the right to suspend the constitution and effectively create what Giorgio Agamben has called 'zones of anomie', states of exception that in Carl Schmitt's terminology are 'beyond the line'. For Schmitt the sudden and immediate incursion of such a state implies a sovereign arbitrariness in the determination and application of *ultima ratio* – a concept which in constitutional law is used of the declaration of war (*ius ad bellum*) or the legalizing of an existing conflict with all the means required to pursue it, even beyond the purview of international law. Against the background of the type of postmodern war that has emerged since the 1990s, the concept of *ultima ratio* has been extended to cover an increasingly wide range of catastrophes, crises, risks and preventive actions, as well as the civil, political, economic and media contexts, whether factual or fictional, in which these impact society; images of an enemy or adversary are a case in point.

The extension of the juridical state of emergency from the field of constitutional to that of civil law amounts to a redefinition of its claim, rooted in the psycho-political paradigm of shock or trauma in its modern form, including terror, domestic or foreign breakdown, and deterrence. As such it has becomes a basic pattern of reaction applied to precarious or marginalized spaces and their communication in the media. No person or platform can be *a priori* excluded from its scope, which embraces both victim and aggressor.

Emergencies are on the one hand wars and catastrophes consumed in real time on our television screens: the suicide bombings, plane crashes, explosions, executions, accidents, and climatic devastation that – above all since the end of the Cold War – primarily constitute news. At a more individual and local level, the concept of emergency extends to job-loss, social impoverishment, wavering prospects, biologically diminishing employability, and the marginalizing of whole classes of the population along with their living spaces. On top of this, the permanent oscillation of the parameters of social inclusion, the fine line between this time's victims and this time's narrowly escaped, frustrates the very concept of a stable norm.

The concept of emergency thus applies to insecurity of whatever kind – from natural catastrophe to war, from national debt through democratic intervention to social decline – that plunges the (subjective) space inhabited by a person, network or corporate entity into a state of exception, with fundamental impact on such institutions and values of daily life as justice, crime and the market.

Sociology – emergency as a new type of urban catastrophe

Emergencies, therefore, embrace what Lars Clausen has called 'crass social change' and 'abhorrent social processes' (2003), indeed the whole gamut of natural, social and political disasters caused by deportation, migration, homelessness, famine, drought, shortage of water, or lack of other essential resources that in our post 9/11 world we bundle under the heading of cultural catastrophe. In this respect the concept of emergency has taken on new post-political and post-institutional meaning complementing its implications for civil law.

In his recent book *Planet of Slums* (2006), as well as in his two earlier works *Ecology of fear: Los Angeles and the imagination of disaster* (2000) and *Late Victorian holocausts: El Niño famines and the making of the third world* (2001), Mike Davis gives this new type of urban catastrophe a local habitation and a name, translating the critical discourse of such opponents of globalization as Noam Chomsky, Naomi Klein, Elmar Altvater and Saskia Sassen to the concrete level of urban anomie represented in the struggle for survival, the slums and the homelessness of modern megacity peripheries. A further contemporary context of emergency arises at the interface between the new war theories of RMA (Revolution in Military Affairs) with its concepts of collateral damage on the one hand and false flag operations with a human face on the other (e.g. covert weapons testing and money transfers), and the growing number of civilian victims on the periphery of the same megacities. The research and publication project *Emergency Empire/Emergency Design* examines these contexts of civil catastrophe from a sociological point of view.

Fig. 1: Poster from German student walkout

Media theory – emergency as the discourse of anomie

The vocabulary of emergency, survival, states of exception and anomie has penetrated the discourse not only of political science and sociology but also of cultural and media studies and their philosophy. Against a background of neo-liberal markets, global business, and the violation of human and constitutional rights, these concepts serve as signposts in the new discourse of eternal warfare that characterizes an advanced post-war era of society. The boardrooms of international corporations (or what John Perkins calls 'corporatocracies' (2004) delineate and stigmatize public space, designing gated zones that are simultaneously zones of anomie whose 'spacing' (Löw 2005) is effected in terms of the biopolitical exclusiveness and exclusion communicated by corporate design and corporate identity. These spaces have in the past two decades experienced the transformation or dissolution of the classically differentiated fourfold structure of private and public areas plus suburbia and the peripheral zones of military (and/or militant) operation 'beyond the line'. Urban space has begun to define itself anew as a museum, an order defined by purchasing power, and hence on a par with private space; but by the same token it is also a marginalized space for those excluded from purchasing power and access, a clandestine realm, home to criminally creative forces that harbour the potential for militant-military operations of terror and counter-terror at all points of the public-private spectrum. In the discourse of media and design sociology the new structural multiplicity of urban space is rendered visible and experientially accessible.

Who does public space belong to? Space denotes a defined interior, a market created by the twin defining forces of domestic purchasing power and governmental immersion. Public space is a corridor where brands and branding proclaim ownership, and diverse uniforms, from Armani to Zara, with the chip cards concealed within them, evince the right to access and participation. This is the preserve of a new combative phalanx: the inhabitants of the living machine, possessors of the bank accounts that for Peter Sloterdijk,

> 'provide access to places, persons, goods and data – opportunities derived solely from the fact that the standard form of subjectivity within the grand installation is determined by the availability of purchasing power' (2005, p. 309).

It is at this point that the problem of spatial sovereignty impacts design via the biopolitics of media iconography in the multiple dimensions of living, dress, physical appearance, bearing and intimacy – an iconography that is at the same time one of separation from the realm of the other, the precarious, superfluous and dispensable, the migrants and watchers from beyond the fence. The worlds of political and economic, technological and media immersion are designer worlds of social polarization where the exclusiveness of the living machine, the *urbs/domus* aggregate, ipso facto generates the marginalization of the excluded, the psycho-political emergency of cultural catastrophe and its inherent market, the zones of anomie and media hysteria, the designer paradigms of management and poverty. What is true of domestic space holds equally for public: house and home have become 'an ignorance machine [...] an integral instrument of defence, where the basic right of non-respect towards the exterior world [has] found its architectonic pillar' (Sloterdijk 2004, p. 540). On the one hand, then, stands the apparatus of sovereign exclusiveness, the crystal palaces of the gated community; on the other the habitat of the masses, the vast living machines of slum, ghetto and suburbia, not to mention the informal settlements of tent city and *favela*. Across all of it lies the smog of sidelining and burnout, for '[t]he case of the 'superfluous' is more than a matter of structural disadvantage in the job market. It is a matter of the nagging, tormenting, self-destructive feeling of not being able to keep up in a world of working to earn and earning for affluence, of being unrepresented in the symbolic system of professional rank and status, in short of being superfluous in a society of superfluity' (Vogel 2008, p. 157).

Design economy – emergency as transformational topos

Emergency design presents itself as a potential model of spatio-cultural production whose strategic features reflect the management techniques of highly efficient living spaces, bringing them to bear on social habitats conditioned by the state of exception. Discussion focuses on the causal relation between the dynamics of geopolitical buying power on the one hand and those of psycho-political displacement and marginalization on the other, along with their specific communications, media, design and marketing strategies. Within this framework analysis is essentially concerned with differentiating economies of power and profit from those of crisis (a term etymologically and psychologically rooted in a western mindset, evoking division, discrimination, either/or). As such it generates a field in which notions of war and economics interact and oscillate, a process that has long since overthrown the classical capitalist axioms of nation-state conflict, replacing them with such concepts as 'teletopology' and 'livetime war' (Virilio), 'asymmetrical wars' (Münkler, van Crefeld), and the business and/or media inspired wars of John Perkins' corporatocracies and Thomas Meyer's 'mediocracies' (2001). Based on purchasing power and powerlessness, the conflict of interests is that between 'offspace' and 'subspace' forces, involving the psychopolitical, socio-political and design dimensions of the urban (both public and clandestine), as well as those of free vs. 'shadow' trade. It is increasingly a context whose spaces and topographies are determined by the dynamics and interests of design and the media, evident in the contrasting cultures of protest and corporatocracy.

The growing medialization of social and political conflict results in what might be called a geography of crisis – of spatial and topographic fluidity, diasporic confusion and insecurity at the heart of the architecture of safety and seclusion, where vital, flowing design can engage in subversive manoeuvres. This is a key to the emergency design project, which sees such critical spatio-dynamic relations as a fitting sociological response to the sovereignty of the corporate-media conjunction that is, after all, responsible for emergency and cultural catastrophe in the first place. But it is not just a matter of response, for the creation of the state of emergency, the zones of anomie, is the precondition for the genesis of a new, innovative social space: the 'spacings' of design politics and sociology. The state of emergency, and the emergency design that masters it, both gain their impact from their contiguity and synchronicity with the principle of crisis that serves them as resource, matrix and competency.

The principal focus of emergency design lies, therefore, on the investigation of the interface between power, space and body in the design context. Here, crisis – or what Luhmann called permanent susceptibility to confusion – becomes the natural default condition of spatial systems. The translation of this principle to the various levels of conflict (religious, economic, distributional, political or otherwise) pertaining in social space, along with the potential for cultural immunity and resilience it entails, might, it is hoped, facilitate the development of a method beneficial to the space of crisis concerned. In the light of the foregoing analysis the inner logic of emergency design reveals itself, therefore, in the axiom that whatever outwardly transcends or subverts the codex of negotiations and the code of security will create a new inward code of resistance and immunity. New relational space will be generated where new immunities successfully shape and deploy their communications management against outworn systems of security.

Emergency design: new semiotic orders of urban survival

Cultures of resistance, protest, refusal, exchange and transformation

The 'superfluous' (Bude & Willisch, 2008) are a new generation of victims of globalization consisting (among others) of migrant labourers, deportees, political and economic refugees, the poor and the homeless, as well as artists, academics and freelancers in general. The sociologists Eve Chiapello and Luc Boltanski argue in *The New Spirit of Capitalism (2006)* that precisely these last three groups have not only faced up to and accepted the anomic conditions of the labour market (part-time work, constantly varying profiles and competencies, permanent on-call duty, unpaid work for the CV, project-based temporary positions etc.) but have created out of them a new type of nomadism: the nomadism of the labour market and the redistribution of capital. These are tribal designs of multiple, rapidly changing surfaces brought into circulation as unadapted capital currency in response to novel situations – which is the very reason they are able to create new cultural capital. This capital, generated out of the precariousness of the situation by the nomadic phalanx, is defined more closely in the first four orders of emergency design.

Forms of society as forms of art

Joseph Beuys has taught us that 'art is capital' (1992) when it sets out to resist accommodation in disposable institutions and markets, when the 'other side' determines and expounds the consequences, when by voicing its protest and intransigence it opens up new interstices of political and social communications design. In this context the acceptance of art and design as capital currency by and on the market – and not just the art market – means the acceptance of belligerent social activism.

The problem of belligerence is connected with the juridical and political acceptance of guerrilla warfare at the international level, where the crucial issue has always been that of parity in the treatment of guerrilla and conventional forces. Belligerence as such – i.e. the recognition of a state of war – is only established in such a context when the political status quo is forced to accept the guerrilla movement as a party to negotiations. This (or equivalent recognition by third party states of international standing) constitutes the foundation for the realization of the group's political aims, as can be seen in the debate about recognition of the PLO. Only after such recognition will guerrilla fighters be accorded POW status in the event of capture. Otherwise they count as unlawful or unprivileged combatants and remain outside the remit of international law.

In his 1962 lectures on the *Theory of the Partisan (1963)*, the German legal philosopher Carl Schmitt developed these issues on the basis of Spain's guerrilla war of 1808-1813. He saw the special status of partisan warfare, its irregularity and immediacy, as related at a theoretical level to the concept of terror both in its modern form and in that of the reign of terror that emerged from the French Revolution (famously legitimated by Robespierre in his 1794 address to the Convention).

Fig. 2: Image intervention action in the name of Nine Inch Nails

Jurists have always carefully distinguished between terror, partisan action and guerrilla warfare. However, all three share certain cultural-political traits: autonomy (central motive), resistance (central means), revolution (central aim), and belligerence (central foundation). These features are reflected in the situational theories of Guy Debord and Derivé (1963), as well as in Michel de Certeau's and

Pierre Bourdieu's deconstruction of the boundaries between art and activism ('art of action' theory), which served as a launching pad for the drive to meld political, legal, media, artistic, theoretical and sociological strategies into a new political and sociological design imperative. This outed itself at the turn of the millennium as the practice of cultural hacking (Düllo & Liebl, 2005). A further trend in contemporary discourse, highlighting social action in both theory and design and dismantling the boundaries between art and guerrilla activity, leads to a similar activist theory networking activism, art and the emerging community under the heading of 'transnational guerrilla' (Kastner 2007). Giorgio Agamben has also written recently on the symbiosis of art and terrorism: indeed his article 'Terrorism or Tragicomedy?' (2008) can be read as a call for transition to 'communications guerrilla' (Blissett & Brünzels 1997) action.

In contrast to modern guerrilla groups (from the *terreur* of the French Revolution to the urban activism of the Red Army Faction in 1970s Germany and after), postmodern communications guerrilla activity dispenses with the traits of revolution and belligerence in favour of clandestine tribal strategies of cultural transformation. As such it fulfils a central demand of Beuys' extended concept of art as 'social sculpture' (*soziale Plastik*). Today we have added a further dimension of design to this anthropological concept, entailing the fusion of social action in theory, semiotics and media practice into an art-form of society in which the dissolution of boundaries between the establishment, politics, art, design, social work, theory, representation and the market leads to a revaluation and repositioning of nomadism. New forms of cultural capital, new currencies are germinating in the deconstructive grassroots dynamics of migration and diaspora. It is here that the five orders of emergency design have their origin.

Emergency design as precarious, nomadic adaptation of living space in five orders

Emergency design represents a form of society-as-art (Beuys). It understands itself as:

- art-less art;
- non-artificial organic living;
- a precarious, nomadic approach to living space;
- the non-aestheticizing production of objects and surfaces;
- anti-design in marketing and advertising;
- detached from the economics and distribution parameters of the art market;
- triggering crises within the economy and distribution structures of the art market;
- triggering crises within the logistics of markets and institutions;
- transformational action beyond marketing and the culture/art industries;
- post-democratic, post-political, post-economic, post-religious, post-sovereign;
- invasive of politics, markets, institutions, economies, industries;
- new cultural capital, the currency of crisis capital;
- queer, queering, querying transdisciplinarity in queer economics, queer politics, queer theory;
- resource-based, core-energetic, emotional, interneuro-physiological, kinsai-aesthetic, body-based, auto-energetic movement;
- an untouchable, invincible, non-exploitable microtope: an immune space of exception amidst induced states of exception.

First order: survival space / living space

The increase in phenomena associated with the first order of emergency design, which we have defined as urban-semiotic designs of survival and living, is directly due to the globalization and urbanization of precariousness, poverty, exclusion, marginalization and human superfluity that goes hand in hand with the globalization and urbanization of private and profit interests. This fact in turn impacts and multiplies the statistics of global population growth, of the daily load added to the mountain of garbage and toxic waste, to the housing shortfall, to those barred from the satisfaction of basic needs, to cheap products and media trash, to exclusion from a public space whose events are either coded or overpriced, to the dearth of resources, geopolitical migration, urban expansion, the explosion of urban populations, the extension of free markets etc. The consequences stand in the chapter headings of critical discourse, in Peter Sloterdijk's 'global sea of poverty' (2005) and Mike Davis's Planet of Slums: 'According to the conservative calculations of the report [of the UN Habitat organization] a billion people currently live in slums, and more than a billion struggle for survival in irregular employment conditions. The spectrum ranges from street traders through casual labourers, child-carers and prostitutes to people who sell their own organs for transplantation. These are shocking figures, all the more unsettling for the fact that our own children and grandchildren will experience humanity at its quantitative peak. Sometime around 2050 or 2060 the human population of the Earth will reach its maximum, probably at about ten or ten-and-a-half billions. This figure is admittedly well below the apocalyptic prophecies of the past, but no less than 95 percent of this growth will take place in the cities of the south. This means that the entire future growth of the human race will occur in cities, predominantly in poor cities and to a great extent in slums' (2006, p. 2).

The global employment and housing crisis so impressively and consistently presented by Mike Davis represents, as it were, an emergency that in a sociological perspective can be seen as the result of neo-liberal industrialization. Further contemporary emergencies are climatic change, with its increasingly catastrophic scenarios, new asymmetrical wars and hyperindustrial proxy wars, as well as service sector wars under the cover of UN aid organizations and UN emergency forces.

The phenomena of emergency design in this first order consistently reveal techniques of survival management in conditions of direct impact through the emergencies of 'crass social change' and 'abhorrent social process' such as garbage housing or squatting. The new cultural capital, the currency of this situation is first and foremost the immunity that grants resilience. Medical sociology sees resilience as the ability to react flexibly to changing contexts, and to cope with stressful, frustrating, traumatic, difficult and otherwise charged situations without major psychological damage. From a perspective of affluence, the strategies developed by social systems whose members consistently suffer from acute deprivation with respect to housing hygiene, nutrition, privacy etc. remain a matter of astonishment. The survival economies of this first order are slum economies inhabiting and transforming the exclusive trash of the cities to engender the anthropological humus of planet Earth.

Second order: legal space / resources space

The (human) rights space, suffering collateral damage, is not just a focus for economists and political scientists, but also for political activists on a worldwide scale. Organized in blogs, projects and platforms, the most well known from this group are Human Rights Watch, Greenpeace, attac, AVAAZ and Amnesty International. Social exclusion, poverty and human rights abuses such as illegal arrests, surveillance and torture, deportation dramas, migration dramas, environmental catastrophes such as CO_2 emissions and their consequences in melting glaciers and polar caps, world-wide water and garbage disasters as well as discrimination of women, female circumcision, forced prostitution, stoning of women, no punishment for marital abuse of women, etc., are all the object and the reason for Emergency Design's 2nd Order.

As a direct reaction to random abuse of rights and resources, caused above all by states, governmental agencies and business corporations, activists react world-wide with a differentiated network of instruments such as boycotts, strikes and media work. Flashmob events, for example the most recent one by AVAAZ, 'Climate Wake Up Call' on September 21st 2009, but also film productions, for example the sensational production Waiting for the Guards by Marc Hawker and Ishbel Whitaker, commissioned by Amnesty International, are a part of this phenomenon.

The borders between politics, theory, street art, protest and strikes such as the squatting event by the 'Enfants du Don Quichotte'[1] in Paris 2006/2007, between political campaigns, net activism and the media and narrative interventionism of Culture Hackers, are often unclear.

Publishing, medialization and enlightenment go hand in hand. Heinz Bude, professor at the Hamburg Institut für Sozialforschung, and author of the two books *Exklusion*[2] and *Die Ausgeschlossenen*[3] , not only delivers the current status quo for sociological discourse, but also for activism in the social-political field.

In a similar way the worldwide problem of habitats and human rights is addressed in Das Bild der Menschenrechte, which is the current standard reference work for architecture and design activists.

Fig. 3: Image by Amber Frid-Jimenez, © 2008 MIT

The lively connection between political sociology and political practice in the social space as well as within the post-war institutions gains an impressive protagonist in the French sociologist Pierre Bourdieu. His solidarity with railway workers on strike – voiced at a meeting in December 1995 – is well known. In 1998 he supported the movement for the unemployed in France, was co-founder of the critics of globalization attac and in May 2000 he was engaged in forming a network for social movements against neo-liberalism. 'Sociology is a martial art,' was the polysemic slogan for a Bourdieu position that shifted between research, solidarity and mediation.

Third order: data space / brand space Grid hacking, culture jamming

The third order of emergency design is summed up in Roland Barthes' question: 'Isn't the best form of subversion the distortion of codes rather than their destruction?' (Barthes 2000) Like Martin Kippenberger's slogan 'The aim of design is to define space' and Henk Oosterling's 'Design is *Dasein* [being/presence]', Barthes' aphorism highlights the transformational quality of socially immanent design. In contrast to the political and economic trend of recent decades, which has been to seek a secure foothold in the inner world of capital, in the living machines of comfort and consumption, crisis capital is the new currency that opens the door to the systems and cultures of crisis – a thesis and a perspective that turns the discourse of access and opportunity, hitherto monopolized by purchasing power, on its head. Emergency design is the transformation of capital on the basis of crisis economies, concretely effected in the performative link between the currencies of established capital and crisis capital. Here new spacings (or spatial productions) arise that unequivocally incorporate a transformation of the established currencies of rank, money, image, purchasing power, consumption, access to opportunity, prestige, beauty, knowledge, security etc., as well as a shift in the scale of power and systematic dominance that results from that upheaval. Emergency designs are to be found to a significant degree in emerging systems, networks, platforms and domains. New topologies of art are new topologies of cultural production, and at the same time new spaces for the redistribution of cultural capital. They function queerly, as critical microtopes of the inbetween queering and querying media, disciplines, politics, economics, and semiotics.

Culture Hacking, grassroots capitalism, communications guerrilla

Billions are spent every year, specifically in the European countries of the Schengen Agreement, on interior design and related events, trade fairs, publicity and PR productions, media and advertising in general – all of it devoted solely to the marketing of exclusiveness in terms of advanced and innovative work-worlds and surfaces. Nor is it innovation and creativity that are being marketed here, but power and dominance. Here parasitic strategies are employed by what is termed a 'poor' clientele – on the analogy of flash-mob and smart mob concepts – to interrupt and subvert the goals and methods of prosperous competing market currents. Parasitic strategies are unannounced and unprepared participations in expensively produced events and interiors and the appropriation of these for a divergent counter-message. They differ from recycling strategies in not defining the specific tracks of market circulation they break open for business; and their proximity to clandestine techniques gives them a guerrilla quality. As such, they are, as it were, third order emergency designs, and hence strategies of civil disobedience.

Civil disobedience is a weapon. Whilst the state does all it can to nip protest in the bud, the disobedient are a constant irritant outside the framework of the law. Whether blockading streets at the G8 summit or genetically manipulated maize fields at harvest time, civil disobedience can be relied upon to generate spectacular pictures and any amount of polemics (*radio FRO* 2008). For parasitic strategies are first and foremost designs of resistance in public space: anti-design, anti-publicity, consumption-critical, critical of existing policies of asylum and deportation, of the World Economic Forum and G8

Summit, of state financial packages for banks, of the sacrifice of large tracts of land to urbanization and its accompanying infrastructure of motorways and airports. And because they act from an impulse of protest, because they seek to break through or undermine established strategies of power, because they are moulded to a specific situation and uninhibitedly meld art and politics in their expression – for all these reasons they are emergency designs of the third order.

Parasitic and civil disobedience strategies engender new discourse and new publications – for example *Culture Hacking (2005)* by Franz Liebl and Thomas Düllo, *Konsum Guerrilla* by Diedrich Diederichsen (Richard & Ruhl 2008), *Netzkulturen (2002)* by Inke Arns, *Wir nennen es Arbeit (2007)* by Holm Friebe and Sascha Lobo, *Handbuch der Kommunikationsguerrilla (1997)* by Luther Blisset and Sonja Brünzels, *Anti-Design (2006)* and *Culture Jamming – Das Manifest der Anti-Werbung (2005)* by Kalle Lasn – and formulate, each in their own way, subversive models of action and manoeuvring in real living space.

Cultural hacking is a concept that links and develops the techniques of *Culture Jamming* (Lasn 2005), situationism and its derivatives and adbusting. The editors of *Culture Hacking*, Franz Liebl and Thomas Düllo, write as follows in their foreword:

> Cultural hacking, the art of strategic action, illustrates the opportunities for cultural innovation available today. From Dada through situationism to punk a direct line of development leads to current forms of subversive strategy. These follow the hacker logic of penetrating alien systems, grasping their frames of reference and supplanting these with new and surprising orientations of their own. Thus cultural hacking is the contemporary realization of the art of action as advocated by Michel de Certeau (Liebl & Düllo 2005).

Cultural hacking is practised in many different areas and contexts and incorporates a network of designers, artists, managers, activists and academics. Liebl and Düllo plot the movement's strategic arsenal with new concepts such as 'placebo products', 'uniformed brand communication', 'terrorist appropriation', 'coolness competency', 'deconceptual coding', 'hysteria-based market segmentation', and 'brand hacking'. 'Communications guerrilla', a concept introduced by Gerald Raunig at the end of the 90s in the context of the European Institute for Progressive Cultural Policies' (eipcp) 'Transversal' program, stands for a cultural technique sharply distinct from the political actionism of the 70s and 80s. Here art and politics merge in an action system of protest culture that aims to combine political action with performative, semiotic, narrative and media interventions. The interplay of representations, identities and power strategies gives rise to absurd, paradoxical and hybrid constructs that explicitly reject the epithet 'art-in-action', though their public performance often involves artists. Yet 'in the business world of art that is scarcely possible':

> The very concept of art functions as a lubricant enabling the audience to ingest the most blatant provocation without choking. Radical obloquy directed at the established art scene, for example, has long been canonized and neutralized by the artistic avant-garde. The storm of signs and images launched by the mere employment of artistic techniques creates tension only when it has left the integrative framework of the art world behind (Raunig 2003, p. 2).

In this sense, communications guerrilla can rank as a new hybrid form of protest culture because and inasmuch as its *guerilleras* inhabit ordinary work worlds and institutions, from which they do not seek to distance themselves militantly:

> For communications guerrillas it is not enough to know their enemy: they must themselves master the forms and signs that constitute, so to speak, the language of power. Communications *gueriller@s* are neither spies nor undercover agents in the worlds of work and bourgeois consent. At an everyday level they are often part of both worlds: they accept roles as teachers, colleagues, colegitimates, and assume functions within the capitalist system. It is this that makes the oscillation between radical critique and camouflage possible (Raunig 2003, p. 6).

Emergency designs of this sort are produced in communicative microtopes of delimitation, expropriation and over-identification. The third order of emergency design is exhibited concretely in examples of communications guerrilla activities, cultural hacking, *Culture Jamming* and adbusting.

Fourth order: media space / viewing space architecture, shelter housing, advertising, art

Emergency designs of the fourth order are forms of cultural production which, like those of the communications guerrilla, also create new interventionist microtopes in social space, the difference being that they represent art forms as forms of society. Admittedly the distinction between art and the activities of a communications guerrilla is a fine one, not least because artists, too, belong to the ranks of the precarious and of protest – in their case directed against the art market and industry. Many artists have liberated themselves from the classical concept of art, the art market and the dictation of artistic reputation by international capital; for, like other highly qualified and flexible (unemployed) freelancers, they often live in conditions of minimum security, where they nevertheless (or for that very reason) generate highly creative micropolitical systems of survival.

Fig. 4: Logo of REINIGUNGSGESELLSCHAFT
Martin Keil & Henrik Mayer

No wonder artists of this kind prefer to call themselves activists: as such they are represented in various roles on many platforms; and it is in such contexts – in the forms and dynamics of alternative and anti-art – that one should look for fourth order emergency design. Banksy, for instance, exemplifies the techniques of *Culture Hacking* and *Culture Jamming* – and also their sanctioning by the art market. His high profile actions have brought him public notice; others are first noticed by fellow artists of the establishment – either out of genuine sympathy or out of coquetry with the more powerfully driven scenes of protest, street art and hacking. Emergency design as an art form can be understood in these cases as an answer to emergency design as the space of survival defined in the first order.

New issues in art, architecture and advertising are frequently based on research into social and political dynamics in the critical media. Thus a recent topic to sweep the art scene was security – evidenced in the Berlin exhibition on 'Embedded Art' – whereas habitat, survival and war are relatively stable and recurrent aspects of that scene. But the market is also interested in the grassroots scene, and here the fourth order of emergency design presupposes a certain mimicry of the existentialist orders 1-3 with a view to asserting its own novelty on the market. Yet the space for movement between new directions, interventions, adaptations, annexations, or indeed colonializations, is often small. Nor should one forget that the Marco Polo syndrome thematized by Catherine David remains critical in the arts – including architecture, advertising and film. In a region of such rapidly flowing borders the questions 'When is art critical?' 'When is it synchronous with communications guerrilla action?' 'When does it subject deprivation and need to its own craze for innovation?' are hard to answer. After all, the problematic of such transformational activity reaches across the borders of aesthetic, sociological and ecological categories, inasmuch as its key concepts – precariousness, capital currency, redistribution of cultural capital etc. – are on the one hand sociological topoi and on the other factors impacting cultural strategy predominantly as techniques and forms of survival on the labour market.

Fifth order: knowledge space / program space

The fifth order of emergency design consists of the culture and design economies that generate and manage critical microtopes of the post-institutional, post-political and post-economic world. Significant characteristics of such microtopes are in the first place the active disruption of established political and economic urban mainstreams, and their diversion and utilization for the social, intellectual, media and energy interests of the microtope. A further characteristic is the existence in such microtopes of aggregates of resistance and refusal in terms of culture and design research. Concretely this means that the production segments of the new critical microtopes operate not only with many design strategies from emergency orders 1-3, but also lead to new types of fusion, and to new platforms, programs and institutes of culture and design research, as well as culture and media activism.

Critical microtopes of this type incorporate, for example, design strategies for the redistribution of cultural capital, for *Culture Hacking* and *Culture Jamming*, indeed for design and media anarchy in the widest sense – including squatting, blackspot philosophy, culture and media theory, and brand management in free-label stores – as well as for publications, platforms (blogs), festivals and conferences. For in the urban space of global metropolis and megapolis a new flexible migratory and nomadic market system has emerged. Divorced from the modern institutions of the academy, art market and free market in general, it is a grassroots movement whose dynamics generate the blackspot zones I have called microtopes – a name that reflects their complex organic structure. Here stores and showrooms disseminate, together with their labels and products, the post-political theories and blackspot philosophies of *Culture Hacking*, grid hacking and their derivatives; and behind them are whole scenes that not only conspicuously wear anti-fashion but also organize conferences, produce sounds and exhibit art, quite apart from gratifying their members' appetites for dumpsterware. Behind the visible showrooms and label stores in the cities, their action spaces – whose logos often represent only a www-domain – are responsible for network platforms, blogs and physical squats, raves and noise parties, but also for living, office and studio space, as well as independent institute platforms. In this environment urban mass aggregates are hacked across the board: from the pay-check stream of consumers and brand-shoppers, through the information flood of pop and trash consumers, to the asphalt river of employees, nine-to-five office workers gracing the streets in company cars and city suits.

The goal is fourfold: independent urban space (squatting), independent data space (grid hacking), independent knowledge space, and, of course, location independence, and with it the opportunity for label-adequate networking. The following platforms, programs, festivals and institutes represent the sort of critical microtope I mean.

Conclusion

Microtopes – new zones of geo-energy (local and global)

An example of a microtope as a new zone of geo-energy at the local level is the premises of the old cotton mill in Leipzig in its initial avatar as a squatting enterprise – a self-governing blackspot zone independent of the academies and institutions, devoted to symbiotic, micro-topic cultural production. Discovered and purchased at a spectacularly low price by an entrepreneur from the German state of Lower Saxony at the end of the 90s, its 70,000 sq. m. were let at even lower prices to artists, architects, IT specialists, craftspeople, designers and theoreticians. Initially vested as a sort of trust, it proved a sustainable model for a new symbiotic cultural economy, and eventually broadened out into being a media model for the entire culture industry.

At a global level, Auroville (located south of Chennai in the Indian state of Tamil Nadu) exemplifies the new micro-topic zones of geo-energy. Founded by Mirra Alfassa ('the Mother') on the basis of the social theory of the Indian philosopher and yogi Sri Aurobindo, it is planned as a universal city, a planetary habitat – not in the sense of urban or architectonic planning, let alone of the international construction business, but as the free occupation and possession of unowned land (in other words squatting). Instead of lifestyle and consumption, or institutional careerism and private ownership, this microtope is dedicated to spiritual practice and development. Thus there are as many different types of house and building there as there are people – and these range from artists, craftspeople, IT specialists, designers and theoreticians to research institutes. The town has grown organically in the form of a spiral, but not one designed on the drawing board. Currently it is home to a manageable 1829 people. Viewed geo-politically, it is an autonomous enclave in which, amid a global sea of poverty, globalization profiteers, multinationals, dictatorships, designer wars, democracies and tax-havens, a new sociological, semiological and mediological project is emerging.

Whilst in comparison with other experiments observed by the Emergency Studies Project Auroville (founded 1968) can already look back on a considerable history, there is another microtope I should like to mention here, also generated by a symbiotic cultural economy, that is of more recent date. The Urban Typhoon project, a travelling design forum located last year in Dharavi, near Mumbai, investigates the future of alternative societal forms, merging first and fourth order emergency designs.

Notes

1 Les enfants de Don Quichotte (Don Quijote's Children) was the name of the association that grouped over 280 homeless in this unusual demonstration. The idea originated in an art project. In the fall of 2006, the actor Augustin Legrand, constantly accompanied by cameras, spent three months among the SDF (the French term for the homeless: 'sans domicile fixe'), Wiener Zeitung, Saturday, 17. March 2007

2 Heinz Bude, Andreas Willisch (Hgg.), Exklusion. Die Debatte über die ‚Überflüssigen', Suhrkamp, Frankfurt/Main, 2008

3 Heinz Bude, Die Ausgeschlossenen. Das Ende vom Traum einer gerechten Gesellschaft, Hanser, München, 2008

References

Agamaben, G 2008, 'Terrorism or Tragicomedy?' first published in *Libération*, 19 November.

Arns, I 2002, *Netzkulturen*, EVA Europäische Verlagsanstalt, Hamburg.

Barthes, R 2000, *Sade, Fourrier, Loyola*, Suhrkamp, Frankfurt/M.

Beuys, J 1992, *KUNST = KAPITAL: Achberger Vorträge*, (text of 2 lectures and discussion at the International Cultural Center, Achberg, 1974 and 1978) FIU-Verlag, Wangen/Allgäu.

Blissett, L & Brünzels, S 1997, *Handbuch der Kommunikationsguerrilla: wie helfe ich mir selbst*, autonome a.f.r.i.k.a.-gruppe, (eds) Verlag Libertäre Assoziationen und Schwarze-Risse/Rote Strasse, Hamburg/Berlin/Göttingen, 1997.

Boltanski, L, & Chiapello, E (eds) 2006, *The New Spirit of Capitalism*, Verso, London.

Bude, H 2008, *Die Ausgeschlossenen: Das Ende vom Traum einer gerechten Gesellschaft*, Hanser, Munich.

Bude, H, & Willisch, A (eds) 2008, *Exklusion: Die Debatte über die Überflüssigen*, Suhrkamp, Frankfurt/M.

Clausen, L, Geenen, EM & Macamo, E (eds) 2003, *Entsetzliche soziale Prozesse: Theorie und Empirie der Katastrophen*, Literatur Verlag, Münster.

Davis M 1998, *Ecology of fear: Los Angeles and the imagination of disaster*, Metropolitan books, New York.

Davis, M 2000, *Late Victorian holocausts: El Niño famines and the making of the third world*, Verso, London.

Davis, M 2006, *Planet of slums: Urban involution and the informal working class*, Verso, London.

Davis, M 2006, 'Dossier Megastädte', in *Planet der Slums: Urbanisierung ohne Urbanität*, p. 2, accessed 20 March 2010, <http://www1.bpb.de/themen/SB18M2,0,0,Planet_der_Slums.html>.

Düllo, T & Liebl, F 2005, *Cultural Hacking: Kunst des strategischen Handelns*, Springer, Wien/New York.

eipcp, European Institute for Progressive Cultural Policies, Transversal program, Vienna, accessed 20 March 2010, <http://eipcp.net>.

Friebe, H & Lobo, S 2007, *Wir nennen es Arbeit: Die digitale Bohème oder Intelligentes Leben jenseits der Festanstellung*, Heyne Verlag, München.

Kastner, J 2007, *Transnationale Guerrilla: Aktivismus, Kunst und die kommende Gemeinschaft*, Unrast Verlag, Münster.

Kippenberger, M in interview with Y Milev, accessed 30. March 2010 <http://www.aobbme.com/presse/ED_INTERVIEW_M_v_Lupin.pdf>.

Lasn, K 2005, *Cultural Jamming: Das Manifest der Anti-Werbung*, Orange Press, Freiburg.

Lasn, K 2006, *Anti-Design*, Orange Press, Freiburg.

Liebl, F & Düllo, T 2005, *Culture Hacking – Die Kunst des strategischen Handelns*, Springer, Wien/New York.

Löw, M 2005, *Raumsoziologie*, Suhrkamp, Frankfurt/M.

Meyer, T 2001, *Mediokratie: Die Kolonisierung der Politik durch die Medien*, Suhrkamp, Frankfurt/M.

New Oxford Dictionary of English 1998, Clarendon Press, Oxford.

Oosterling, H, *Henk Oosterling website*, accessed 20 March 2010, <http://www.henkoosterling.nl/.

Perkins, J 2004, *Confessions of an economic hit man*, Berrett-Koehler, San Francisco.

radio FRO 2008, 'Ziviler Ungehorsam: Teil 3', *FROzene, Monatsschwerpunktsendung*, 28 Mai, accessed 20. March 2010, <http://www.fro.at/article.php?id=1610>.

Raunig, G (ed.) 2003, 'Transversalität im Alltag?', in *Transversal: Kunst und Globalisierungskritik*, Turia & Kant, Vienna, accessed 20 March 2010, <http://www.republicart.net/disc/artsabotage/afrikagruppe01_de.pdf>.

Richard, B, & Ruhl, A (eds), 2008, *Konsum Guerrilla: Widerstand gegen Massenkultur?*, Campus Verlag, Frankfurt/M, New York.

Robespierre, M 1794, *On the Principles of Political Morality*, accessed 20 March 2010, <http://www.fordham.edu/halsall/mod/1794robespierre.html.>

Schmitt, C 1963, *Theorie des Partisanen: Zwischenbemerkung zum Begriff des Politischen*, Duncker & Humbolt, Berlin.

Sloterdijk, P 2005, *Im Weltinnenraum des Kapitals*, Suhrkamp, Frankfurt/M.

Sloterdijk, P 2004, *Sphären III*, Suhrkamp, Frankfurt/M.

Vogel, B 2008, 'Überflüssige in der Überflussgesellschaft? Sechs Anmerkungen zur Empirie sozialer Ausgrenzung', in H Bude & A Willisch (eds), *Exklusion: Eine Debatte über die ,Überflüssigen'*, Suhrkamp, Frankfurt/M.

THE ART IN WASTE

Denise Scott Brown

In the 1960s at the University of Pennsylvania, my students and I watched a lecture in landscape architecture where the growth of roses was demonstrated through time-lapse photography. We enjoyed the beauty of the movement from bud to bloom, twice, three times – then I realised that we were seeing only half the pattern. After bloom comes blight; the rose wilts, withers and dies. But our sequences ended with full flowers. They omitted the wasting that followed.

Wilting, withering and dying

The cycle of nature is seed, bud, bloom, blight, death, rebirth and another cycle. This figures in all life and all mythology and should be the context for discussion of human processes, including those of urban life. During the 1950s, urbanists who watched American city centres deteriorate as their occupants left for the suburbs, took a cue from nature and called this wastage 'blight'. When it spread, some urban thinkers began to reassess their notions of change, to consider whether decline could not be part of the cycle of life in cities. A view of wasting as part of this cycle is background to my thoughts on the art in waste.

Defining waste

Human beings see waste, particularly wet waste, as dirty. Dust is dry and relatively clean but garbage is damp, clinging and smelly. We find it disgusting. For this reason a pursuit of links between art and waste may lead down paths that people find indelicate, especially when the enquiry goes to human basics. Imagine a baby who has escaped from a diaper of faeces. If she has the chance, she will play with them. They are part of her and she loves them. But the mother will not survive. Nor will the society. We must deal with these faeces, because they can bring disease. Yet when the child is controlled too much and without tact or knowledge, the result may be inhibition, perhaps particularly of artistry, because the need to play with waste seems to relate to creativity. A good mother will transfer this need by helping the child to play in the mud; to make mud pies or castles of sand; to do something in dirt that is safe.

Our definitions of waste are culture based. A peasant would have a different outlook from an urbanite. The floor of a Cape Dutch farmhouse I visited in South Africa was made of cow dung. It was polished and smelled fresh. Peach pits had been inserted into the dung and, when walked on, it felt like the softest rubber. Dung and pits were seen as valuable resources, not waste, in that society. African kraal houses also have dung floors and Africans make shoes from old tires. (see Colour plate xxxi, Fig. D) They are excellent for rough roads. Tin cans serve as wheels for African children's toys and larger containers act as seats, fire grates and sounding boards for musical instruments. Rem Koolhaas's research in Lagos, Nigeria found urban expressway interchanges recycled on the same principle.

And our definition is class based. Upper-class people tend to see lower-class tastes and preferences and the facilities that serve them as vulgar and wasteful. They call them 'visual pollution'. Yet the analogy to chemical pollution is not supportable. Chemical substances can be proven to be harmful to health and their presence in the air is measurable in particles per cubic centimetre. How is visual pollution measured? We apply the term to objects and areas that look ugly to us, especially if they have lower-class connotations. For example, we call lower-middle class suburban housing and its environment 'urban sprawl' and define run down inner-city neighbourhoods and industrial areas as 'blight'. But urban sprawl is a condensed version of the suburban or exurban settings many critics of sprawl choose for themselves and, for want of anything better, dilapidated old buildings provide low-rent housing for poor families, students and artists and incubation space for start-up enterprises. Because no society provides enough social housing for its population, in an entirely new or 'gentrified' city there would be no place for growth for people and ideas. Waste may lie on many points along spectra from avoidable (recyclables that are not recycled) to unavoidable (wilted flowers) and harmless (spilled milk) to harmful (toxic waste). Artistry may reside in the reuse of waste products, or in clearing up the mess, or in doing some of each.

Getting to waste via its archetypes

In 2005, members of a project called Basurama – 'basura' means 'waste' in Spanish – (see Fig. 1) asked me to lecture on this subject in Madrid. Their invitation, derived from our studies of the Las Vegas Strip (Venturi et al. 1972) and Levittown[1], suggested intriguing new ways to learn from the everyday landscape. A view from the garbage dump might suggest more phenomena to see with fresh eyes, other needs to meet creatively and further ugliness to draw beauty from. I narrowed the topic to 'The Art in Waste' (2006).

Las Vegas is an apotheosis of the commercial sprawl found on highways outside American cities (see Colour plate xxix, Fig. B). Levittown, built largely for returning World War Two veterans, epitomises lower-middle-class suburbia and was the model for the song 'ticky-tacky boxes' made famous by folk singer Pete Seeger (Reynolds 1962). To upper-middle-class architects Las Vegas is irredeemably vulgar and Levittown is definitely someone else's house. Such architects thought that if we analysed Las Vegas we must be socially irresponsible. But just as I need not believe in the Crusades to study gothic cathedrals, so I don't have to approve of gambling to learn from Las Vegas. As for Levittown, the information is far from complete; antagonists are still arguing on whether and when 'sprawl' constitutes wastage. Meanwhile it behoves us architects to understand the needs and aspirations it satisfies. And some lessons learned in our research can apply (with provisos for differences of culture and circumstance) to low income and social housing globally. (see Fig. 2)

Via Africa

Another route to the art in waste led me via South Africa. Growing up in Johannesburg, my cultural life was dominated by England. Although no longer a colony, we were still, culturally speaking, colonials of the mind. Our daily news came from the BBC. Books at home and in school were from England. English expatriates told us our culture was inferior to theirs. Disdaining our khaki-coloured vleis and koppies they looked beyond our landscapes to the

Fig. 2: An American cartoonist's take on 1960s Levittown (a). Public housing 'sprawl' (b) in a township of Johannesburg South Africa,1950s. Squatter housing (c) nearby, constructed of mud and scrounged waste materials. (Denise Scott Brown and VSBA)

Fig. 1: Spanish language recycle sign outside VSBA office in Philadelphia (VSBA)

Fig. 3: Painted fronts to housing (a) of the Mapoch tribe. Note the western suburban houses painted at the entry ways. Some art-from-trash objects produced for Europeans and Americans are neatly polite. This car (b), made from a discarded paraffin can, has rubber wheels. The African people working on it are dressed in beads. A soda pop bottle decorated in a traditional mode (c). Western urbanism interpreted in wood in an African way (d): buildings of the city of Bulawayo, Zimbabwe, with its train station, dated 1934. (Denise Scott Brown and VSBA)

green slopes of Surrey. As a child I questioned why my beautiful highveld had to look like England and railed against the importation of other cultures – objecting perhaps too much, because I now believe in multiculturalism.

My outlook was shared by many around me as debate raged on how Africa might be expressed artistically. In this context, indigenous art was revered but, when folk artists broadened their traditions to encompass industrial Johannesburg, the purists objected. Yet I felt these African responses, especially when they recycled industrial waste, were more interesting than the high artists' interpretations of Africa. One example: Africans used hollowed out gourds for drinking and frequently decorated them with beads tightly clustered around the original shells. But in urban areas soda pop bottles were substituted and these might be beaded too. (see Fig. 3c)

In essence we were caught between the 'oughts' of a far away country and the 'is' of Africa. I believe that artists who ignore the 'is' around them and respect only the 'oughts' of a distant place risk losing their creativity. This African outlook coloured my view on Las Vegas. It implied seeing the everyday environment as an artistic and cultural resource. And questioning the rules: if they come from another place or time do they apply here, now?

Via Europe

In 1952, as an architecture student in my fourth year, I moved from Johannesburg to London and entered the Architectural Association (AA) Final School. I arrived at a time when post-World War II policies were changing the English political economy and causing intense social polarization. This was reflected at the AA when the admission of scholarship students caused the school to split into two major, class-based schisms. Although each looked disapprovingly on the other, neither had standards for members of out-groups – ex-service, foreign and 'colonial' students like me. We could move among (though at some distance from) our classmates in either of them.

The most vital architectural debate was occurring among brilliant rebels in and around the scholarship group. The New Brutalists, led by architects Alison and Peter Smithson, caught their interest. Coming from the North of England, the Smithsons were also members of an out-group. They, Robert Scott Brown and Rem Koolhaas (who lived as a teenager in Indonesia and studied later at the AA) arrived, like me, at the site of origin of our now divergent cultures, as outsiders. Perhaps our skewed views helped us understand the debate.

However, for the Brutalists the argument was not, as in Africa, between colonial and metropolitan cultures, but among class groups and their values. The Smithsons joined with Team 10, rebel European architects, in discarding the principles of urbanism codified in the 1930s by the Congrès International d'Architecture Moderne (CIAM) and turning for lessons to the street life of neighbourhoods where the poor lived. They heeded sociologists' warnings that people bombed from the London East End should not simply be moved to suburban new towns, because they would lose the support of family and friends – of the 'life of the streets' so necessary in low-income neighbourhoods (Young & Willmott 1992 (1954)). The Smithsons hoped to evolve ways of relating social and community patterns to the form of cities and buildings, via what they called an 'active socioplastics'.

But incorporating sociology into design proved difficult. For this the Smithsons blamed the sociologists who, they declared, should extend their discipline to meet the needs of architects. I felt that the problem lay with differences of mind set between the two disciplines and that, for many reasons, the Smithsons should be the ones to extend. But they gave up. I kept trying (Smithson 1962).

The Brutalists shared in the English proto-Pop Art movement that originated in the 1940s long before Pop Art in America, and that included Eduardo Paolozzi, Ian Hamilton and others of the London Independent Group. These artists were intrigued by popular culture, particularly American pop culture, and they looked creatively at 'throw-away' phenomena, at 'kitsch' and 'schlock'. They consciously broke the rules of salon art and Brutalists among them rebelled against the laws of architectural composition inherited from the Greeks and Romans via the Renaissance. This rule-breaking piqued my Africa-inspired need to question so when the Smithsons turned to the subtly sabotaged Classicism of Mannerist architecture, I followed.

However rule breaking was not to be arbitrary; rational thinking was to prevail. The Brutalists revived the early Modern doctrine of Neue Sachlichkeit, new objectivity. 'Forget 19th century architecture' their argument went, 'face the challenge of modern industry. By solving problems directly without reference to dogma, we will discover solutions right for the project and the times.' And if the resulting architecture was ugly with jarring juxtapositions between, for example, the scales of industry and people – then so be it. The young revolutionaries felt that, although the built results of objective thinking might seem outlandish at first, architects and the society would grow to love them because, in economic and social terms, they were the way they had to be.

Our experience matches theirs. We have on occasion come to a 'good' design solution that looked ungainly enough to discard, yet that led, when accepted, to an altered sensibility. Like everyday architecture, it jolted us from aesthetic grooves into new ways of seeing in line with new times and technologies. Therefore I believe in the Brutalist version of Neue Sachlichkeit and aim, for both moral and aesthetic reasons, to be a Modernist and functionalist.

But the definition of functionalism must change. This conclusion derives from studying another phenomenon fascinating to Brutalists: urban change. To discover how the massive increases of industrialistion could be accepted in cities without brutalizing or sentimentalizing them, the Brutalists investigated urban growth, particularly in central areas. Their thinking and my experience with historical cities, made me question Modern architecture's succinct maxim: form follows function. In Venice, for example, some buildings had served as housing since the 12th century, though the plumbing was not 800 years old, and the uses, even when still residential, had varied widely over time. A palazzo, built as a dynastic family house and warehouse, might recycle as a bank, museum, governmental agency, or apartment building.

This suggested that we not see the requirements of the first client as the only brief to be accommodated in a building, but design to expedite activity changes that almost all buildings will undergo over time. The definition of function should encompass physical change from stasis to demolition and allow for subtle interplays between activity change and physical change. Culture-bound attitudes should be accommodated – can we, for example, imagine American cities maintaining and renewing themselves as European cities do?

As an aid to design, we might broaden our ways of categorizing building uses, including cultural variety in the definition – consider humanity's myriad eating customs, for example. Or we might generalise activities into public and private. And, as sophisticates, we should understand that built form does not derive directly from function but, like the writing of sentences, requires vocabularies and grammars to put it together. However the rules of language should be frangible, to prevent constraint upon other important values (Scott Brown 2004a).

Via the USA

With my head full of questions from Africa and Europe, I arrived in America just as the civil rights movement was starting. For me, the New Left began in 1958 during debate on urban social and racial issues in city planning departments at the Universities of Pennsylvania and California (at Berkeley). I had come to the United States because I wanted to study urbanism, as did many committed young architects in Europe during the years of post-war rebuilding. And America was the place to do it. But Robert Scott Brown and I had a further reason: we were going home to work for a better Africa.

Then Peter Smithson recommended that we attend the University of Pennsylvania where Louis Kahn taught. When we arrived, we were amazed to discover that Kahn did not teach in the city planning department. But our student advisor, David Crane, urged us to stay, observing that Penn's interdisciplinary approach to urbanism would help us face the great planning problems of Africa. In our first semester we studied city planning history and theory, urban sociology, urban economics, housing economics and statistics – no studio. Listed as reading for our sociology course was the London East End study whose findings had intrigued the Brutalists (Young & Willmott 1992(1954)). Our professor, Herbert J. Gans, had researched the low-income West End of Boston and was initiating his famous study of Levittown (Gans 1982(1962)) (Gans 1982 (1967)). We found that the architectural urbanism of the 1920s and '30s, which was so exciting to us in England, was sitting in staid textbooks, while the subjects of our courses covered real and present urban conditions and problems, and suggested strategies for achieving the active socioplastics that had escaped the Smithsons.

In planning school we learned that government urban renewal, so highly welcomed by architects had, in fact, converted architectural visions for cities into nightmares for low-income urban people. American and European images of the renewed city looked similar, but the US housing was occupied by the rich. The poor were forced from the site into dense existing slums. This was one reason for the 1960s civil rights uprisings and it resulted, in part, from what architects had designed. When I told a group of fourth year architecture students at Berkeley that they were potentially part of the problem, they were horrified. 'What are you doing about this?' they asked. Some years before, at Penn, I had asked the same question of my professor of housing, William Wheaton: 'You describe this terrible problem but you show no solutions. What are you doing about it?' He replied: 'I don't know. What are you doing about it?' His question has remained with me. What am I doing about this problem that I did not cause but inherited? What were the students doing about this problem that no one had told them about in the first four years of architecture school? When architects of the 1960s considered the city they looked inwards, at the work of other architects. They read Le Corbusier on the Ville Radieuse, not in itself an unworthy activity, but few examined aspects of the city around them that were not of architectural interest, or read in urban fields beyond architecture, where the solutions to some problems lay.

I am a circus horse rider whose twin horses, architecture and planning, are galloping in diverging directions. I try to bring them together. I learned from planning school to consider the 'is' of the city, before propounding its 'oughts'. When I studied the sociology of class structure in America, I tried out on Gans an observation by my old Communist professor at the AA, Arthur Korn (who, like Gans, was a German refugee) 'We are all workers'. Gans replied that middle class people did not like to talk about class, but that architects, whatever they said, generally had upper-middle class values and lifestyles. He complained that architects who considered themselves experts in urban physical planning, did not have training in urban social issues, and did not understand that, as planners, they should respect other people's tastes and values. How, he asked, could we plan for people without understanding their needs as they saw them? Planners in a democracy should learn the views of the many people of diverse cultures who live together in a city. Penn's social planning professors recommended that we architects visit cities of the American Southwest, those that people flocked to because they enjoyed themselves there. We should try to understand what people loved in these places – and what qualities were lacking in the ones architects created. These were major reasons for our studying Las Vegas and Levittown.

My first studio topic at Penn was a new capital city for Chandigarh, in the Punjab, based on the one designed there by Le Corbusier in the 1940s. Our studio critic, David Crane, adopted Le Corbusier's program but asked us to consider the city primarily from the viewpoint of rural families flocking there to work. These migrants would depend for shelter on urban cast-offs and waste. How could a city with little money help them build?

Guided by Crane, we decided that government's first infrastructure for them should be subdivided and drained land. In a monsoon climate drainage would come before roads. Thereafter, housing construction could be a public-private venture. Families would provide their own labour and materials and government would contribute utilities, community facilities, and perhaps some roof and wall elements[2] (see Fig. 4).

Planning for change was another concern. Given the city's rapid growth there would be many, mostly unpredictable, transformations. Indeed, for a given time period, the population expansion of the nation may be forecast more accurately than that of an outlying suburb in one of its cities. In unpredictably changing situations, planners often design for a selected datum, perhaps midway between high and low projections. But a solution for one point will be wrong for all others. An approach that built in flexibility would be more appropriate. Kevin Lynch (1958)[3] recommended several ways of planning for change without predicting what form it would take. One was to leave enough room for different activities

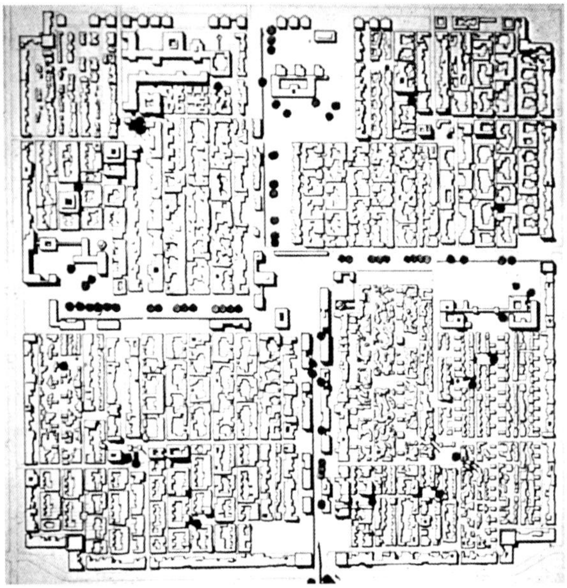

Fig. 4: The New City Punjab Studio, (University of Pennsylvania, 1958) In this plan for the 'City of 1000 Designers', government provides a grid of drainage, roads and facilities, which establishes a framework for housing development by low-income migrants, using scrounged material and found objects. 'Don't confuse prediction, recommendation and design' say the planners, 'and remember that you can't design the whole city.' (Denise Scott Brown)

to occur over time. But that is expensive, and so is frequent renewal via demolition – the 'Kleenex City' solution. A building designed with ample structural support and column bays wide enough to accommodate a broad range of activities would be practical for many purposes. If as well, structural and mechanical elements were separated from activity spaces and windows were set evenly and frequently in perimeter walls, then future change would not be impeded by existing building systems or lack of light.

Lynch's thought applies to both urban and architectural change. But it focuses on relatively permanent structures and ignores the role of waste in building for change. In poverty areas world wide, urbanising migrants scrounge for shelter, seeking impermanent or discarded materials for shanties that will be affordable in the short run and can be upgraded as their economic circumstances improve (see Colour plate xxx, Fig. C). But during the 1960s social planners saw the relevance of this approach to American urban poverty and in subsequent decades 'enterprise' zones were pinpointed in city grey areas. Here some building and other regulations were lifted to help low-income entrepreneurs or workers gain a foothold in the urban economy.

In the early 1960s planners began to approach the city as a set of systems, using adapted military computers and technologies. These were first applied to studies that combined urban regional economics and transportation, both subjects that lent themselves to statistical analysis. I attended several courses on computers and computer-based urban theory at that time because I felt their evolving mathematical models could offer planners a multidisciplinary understanding of the city as a set of complexly overlaid systems. Although their viewpoint was different from ours the model makers attempted, like architects, to be holistic in their concerns and to avoid uni-disciplinary thinking. As a designer, I saw in their beautiful and evocative urban maps and diagrams an example of how science could be muse to art. However the regional transportation studies were growing complex, and main-frame computers of that time were neither understandable nor user friendly to planners. So when researchers, as they worked, made assumptions about urbanism that were at least as over simplified as those of architects, few planners trained in traditional methods were able to spot their mistakes. One of the worst was that any factor that could not be measured could be ignored. Educated and creative systems people, like Walter Isard, the regional scientist, (1956) were well aware of the importance of including phenomena that weren't manageable by their techniques, and understood the value of human judgement and experience and the applicability of old-school planning skills. But I worried about the computer's zealous neophytes, my students. I hoped to learn to detect their stupid first assumptions. Key for designers and humanists in planning, I felt, was that we open-mindedly welcome the computer for what it could do but not lose our judgement in face of it. A creative role for us could be to derive artistry from the juxtapositions of systems, focusing perhaps on those places where they collide. This view helped me to apply my interest in mannerism to the city. If mannerism is a way of breaking architecture's rules, could it, in urban design, concern breaking the rules of urban systems? This was unavoidable, given the city's myriad systems, each with its own rules and the many conflicts between them. Juxtapositions, even conflicts, among systems can be beautiful, and the waste they create – irreconcilable junctions between road, rail, topography and settlements, slivers of land with difficult dimensions and no clear purpose – can be places of freedom and challenge for urban populations. Urban artists should operate deftly on such points. And where breakdown is greatest or need most dire, highest imagination is called for.

When Robert Venturi and I met in 1960, we shared an enthusiasm for mannerism, and he soon came to share my fascination with popular culture and the everyday landscape. We watched with interest as Pop Art began to put 'waste' in a new context, to place a Campbell's soup can in a museum. The Pop artists discovered new 'found objects'. Modern artists of the early 20th century had their objets trouvés. Henry Moore looked to primitive sculpture and water-worn pebbles, and early Modern architects scoured industrial lofts and silos to find the cubist shapes they liked. So Bob and I had been taught by the Modernists to look and learn in unusual places, but we turned away from their places. With help from the Brutalists, the Pop artists, several art and architectural historians and some social thinkers, we found our inspiration in the historical city and the commercial and residential environments of sprawl. Rome, the Las Vegas Strip and Levittown were our found objects.

'Wasting Well'

Lynch's last book, Wasting Away, (1990) is poetic and philosophical. He talks about waste on many levels, using words unusual in scholarly writing and certainly getting our attention. He refers to the need to 'waste well'. For me this implies cycles of birth and death, the concept of recycling, and its application in the 'adaptive reuse' of buildings. The preservation movement is popular today, but a first question should be: to preserve or not? Venturi points out that no Renaissance palace was built on a parking lot. Many were erected on the sites of destroyed medieval buildings. At times we must destroy, at others save, depending on the situation, but destruction must be for good reason. And when preserving, we must decide on the period to be favoured. Returning to a medieval beginning in Europe or an 18th century one in America may destroy a beautiful 1830s or 1930s addition. So the choice of a time period or periods to preserve should be a situationist one. Taking too purist an approach will lay waste unnecessarily and produce a dull and limiting environment 'preserved beyond repair', one shunned by artists and the public. This, ironically, will induce need for further change (see Fig. 5).

Fig. 5: Provincial capitol building, Toulouse, France 1999. This governmental complex sits on the Canal du Midi, beside an arterial highway, in a busy but intimate, lower-middle class neighbourhood. Only during construction did we learn that we had re-established an ancient road, a palimpsest, visible on historic maps but demolished before we started work. This forms the main pedestrian access to our project and continues to serve its historic role of linking two areas of the city. Other palimpsests: the facades of the complex contain allusions to the historic styles and red brick of Toulouse and to a pair of columns beside the site that once heralded the entrance to the area. The photographs were taken to show how a structure that combines the scales of urban waterways and bridges, civic buildings and private houses can find its place in an intimate and multi-layered context (Matt Wargo).

A living city remains forever subject to pressures for adaptation. When these grow too great for the historical fabric, *ersatz* preservation may result, where the semblance of history is maintained but not its meaning. For these reasons, Barbara Capitman, the great preserver of the Miami Beach Deco District, used to say 'preservation is so temporary.'

There is also the reuse of old ideas. A palimpsest is a text that covers an earlier text. Go beneath the first and you find the second. Architects, before computers, knew some palimpsests well. They were our working drawings, done in pencil on velum paper. If a design detail changed we erased and revised the drawing, and if it changed again we drew over once more. The list of revisions appeared in the title block, and each erasure revealed white lines etched where drawing had been. There are also urban palimpsests. Under Renaissance Rome is medieval Rome and under that Early Christian and Classical Rome. Traces of all Romes lie in modern Rome. Although on the Las Vegas Strip in the 1960s there was only the recent commercial vernacular architecture and the desert, in most cities we live on palimpsests, and the palimpsest could be seen as a metaphor for the processes of recycling of ideas and influence in art.

And there are old methods. 'Palaeotechnology', (Papanek 1972) refers to the use of earlier or more primitive, but still appropriate, technologies: old car tires for shoes, for example. This is common in the Third World, where people must make do with what they have. Cubans creatively use waste in the maintenance of their old American cars for which there are no new parts. The driver of a taxi that has lost its cab light substitutes a bulb set in a yellow plastic soap powder container, and day and night you still recognize the familiar taxi symbol. But there is also the idea of avoiding the palaeotechnical development of others and learning from their present experience – of Third World populations going directly to cell phones, omitting land line telephones altogether. A searing image I brought from China was of an elderly urban villager, squatting on a city side walk in the pose used throughout the rural world for working, conversing, eating, or excreting - with a cell phone to his ear.

There is also 'satisficing'. Traditional economic models assume that all people are perfectly and uniformly rational and that they have all the information they need to make a decision. Herbert A. Simon observes that in the real world limits on efficiency and rationality affect decision-making. His model (1957) assumes that people must decide within restricted time periods and on the basis of imperfect information. He posits the Taxi Game as an example of this reality. In a taxi with the meter running, time is money; you make the best decision you can within the time limit your money allows.

And morphology, the study of form as a result of process. Technical processes have helped form the city in all eras. Consider the effect of mediaeval defence systems on the form of European cities, or of 20th century technologies of movement and neon on the Las Vegas Strip. And today cities must harness the new technologies of the computer. This behemoth revolution has moved beyond my brain power. Its tentacles must be plumbed by another generation. But wire-free hand-held iPhones, for example, offer more than on-the-spot recreation and altered possibilities for living and working. Their emotional concomitants are rich. Simple but deep pleasure can lie, for instance, in wandering in a place you love and sharing the experience, audio-visually and in real time, with a friend a thousand miles away.

Meanwhile, the 'paperless' computer revolution has submerged me in a sea of paper. Even when introduced in the name of savings, technological innovation seems to accelerate waste, partly because its convenience induces increased use. And every change creates new types of debris and demands new forms of recycling. By pressing the 'delete' button today's electronic technologies generate virtual waste. But a search through my delete files may reveal information useful to someone.

Basurama's interest in the creative use of virtual waste suggests new ways of 'wasting well'. My conceptions, described above, derive from social, economic and technological views of the 1960s when I studied them, but social scientists have evolved theories today that address global changes in life patterns, technology and the issues of sustainability. And burgeoning media bring events to our screens almost as they happen, especially if they are visually gripping. New ideas of wasting must take these new findings into account and the Basuramas of architecture must proceed down paths where we can't follow. If our earlier experience can help them, our work may become palimpsest to theirs. (Song 2009)

Tragic waste

The media bring natural and human-made disasters to us particularly well and in almost real time. Lynch died before Wasting Away was published. I would have liked to hear his ideas on Katrina and the World Trade Center. Their wastes can in no sense have been done 'well' but can their resuscitation, short term and long term, involve our best planning arts? Disasters reduce even civilised societies to palaeotechnics. Lives are lost. Debris overwhelms. Before organisation arrives (which is sometimes scandalously late) trapped people try frantically to escape, passers by rush to help. Improvisation is the order of the day and will be even when fire fighters and emergency workers arrive. At Ground Zero, these saviours set up their own operations for rescue and support, developing information for the benefit of all, on available facilities, remaining food sources and operating toilets. Patterns of rescue linked the site with these facilities. Friends and families of victims formed their own patterns, primarily communication systems – printouts with photographs and descriptions, asking 'Have you seen my wife/son/ friend?' These were posted on rubble-strewn streets where New Yorkers still passed.

Although trained disaster technicians lift rescue to a more efficient level, the chaos still requires that support be garnered from the wasted environment itself. I read of a young architect who journeyed to a hurricane-hit Asian village to help its occupants build shelter from planks and shards in the detritus at hand. Can such palaeo-planning, while solving immediate urgencies, form the embryo of the new to come? I feel that, for practical and symbolic reasons, even the most modest first steps of emergency planning should be directed toward goals for the future. But this calls for a multidisciplinary understanding of how different patterns in the city, even in their early stages, can help to reinforce each other – the same planning skills as needed in developing areas.

As the bombed remains of Berlin's Kurfürstendamm formed the nucleus of West Berlin's post-war retail centre, so existing activity and movement systems around the World Trade Center could have directed plans for its new ground floor. And planners could have adapted the early patterns of rescue as a memorial and nucleus for growth. Converted to stone or steel, the Xeroxed search sheets could have been like remembrance plaques to individuals that line walls of European churches. Affixed where they were originally posted, they would have formed a quiet walk along bustling routes, and a compassionate memorial to people cut down in the urgency of their lives. And the twisted remains of the Trade Center buildings, too prettified and sentimental for my taste when alive, looked starkly agonized, post-disaster on TV, their powerful distortions symbolizing death. Where are they now? It would be inconceivable that neither plaques nor structure have a part (not necessarily together) in a memorial (Scott Brown 2002a, Scott Brown 2002b)

In post-Katrina New Orleans, the same principals apply but at a different scale. As survivors were literally and figuratively washed up on shore, the central need was for emergency sustenance and shelter. This the federal government mishandled signally. Thereafter, and in view of the scandal, a compassion for local government, an understanding of the population's limited resources for renewal, and some modesty in initial plans would be wise. Some rebuilding in New Orleans seems to have followed this almost inevitable low-energy pattern, starting where construction was easy, on flat, relatively inexpensive residential land at the outskirts of the city, away from flood danger and the rebuilt but not trusted levees. This typical developing-area option would be appropriate for early stages. But it should, in the process, pay particular attention to the needs of the poor, who suffered more than all others in the disaster. In my opinion, rehabilitation of city neighbourhoods should wait until resources return and rebuilding can meet correct standards, including those of flood protection. At that time, the difficult issues of equity, heritage and sustainability can be tackled from strength.

Meanwhile central New Orleans, and particularly the entertainment district, could be considerably shored up, right now, if major regional industries kept in mind the needs of the city as they reasserted their world-wide and national linkages. Connections that support the regional and national economy will already have been re-established. Oil will survive. But these should be reassessed with the aim of supporting others beyond themselves, of helping to revive the city, its citizens and businesses and the cultural richness of the 'big easy'. Loss of skills and evaporation of atmosphere are among the tragic wastes of urban devastation, and there is no way to do them well. But mass movement away from the city may have induced dissemination rather than loss of culture. I can imagine future historians of jazz tracing Katrina-induced migrations west as part of the story that leads from slavery and the cotton fields via the Mississippi to the world. Nevertheless, regenerating urban art and culture requires density, intensity and layers of history and will take time. This applies perhaps particularly to the racy, edgy atmosphere of the entertainment district. As one artist put it, 'the hardest thing to replace will be the evil' (Scott Brown 2005).

In sum, any doing (not wasting) well after horrific devastation involves combining an interdisciplinary overview and on-the-spot emergency strategies. It lies in foreseeing future possibilities for good in plans whose immediate aim is to deal with the here and now. Perspicacity is required to watch the horizon for the future without missing a beat in the present. And artistically, the first rescue efforts and pieces of the ruins should be embalmed in our memories and in the forming of our heritage. Our best talents, deepest insight and warmest hearts should be employed to combine compassionate rescue, the passion of the moment, and broad options for the future. You offer deepest respect by doing your best.

Artistry in waste

Mention art and waste together and Simon Rodia's Watts Towers come to mind or the Nevada house of Chief Rolling Thunder In The Mountains[4]. Built by lone visionaries to the glory of their gods, the soaring teacup shards and auto parts of these 'piles of junk' typify Outsider art world-wide. They relate to the impure African folk art and high culture objets trouvés described above, and to Trashion Art today, and they seem to epitomize artistry in waste.

Yet what of the broader artistic possibilities of waste? Who is taking them up? In Beijing in 2005, on an architectural jury at Tsinghua University, I asked a young woman whose project I admired what her major was, and she replied waste water management. I was surprised: she was so bright but her topic sounded dull. So I asked whether she was studying waste water management as an engineering discipline, and she answered, No, as an artistic discipline. Basurama also works in this discipline. Their thrust is melding the randomness of waste with the most modern abilities of industry.

They aim to produce goods and services more systemic than outsider art – ones able to gain markets, improve economies and move people. Although, when they invited me to lecture, they did not know the context I have sketched here, they felt *Learning from Las Vegas* took a creative view of the art of waste. I agreed that our Las Vegas and Levittown research projects were undertaken in the service of art but added that cultural, social and methodological concerns had been as important in leading us to examine the cities of the American Southwest. And an interdisciplinary approach was as significant to us in this research as it would have been in design.

But why Las Vegas? Because it was the clearest example, its signs were bigger than those of the average strip; it was the archetype not the prototype. And its context was simpler. No Colonial or 19th century city intervened between The Strip and the desert. Although Los Angeles is a greater, more extensive automobile city, the phenomenon is obscured there by an earlier pattern, the railroad city. In Las Vegas we could measure it pure.

The purpose of our study was outlined by Karin Theunissen:

> 'This studio was entitled "*Learning from Las Vegas*, or Form analysis as design research" and was introduced as "a study that will help to define a new type of urban form emerging in America[...], that from ignorance, we define today as urban sprawl." The object of the study is given as "to understand this new form, and to begin to evolve techniques for its handling". From this we understand that *Learning from Las Vegas* is a study in observation of the form of the city, followed by the recording, analysis and processing of the data to be made useful as design tools for urban designers. The original publication contains marginal notes in bold text referring to aspects of the technical analysis, such as "This has been a technical studio. We are evolving new tools: analytical tools for understanding, new space and form, and graphic tools for representing them".' (Theunissen 2006).

What did we learn?

So for us, Las Vegas was not signs alone. We studied its symbolism and iconography but we were equally interested in its urban form, processes and systems; in social issues, social diversity, taste cultures, popular culture, folk and Pop art; in the uses of history, and in urban mapping as a design technique. Travelling, literally and figuratively, from Rome to Las Vegas and back to Rome, we tried to tie the present to the past, and to fold the everyday landscape into the traditions of architecture and our modern experience. The Modernists had broken with the past. We hoped to re-seam modernity with history without doing violence to either. And yes, we wanted to learn about signs; about how Las Vegas communicated with people in cars as they travelled The Strip at 50km an hour. Later we realized that the city had taught us a major lesson on the role of communication as a function of architecture and as a means of supporting community in urban life. These aspects had been ignored by Modernists, even as their designs used cubist shapes to communicate their outlook on industry and a changing world.

As doers and makers, our aim was also to augment our skills and tools. Adapting concepts from other fields was one method. We looked in history, iconography, economics and sociology for ideas apposite to building and the physical city, seeking logical and creative ways of evoking physical designs from the verbal information of these fields. In *Architecture as signs and systems for a mannerist time*, (Scott Brown 2004b) I explain some concepts and discuss means of applying them. Perhaps near the end of our careers the body of our work can reveal what we learned from Las Vegas. I hope it shows that our research had both moral and artistic purposes. Far from lowering expectations, stressing the 'is' and the everyday was intended to bring greatest imagination to the hard reality of cities. 'Playing in the mud' seeking an uncommon beauty in its grit and glitter, meant consecrating waste, making the secular sacred. We see ourselves as Modernists continuing the Modern tradition but adapting its philosophies to new conditions, hoping to discover architecture appropriate to our times.

Meanwhile Las Vegas has changed. Dragged by a few strong minds beyond its single industry focus and towards the broader role of cities, it has shot like a teenager through various phases, some more gormless than others – Post-modernism, Disney-for-adults, Neomodernism, Photoshop collage (Scott Brown 2009). There was a grand abolition of neon and its readmission several years later. The wastage that accompanies rebirth was celebrated in the filming of the implosion of the Dunes sign, which ironically, was allowed to deteriorate before its demolition and had to be refurbished to look good for its public execution.

What should others learn?

Today young architects and scholars are recycling our ideas, studying their relevance more than 40 years later, drawing implications for their own time. There are follow-up studios on Las Vegas and Levittown and projects whose names start with 'Learning from ...' Changing social and economic paradigms and new technologies, especially of communication, are emphases of others. Creatively tackling the problems of sustainability and challenging the world outlook on waste is a mandate assumed by increasing numbers[5]. All have accepted for their generation architecture's perpetual task of rediscovering Modernism – of establishing its new centre in a changing world. As a result of their efforts, this rediscovery must now include a wide-eyed visit to the waste dump.

The neon bone yard

In June 2009 we made such a visit to the 'Neon Bone Yard' a sign museum that sits at the outskirts of Las Vegas. Here grand signs that we described in *Learning from Las Vegas* lie open to the elements. Literally 'laid waste', they have been sawn into movable sections and dumped in the desert along alleys defined by the trucks that brought them (see Colour plate xxviii, Fig. A).

News has got out and visitors from across the world come to see them. Architectural Hamlets stand there to say 'Alas, poor Vegas!' (Witcher 2009; Scott Brown 2009) Lines of signs gathered around a central opening form naves off a plaza. I cannot convey the force and fascination of the sight. Its agony calls for artistry, for opera to be performed before it. And it demonstrates a primary reason for turning waste to art -- to reduce the loss.

Notes

1 Venturi, R Scott Brown, D & Associates 1992, 'Remedial Housing for Architects, or Learning from Levittown', a studio given at Yale School of Architecture in 1970. The studio work topics were published in, Venturi, R, Scott Brown, D & Associates 1992, *On Houses and Housing*, Academy Editions, London, pp. 51-57. A further development of the Levittown study was illustrated in the 'Home' section of the *Signs of life: Symbols in the American city* 1976, exhibition, held in the Renwick Gallery of the National Collection of Fine Arts, Smithsonian Institution in Washington, D.C. in 1976.
See also VSBA bibliography, accessed 22 March 2010, <www.vsba.com>.

2 Crane, DA 1965, 'Chandigarh reconsidered: The dynamic city', *Journal of American Institute of Planners*, vol. 31, November, pp. 280-292. At the end of that semester Robert Scott Brown was killed. Such wastage cannot be assuaged, but I try, in my life, to make up for the work he would have done in his.

3 Lynch, K 1958, 'Environmental Adaptability', *AIP Journal*, vol. 24, no. 1. Lynch, writing for planners, couches his recommendations in terms of urban form. My description here adapts his to apply to buildings as well.

4 Trent Harris, Chief Rolling Thunder In The Mountains and his House, DVD-R Trent Harris Productions, 1978?

5 The 'relearning' studies are too many to list, but they include: Koolhaas, R & Obrist, HU 2001, 'Re*Learning from Las Vegas*, an Interview with Denise Scott Brown and Robert Venturi', CJ Chung, J Inaba, R Koolhaas, S Tsung Leong (eds), *Harvard Design School Guide to Shopping*, vol. 2, Taschen, Köln, pp. 590-617. This contains illustrations of the Las Vegas 2000 Studio at Harvard. Rattenbury, R & Hardingham, S (eds) 2007, *Supercrit #2 Robert Venturi and Denise Scott Brown: Learning from Las Vegas*, Routledge, London. Based on the symposium, 'Learning from *Learning from Las Vegas*', University of Westminster, March, 2004. Stierli, M 2007, *Ins Bild gerückt: Ästhetik, Form und Diskurs der Stadt in Venturis und Scott Browns Learning from Las Vegas*, (Put into perspective: Aesthetics, form and discourse of the city in Venturi and Scott Brown's *Learning from Las Vegas*) Ph.D. Dissertation, Eidgenössische Technische Hochschule, ETH Zurich (In German).

References

Crane, DA 1965, 'Chandigarh reconsidered: The dynamic city', *Journal of American Institute of Planners*, vol. 31, November, pp. 280-292.

Gans, HJ 1982 (1962), *The urban villagers*, updated and expanded, The Free Press, New York.

Gans, HJ 1982 (1967), *The Levittowners: Ways of life and politics in a new suburban community*, Columbia University Press, New York.

Harris, T 1970s, *Chief Rolling Mountain Thunder and his house*, DVD-R Trent Harris Productions, website of photos accessed 22 March 2010, <http://www.spyrock.com/nadafarm/html/thnderpix.html>.

Isard, W 1956, *Location and space economy: A general theory relating to industrial location, market areas, land-use, trade, and urban structure*, MIT Press, Cambridge/MA.

Koolhaas, R & Obrist, HU 2001, 'Re*Learning from Las Vegas*: an interview with Denise Scott Brown and Robert Venturi', CJ Chung, J Inaba, R Koolhaas, S Tsung Leong (eds), *Harvard Design School Guide to Shopping*, vol. 2, Taschen, Köln, pp. 590-617.

Lynch, K 1958, 'Environmental adaptability', *AIP Journal* vol. 24, no. 1.

Lynch, K 1990, *Wasting away. An exploration of waste: What it is, how it happens, why we fear it, how to do it well*, Sierra Club Books, San Francisco.

Papanek, V 1972, *Design for the real world: Human ecology and social change*, Pantheon Books, New York, NY.

Rattenbury, K & Hardingham, S (eds) 2007, *Robert Venturi and Denise Scott Brown: Learning from Las Vegas*, Supercrit # 2, Routledge, London.

Reynolds, M 1962, *Little boxes*, sung by Pete Seeger, Schroder Music Company.

Scott Brown, D 2002a, 'Measuring downtown's future', *New York Times*, 16 August.

Scott Brown, D 2002b, 'What shall we do about the World Trade Center?' *MetropolisMag.com*, 8 April, accessed 22 March 2010, <http://www.MetropolisMag.com/html/wtc/wtc_denisescottbrown.html>.

Scott Brown, D 2004a, 'The redefinition of functionalism', in R Venturi and D Scott Brown, *Architecture as signs and systems for a mannerist time*, Belknap Press of Harvard University Press, Cambridge/MA, pp. 142-174.

Scott Brown, D 2004b, 'Architecture as patterns and systems: Learning from planning', in R Venturi and D Scott Brown, *Architecture as signs and systems for a mannerist time*, Belknap Press of Harvard University Press, Cambridge/MA, pp. 105-217.

Scott Brown, D 2005, 'What should New Orleans do?' *Artforum*, vol. 44, December, pp. 10, 264, 266, 268-69, 300, 308. (re-published in Dutch in de Architect, 2006).

Scott Brown, D 2006, 'The art in waste', in *Urban Distortions*, BC Terán & J López-Aranguren Blázquez, (eds), Basurama, Madrid, pp. 14-38.

Scott Brown, D 2009, 'My kind of town', *Architecture Today*, No. 200, July, p. 104-105.

Signs of life: Symbols in the American city 1976, (exhib. cat.) Rennwick Gallery of the National Collection of Fine Arts, Smithsonian Institution, Washington, D.C.

Simon, HA 1957, *Models of man*, John Wiley & Sons, New York.

Smithson, A (ed.), 1962, 'Team 10 Primer 1953-1962', *Architectural Design*, vol. 32, no. 12, special issue.

Song, S 2009, 'Shifting paradigms: Renovating the decorated shed', *Space*, no. 496, March, pp. 117-129. Modified from article previously published online at Archinect, May 15, 2008, accessed 22 March 2010, <http://archinect.com/features/article.php?id=75248_0_23_72_M>, and <http://archinect.com/features/article.php?id=75250_0_23_72_M>.

Stierli, M 2007, *Ins Bild gerückt: Ästhetik, Form und Diskurs der Stadt in Venturis und Scott Browns Learning from Las Vegas*, Ph.D. Dissertation, Eidgenössische Technische Hochschule, ETH, Zurich.

Theunissen, K 2006, 'Re-building as urban tactic: Examining Venturi Scott Brown and Associates' transformation from within the American campus', *The Architecture Annual 2004-2005*, Delft University of Technology, Delft.

Venturi, R, Scott Brown, D & Izenour, S 1972, *Learning from Las Vegas*, revised edn 1977, MIT Press, Cambridge/MA.

Venturi, R, Scott Brown, D & Associates 1992 (1970), 'Remedial housing for architects, or learning from Levittown', in *On Houses and Housing*, Academy Editions, London, pp. 51-57.

Witcher, TR 2009, '*Learning from Las Vegas*, 2.0', *Las Vegas Weekly*, June 25, accessed 22 March 2010, <http://www.lasvegasweekly.com/news/2009/jun/25/learning-las-vegas-20>.

Young, M & Willmott, P 1992, (1954) *Family and kinship in East London*, University of California Press, Berkeley.

BIOGRAPHIES

Brandon Ballengée

Exploring the boundaries between art, science and activism, Ballengée creates artworks out of information generated from ecological field trips and laboratory research. In 2001, He was nominated for membership into Sigma XI, the Scientific Research Society. His lead authored article (with Dr. Stanley K Sessions), 'Explanation for Missing Limbs in Deformed Amphibians' was published in 2009 in Journal of Experimental Zoology and received international media attention from the BBC and others. In 2009, he co-founded Urban Nature Atelier, midtown Manhattan's first dual ecological art and biological research studio. He currently is a visiting scientist in the biology department at McGill University in Montreal, Canada. Three forthcoming books on Ballengée's transdisciplinary art and science projects will debut in 2010 published by the Arts Catalyst, London, England, the Shrewsbury Museum in Shropshire England and Gallery Nowhere, Milan, Italy.

Zvjezdana Cimerman

Was born in Zagreb, where she also studied music and science. For more than 20 years she worked as a scientist at Zagreb University, before moving in 1998 to Zurich. Her work over the past 15 years has focused on projects at the interface of art and science. Her interests are concentrated on the potential and limits of art and science as different modes of knowing, and their impact on the formation of the human environment. In this context she has examined the roles and patterns of art and science, and above all their relations in the course of history. She has written articles in the fields of both science and art, and co-curated exhibitions at the Coninx Museum and Zurich Design Museum (among others), where she worked on such topics as genetic engineering, sense experience, and the limits of human knowledge, or gravitation. She co-authored 'Kunst und Gentechnologie' (Art and Genetic Engineering, 1997), and 'Das Tier in der zeitgenössischen Kunst' (Animals in Contemporary Art, 2002), and since 2000 she has lectured on 'Art and Science' at the ETH (Swiss Federal Institute of Technology) in Zurich.

Nik Gaffney

A systems and media researcher, and a founding member of FoAM. His studies covered the fields of computer science, cognitive science and organic chemistry. Nik has put this research into practice through the artificial-life environment 'mutagen', mixed reality systems for 't*series' and 'groWorld', as well as by leading FoAM's research into artificial companions within the European project LIREC. Since joining FoAM in 2000, Nik has designed and facilitated a number of workshops and master classes, focusing on the role of innovation and technology for creative practices. The results of his work have been published in scientific and cultural journals, as well as being exhibited at international art and design festivals.

Andrea Gleiniger

A historian of Architecture and Art. Her teaching, research and writing concern Theory of Architecture and Media, History of Modern Architecture und Art. Since 2007 a senior lecturer in scenography, history and theory of space at the Zurich University of the Arts. She is also supervisor and editorial advisor of the Z-Node PhD program on art and science at the University of Plymouth, UK. From 1983–1993 Gleiniger worked as a curator at the German Architecture Museum in Frankfurt/Main. Since 1993 she was a lecturer for history of modern architecture, media and art at different Universities and Art Academies in Karlsruhe (Hochschule für Gestaltung, TU Karlsruhe), Stuttgart (Fachhochschule für Technik und Arbeit) and Zurich (Institute of History of Art, University of Zurich). In 1995 she founded the Multimedia Studio at the Hochschule für Gestaltung (HfG) in Karlsruhe, focused on multimedia-projects on the History of Architecture and Space. From 1998 to 2001 she was a guest professor at the HfG; and from 2002 – 2007 a research associate at the Chair for Computer-Aided Architectural Design, Swiss Federal Institute of Technology (ETH) Zurich. Her research focus is 20th century architecture, the relation between the concepts of architecture and new media technologies. She is working as a writer and a critic of architecture for several German architecture magazines. She has received various prizes and fellowships.

Helen and Newton Harrison

In 1967, coming from the University of New Mexico, Newton as an Assistant Professor was one of two founding members of the new Visual Arts Department at UC San Diego. Helen Harrison, also coming from UNM doing research-based work and teaching literature, was Director of Educational Programs at UC Extension. The Harrison collaboration began in 1969–1970 with a mapping they made of endangered species around the world for an exhibition called Fur and Feathers at the Museum of Crafts in New York City. In the early 70's their work was about urban farming. They constructed fish farms, portable orchards and flat pastures in such places as the Hayward Gallery in London and the New National Gallery in Berlin, The Houston Museum of Contemporary Art, The Los Angeles Museum of Contemporary Art and various university galleries. Perhaps their best-known early work is entitled The *Lagoon Cycle*, a complex photo mural 360' long in 60 parts. Internationally they have presented their work in two Venice Biennales, two Sao Paolo Biennales, Documenta 8, the Museums of Modern Art in Chicago, San Francisco, Bonn (Germany), Aachen (Germany), Toulouse (France), Ljublijana (Slovenia), the Museum of the Revolution in Zagreb (Croatia) as well as Kasteel Groeneveld in Holland. Their work took Second Prize at the Nagoya Bienale in 1991 in Japan. They received the Groeneveld Award for doing the most significant work of the year for the Dutch landscape in Holland in 2002. Their gallery representation has been with Ronald Feldman Fine Arts from 1974 to the present.

Angelika Hilbeck

Currently, senior scientist at the Institute of Integrative Biology (formerly Geobotanical Institute) at ETH Zurich. Also holds an adjunct scientist position at Genoek – Centre for Biosafety, University Tromsoe, Norway and serves as Co-Director of Studies, for the Z-Node – PhD program for artists in science fields, University of the Arts, Zurich, Switzerland. Her research focuses on biosafety issues and concepts for environmental risk assessment and post-release monitoring of GMOs. Through numerous research and capacity building projects she is heavily engaged in developing countries in Africa and South America and Vietnam. Her research and conceptual work also contributes to the implementation and shaping of the (UNEP CBD) Cartagena Protocol on Biosafety and capacity building in developing countries. In 2006, she was appointed as lead author of Global Chapter 3 and Synthesis Report on Biotechnology of the International Assessment Agricultural Science Technology for Development (IAASTD). She is increasingly involved in broader issues of technology development towards a democratically legitimated, sustainable global future and actively contributes to the debate on agro-fuels, international agriculture, hunger and poverty alleviation. She is a member of various national and international committees and scientific organizations. She is co-founder and acting chairperson of a newly founded European Network of Scientists for Social and Environmental Responsibility. 1990 Diploma in Agricultural Biology at University of Hohenheim, Germany. 1994 PhD in Entomology at North Carolina State University, Raleigh, North Carolina.

Tiffany Holmes
Her art and research explores the potential of technology to promote positive environmental stewardship. Recent projects include a commission for the National Center for Supercomputing Applications where sequences of experimental animations visualize real time energy loads. Her paper detailing this work, 'Eco-visualization: Combining art and technology to reduce energy consumption,' won a Best Paper award at Creativity and Cognition 2007. She lectures and exhibits worldwide in these venues: Museum of Contemporary Art Chicago, J. Paul Getty Museum in Los Angeles, Digital Salon '99, Viper in Switzerland, Next 1.0 in Sweden, Siggraph 2000, World@rt in Denmark, Interaction '01 in Japan, ISEA Nagoya. A recipient of the Michigan Society of Fellows research fellowship in 1998, Holmes has earned an Illinois Arts Council individual grant, an artists-in-labs residency award in Switzerland, and a 2010 Rhizome Commission. Holmes is Associate Professor, and former Chair of the Department of Art and Technology at the School of the Art Institute of Chicago where she teaches courses in computer programming for artists, interaction design, eco-art, and the history and theory of electronic media.

Maja Kuzmanovic
A generalist, with an academic background in Design Forecasting and Interactive Media, whose professional experience includes design, facilitation & transdisciplinary leadership, Maja is the founder, PI and artistic director of FoAM. Prior to FoAM, she worked with MR & VR in research institutes across Europe (GMD, CWI, Starlab), lectured (HKU), as well as collaborated with technological arts collectives in Europe and North America. Her particular approach to people & technology has been recognised by the MIT's Technology Review & the World Economic Forum, awarding her the titles of Top 100 Young Innovator (1999) & Young Global Leader (2006).

Yana Milev
Media artist and curator, studied scenography, media art and cultural theory in Dresden, martial arts in Kyoto und Berlin, as well as cultural philosophy, media theory and artist anthropology in Vienna and in Karlsruhe, Germany. In 1994, Milev established the AOBBME label, a platform for interdisciplinary and transitive research based in Berlin. In 1997, she participated in Documenta 10 dX, as the first female representative from the former Eastern Bloc countries. Since 2000 she has tutored at various universities, among others at the Karlsruhe University of Arts and Design and the Zurich University of the Arts at the Institute for Design Research Design2context. In 2008, she received her doctorate under Peter Sloterdijk on the topic of political philosophy. Since 2005 she is a professional exhibition curator and writer. Initiator and leader of the international festival and

symposium *Emergency Design – Design Strategies in Zones of Anomie* at the Zurich University of the Arts. Founder of the design, media and artistic-sociological group Emergency Design and initiator of the discussion series 'talks in-between emergencies'. Within the framework of her doctoral research, Milev has, as of 2010, become a visiting research fellow at the research institute of the Karlsruhe University of Arts and Design.

Jill Orr

A media artist who has delighted, shocked and moved audiences through her performance installations which she has presented in cities such as Paris, Beijing, Hong Kong, Amsterdam, Antwerp New York, Toronto, Quebec City, Graz, Hong Kong, Sydney, Melbourne, Adelaide and Brisbane from the late nineteen seventies to now. Orr's work centres on issues of the psycho-social and environmental where she draws on land and identities as they are shaped in, on and with the environment be it country or urban locales. Orr grapples with the balance and discord that exists at the heart of relations between the human spirit, art and nature. *From the Sea* began a body of work that traces overlapping histories of indigenous and non-indigenous relations to place. She has recently completed *The Crossing*, The *Southern Cross – to bear and behold* and *Faith in a faithless land* that express cultural and environmental interdependence.

Andrea Polli

Digital media artist, Associate Professor in Fine Arts and Engineering and Director of the Interdisciplinary Film and Digital Media Program at The University of New Mexico. Polli's work with science, technology and media has been presented widely in venues including the Whitney Museum of American Art Artport and The Field Museum of Natural History. Her work has been reviewed by the Los Angeles Times, Art in America, Art News, NY Arts and others. In 2007/2008, she spent seven weeks in Antarctica on a National Science Foundation funded residency. <http://www.90degreessouth.org> <http://www.andreapolli.com>

Juanita Schläpfer-Miller

Research associate at the University of the Arts in Zurich (ZHdK). She is an artist and science communicator and has developed interactive exhibits for science centers and museums, on particle physics, renewable energy research and protein crystallography. She was an exhibit developer and artist-in-residence at the Exploratorium in San Francisco. Her artwork has included themes of self-organized criticality, water and fossil fuel resources, and has been shown in galleries and museums in the U.S. and Switzerland. Currently a doctoral candidate at the Z-Node of the ZHdK, her research interests are the social parameters of climate-change precipitated alterations in small scale agricultural practices, for example, the cultural effects of planting bio-fuels; and the role of art as a model of ritual communication in science communication endeavours.

Jill Scott

Born in 1952, in Melbourne, Australia, has been working and living in Switzerland since 2003. Currently she is Professor for Research in the Institute for Cultural Studies in Art, Media and Design at the Zurich University of the Arts (ZHdK) in Zurich and Co-Director of the artists-in-labs Program (a collaboration with the Ministry for Culture, Switzerland). She is also Vice Director of the Z-Node PhD program on art and science, duly located in Zurich and at the University of Plymouth, UK. Her recent publications include: 'artists-in-labs: Processes of Inquiry' 2006 Springer/Vienna/New York, and Coded Characters, Hatje, Cantz 2002, Ed. together with Marille Hahne she has written many chapters in international books on new contexts for the arts. She has a PhD from the University of Wales (UK), an MA from USF, San Francisco and two undergraduate degrees in education and art and design. Since 1975, she has exhibited many video artworks, conceptual performances and interactive environments in USA, Japan, Australia and Europe. Her most recent research for her artworks is about neuroscience, embodiment in the environment and brain plasticity involving the construction of interactive media and electronic sculptures <http://www.jillscott.org>.

Denise Scott Brown

Architect, planner, urban designer and educator. As a principal of Venturi, Scott Brown and Associates, she has guided the design of the firm's largest institutional and academic projects and been in charge of those in urban planning, urban design, and campus planning. Her work spans from advocacy planning for Philadelphia's inner city to a provincial capitol building in Toulouse, France. Her projects include plans and designs for Tsinghua University, Beijing; the University of Pennsylvania plus its Perelman Quadrangle; and the University of Michigan plus its Life Sciences complex. Her research projects have set new directions in architecture and her interdisciplinary experience has contributed breadth and innovation to design processes in her firm and the profession. Her publications include 'Learning from Las Vegas' (with Robert Venturi and Steven Izenour,1972; revised 1977); Urban Concepts (1990); 'Architecture as signs and systems for a mannerist time' (with Robert Venturi,2004); and Having Words (2009). Denise has received the Vilcek Award in art and the Topaz Medallion for distinguished teaching. As architecture's 'grandmother' she spends time these days writing for publication and corresponding with students and professionals worldwide.

Therese Steffen

English, art history, and literary criticism were Steffen's subjects at San Francisco State University, UC Berkeley, and at the University of Zurich, where she completed her doctorate on William Shakespeare. She was a lecturer at the English Department of the University of Zurich, published articles on Eudora Welty, the 'New Yorker' cartoon captions, Shakespeare and Rita Dove. Her post doc thesis, 'Crossing Colour: Transcultural Space and Place in Rita Dove's Poetry, Fiction, Drama' (New York, London: Oxford UP, 2001) is the first monograph on the Afro-American former US poet laureate Rita Dove.

Steffen was a Fellow (1995–1996), and is now a permanent associate of the W.E.B. Du Bois Institute for Afro-American Studies at Harvard University. In 1996 she was appointed Oberassistentin, later Assistant Professor of Gender Studies in the anglophone context at the University of Basel. Since 1998 she is also Privatdozentin at the University of Zurich and, since 2002, Titularprofessorin of Gender Studies in the anglophone context at the University of Basel, where she focuses on issues of ethnicity (Afro-American and African literature and culture), ethics, gender, and literary space.